Conspiracy in Modern Egyptian Literature

Conspiracy in Modern Egyptian Literature

Benjamin Koerber

EDINBURGH
University Press

Edinburgh University Press is one of the leading university presses in the UK. We publish academic books and journals in our selected subject areas across the humanities and social sciences, combining cutting-edge scholarship with high editorial and production values to produce academic works of lasting importance. For more information visit our website: edinburghuniversitypress.com

Edinburgh University Press Ltd
The Tun – Holyrood Road
12 (2f) Jackson's Entry
Edinburgh EH8 8PJ

First published in hardback by Edinburgh University Press 2018

Typeset in 11/15 Adobe Garamond by
Servis Filmsetting Ltd, Stockport, Cheshire,
and printed and bound by CPI Group (UK) Ltd, Croydon, CR0 4YY

A CIP record for this book is available from the British Library

ISBN 978 1 4744 1744 0 (hardback)
ISBN 978 1 4744 5583 1 (paperback)
ISBN 978 1 4744 1745 7 (webready PDF)
ISBN 978 1 4744 1746 4 (epub)

Contents

Series Editor's Foreword

Edinburgh Studies in Modern Arabic Literature is a new and unique series that will, it is hoped, fill in a glaring gap in scholarship in the field of modern Arabic literature. Its dedication to Arabic literature in the modern period (that is, from the nineteenth century onwards) is what makes it unique among series undertaken by academic publishers in the English-speaking world. Individual books on modern Arabic literature in general or aspects of it have been and continue to be published sporadically. Series on Islamic studies and Arab/Islamic thought and civilisation are not in short supply either in the academic world, but these are far removed from the study of Arabic literature qua literature, that is, imaginative, creative literature as we understand the term when, for instance, we speak of English literature or French literature. Even series labelled 'Arabic/Middle Eastern Literature' make no period distinction, extending their purview from the sixth century to the present, and often including non-Arabic literatures of the region. This series aims to redress the situation by focusing on the Arabic literature and criticism of today, stretching its interest to the earliest beginnings of Arab modernity in the nineteenth century.

The need for such a dedicated series, and generally for the redoubling of scholarly endeavour in researching and introducing modern Arabic literature to the Western reader, has never been stronger. Among activities and events heightening public, let alone academic, interest in all things Arab, and not least Arabic literature, are the significant growth in the last decades of the translation of contemporary Arab authors from all genres, especially fiction, into English; the higher profile of Arabic literature internationally since the award of the Nobel Prize for Literature to Naguib Mahfouz in 1988; the growing number of Arab authors living in the Western diaspora and writing both in English and Arabic; the adoption of such authors and others by mainstream, high-circulation publishers, as opposed to the academic publishers of the past; the establishment of prestigious prizes, such as the International Prize for Arabic Fiction (the Arabic Booker), run by the Man Booker Foundation, which brings huge publicity to the shortlist and winner every year, as well as translation contracts into English and other languages; and very recently the events of the Arab Spring. It is therefore part of the ambition of this series that it will increasingly address a wider reading public beyond its natural territory of students and researchers in Arabic and world literature. Nor indeed is the academic readership of the series expected to be confined to specialists in literature in the light of the growing trend for interdisciplinarity, which increasingly sees scholars crossing field boundaries in their research tools and coming up with findings that equally cross discipline borders in their appeal.

This title represents a new venture in the study of modern Arabic literature, and particularly but not exclusively the novel, in Egypt. Conspiracy and paranoia, rife in the political arena, both in the political elite's speak and in popular discourse under first colonial and then dictatorial, post-independence regimes, has had its reflections over generations in literature too. But this phenomenon has gone largely without study. Whether its treatment represents a literary 'style', a genre, or sub-genre is a matter for contention, but what is incontestable is that paranoia represents a phenomenon that has run through Egyptian literature over several generations of writers and political periods without receiving scholarly attention; not until the monograph to hand anyway.

The author has chosen a good representative sample of works spreading over the best part of a century and a multiplicity of political eras, including both canonical works, which have been much studied though not from this specific angle, and works by less mainstream authors, reaching down to some blogs in the post-January 2011 era of the Arab Spring.

Professor Rasheed El-Enany, Series Editor,
Emeritus Professor of Modern Arabic Literature,
University of Exeter

Note on Transliteration and Translation

The book follows the *IJMES* system for Arabic transliteration, with several exceptions. Accepted English spellings are used for names of prominent figures (Naguib Mafhouz, Gamal Abdel Nasser). For readability, names of the major authors and characters under consideration have also been rendered without diacritical marks. In all such cases, the full transliteration is provided upon first mention in the text.

Transliteration of texts in Egyptian Colloquial Arabic follow the *IJMES* system, with the addition of the dialect vowels /e/, /ē/, /o/, and /ō/.

All translations from the Arabic are mine unless otherwise noted.

Acknowledgements

This book began as a string of shy whispers and incantations, spoken to a wall in a dark room near Abdeen Square, Cairo. It has attained coherence and felicity only through the support of numerous individuals and institutions whose generosity is surely great enough to allow them to bear, beyond what they already have, these belated expressions of gratitude.

After Abdeen, harbingers of this project would next appear in a series of footnotes to my doctoral dissertation, which found fruition thanks to an inspiring group of mentors at The University of Texas at Austin. Tarek El-Ariss has guided me since my first stammerings about public culture, parasitism, rumours, and *radh*; his abundance of *wahy* has proven to be an enduring antidote to *wasāwis*. Kristen Brustad, with her *bayān* and *tabyīn*, taught me to strike the right balance between *lafz* and *maʿnā*; when I have since erred, it is due to my own *lahn*. Mahmoud al-Batal's dedication to Arabic as a language of knowledge production, even and especially in the United States, has and continues to inspire many exciting trajectories for my research and writing. Samer Ali has shown me how *adab* becomes wordly, and how worlds come into existence through *adab*.

Most of the research behind this book was made possible by a generous grant from the US Department of State Bureau of Educational and Cultural Affairs (ECA), provided through a fellowship at the American Research Center in Egypt (ARCE) (October 2015–April 2016). I am extremely grateful to all the staff at ARCE for their warm hospitality and assistance with matters large and small. I am particularly grateful to Djodi Deutsch for her constant support for my research needs, and for making me feel comfortable during an otherwise very stressful period in Cairo.

I would like to express my gratitude to Anny Bakalian and Christopher

Stone at the City University of New York (CUNY) for inviting me to deliver a talk at the Graduate Center, based on an earlier version of Chapter 5 of this book. The Institute for Language Education in Transcultural Context (ILETC) at CUNY was a generous co-sponsor. Many thanks are also due to Orit Bashkin and the Near Eastern Languages and Civilizations (NELC) Department at The University of Chicago for inviting me to speak on themes related to this book, and for their generous hospitality. I extend many thanks to my colleagues at the Department of African, Middle Eastern, and South Asian Languages and Literature (AMESALL) at Rutgers, The State University of New Jersey for providing me with my academic home. I would especially like to thank my department chairs – Alamin Mazrui, Charles Haberl, and Anjali Nerlekar – for their warmth, wisdom, and constant support.

Many friends and colleagues have aided me at various stages of this project. Zeina Halabi has fashioned for me the trestles and trellises necessary for the blossoming of my ideas in numerous forums in both English and Arabic. Suneela Mubayi shone a light that birthed glitters and gleams. Ehab Elshazli chased away evil spirits, while also looking after the cats. Ahmed Naji, with his uncanny knowledge of the cultural teratology, literary speleology, and architectural parasitology of Cairo, has been an *agent provocateur* behind many of my projects. Mohammad Rabie has bestowed wisdom and mirth through our conversations on modern Arabic and American literatures, and patiently listened to some of my earlier ideas for this book. Ahmed Nada has generously shared with me his encyclopaedic knowledge of the *ᶜajāʾib* and *gharāᶜib* of Arabic literature in all periods. Talal Faisal helped generate my interest in Naguib Surur. I would also like to thank the many booksellers of Azbakiyya and Sayyida Zaynab in Cairo, and Nabi Daniyal in Alexandria – especially Mahmud and Nasr – for guiding me to many delectable *kutub ʾadžīma*.

An earlier version of Chapter 4 appeared in the volume *The Beloved in Middle Eastern Literatures: The Culture of Love and Languishing*, edited by Hanadi al-Samman, Michael Beard, and Alireza Korangy (London: I. B. Tauris, 2017). I thank the editors for their kind permission to reuse some of that material here. I also thank the editors of the *Journal of Arabic Literature*, Volume 46, for allowing me to reuse portions of my article 'Reading the Plot:

The Psychology and Poetics of *Pārānūyā* in Yūsuf Rakhā's *Kitāb al-ṭughrāʾ*, which I have incorporated into Chapter 5 of the present book.

Many thanks are due to everyone at Edinburgh University Press, especially series editor Rasheed El-Enany for his insightful comments and recommendations, as well as Nicola Ramsey and the editorial team for their constant help through all stages of the project.

Introduction

It is a strange coincidence, to say the least, that three versions of this book have fallen into my hands in the last few years. Each version pertains to a different edition, and each I obtained without requesting from the bookstores that are known to carry it.

The first version was lent to me by a gentleman from among our military leaders – those who pursue rare books about war, strategies for invasion and conquest, and suchlike. I returned it to him after reading it and copying down miscellaneous chapters.

The second version, redacted and abridged, I purchased from a bookseller who knew neither its title nor what it was about. This version, along with the portions I had copied from it, disappeared along with other papers and books that I accused my household servants of stealing.

The third version, which pertains to the fourth English edition, I found among the belongings of a great physician. Inside was written the date May 1, 1921 and the French word for 'gift' – Souveni [*sic*]. In view of the odd fates met by these various versions, I was nearly convinced this book was destined to be lost.[1]

T he Egyptian littérateur ʿAbbās Maḥmūd al-ʿAqqād (1889–1964) relates this anecdote in his foreword to *al-Khaṭar al-Yahūdī: Brūtūkūlāt Ḥukamāʾ Ṣihyūn* (1961 [1951]), the first 'faithful and complete' Arabic translation of *The Protocols of the Wise Men of Zion*. The 1903 Russian 'original' of this text – in fact, a forgery patched together from a fictional French political satire and a German novel – had already been translated into most languages of Europe, where its violent anti-semitism had great appeal among ideologues and extremists of varying political persuasions.[2] Its Arabic translation would reach a similar readership. Not only in Egypt, but around the world, *The Protocols* continues to evoke associations with the groups summoned in the passage above: military men obsessed with unconventional warfare; second-hand booksellers on city sidewalks; servants or subalterns suspected of purloining letters; otherwise respectable professionals with a secret passion for the esoteric and the occult; the peripheries, the backrooms, and the dark spaces of the social imaginary. What, then, was it doing on the desk of ʿAbbās al-ʿAqqād?

Al-ʿAqqād is best known today for his series of biographies of famous men, his poetry of uneven quality, and his 'salon' that helped socialise a generation of Egyptian journalists and cultural critics. The largely self-educated star of the Egyptian cultural sphere also entertained more recondite interests, among which *The Protocols* stands out for its decidedly anti-intellectual bias. Yet his attraction to this text derived not from any rigid totalitarian ideology – al-ʿAqqād vociferously opposed Nazism and Communism, for example – but from a radically suspicious reading of history as a theatre of hidden plots, 'satanic' groups, 'destructive' sects, 'sick' philosophies, and, above all, 'great men'.[3] Above and beyond the immediate historical context of his writing – for example, the creation of the state of Israel just three years earlier – al-ʿAqqād maintained a penchant for what today would be called *naẓariyyat al-muʾāmara* or 'conspiracy theory'.

Scholarship on conspiracy theory has often been limited to the rhetorical practices of actors in the political field, whether at the centre or along the margins. Historian Richard Hofstatder's investigation into what he termed the 'paranoid style,' to give one famous example, focused largely on texts circulated along the fringes of the American political and religious right.[4] In a more recent study concerning the Arab World, Matthew Gray has called attention to the role played by authoritarian regimes in promoting conspiracy theories and 'conspiracist' discourse in order to demonise opponents, distract from policy failures, and/or mobilise popular support.[5] Yet the interest expressed by al-ʿAqqād in the *The Protocols* indicates that stories of conspiracy may also have currency in the worlds of poets, novelists, literary critics, and *salonniers*. More specifically, the principle motifs of *naẓariyyat al-muʾāmara* – omnipotent secret societies, protagonists overcome by paranoia and suspicion, quotidian itineraries thwarted by uncanny coincidences, dystopian or apocalyptic *denouements*, the hidden interconnectedness of everything – have a significant, while unexamined, presence within modern Arabic literature. This presence is not limited merely to the low-brow thrillers or 'pocket novels' of authors like Maḥmūd Sālim (1931–2013), Nabīl Fārūq (b. 1956), and Aḥmad Khālid Tawfīq (b. 1962). Nor is ʿAbbās al-ʿAqqād an entirely peculiar case. The motifs of conspiracy theory may also be found, in different portions and with varying degrees of attachment, in the novels of Sonallah Ibrahim (Ṣunʿ Allāh Ibrāhīm, b. 1937), Gamal al-Ghitani (Jamāl al-Ghīṭānī, 1945–2015), and Youssef Rakha (Yūsuf Rakhā, b. 1976), the poetry of Amal Dunqul (1940–83), Naguib Surur (Najīb Surūr, 1932–78), and Aḥmad Fuʾād Nijm (1929–2013), and the plays of Ali Ahmad Bakathir (ʿAlī Aḥmad Bā Kāthīr, 1910–69), Tawfiq al-Hakim (Tawfīq al-Ḥakīm, 1898–1987), ʿAlī Sālim (1936–2015), and Saʿd al-Dīn Wahba (1925–97), among others. Across these many texts, conspiracy theory has seldom remained a fixed and univocal phenomenon – at times, it aligns itself with narrow expressions of political committedness, while at others it offers itself as a uniquely rich fountain of imaginative trajectories, counter-cultural currents, and non-ritualised play. Yet it remains coherent and recognisable nonetheless.

This monograph examines some of the diverse uses and meanings of conspiracy theory in the Arabic literature of Egypt, beginning in the mid-twentieth century. It presents a series of interlinked case studies on both canonical and previously neglected authors, in whose work conspiracy – often 'the Conspiracy' (*al-muʾāmara*) writ large – appears as a salient object of concern: a robustly agentive antagonist, a symptom of psychological distress, a lens for interpreting a chaotic universe, a system and a seduction, an obsession of irreducible complexity. Inasmuch as conspiracy theory has been conceived as a mode of *political* discourse, the monograph follows the countless previous studies in the field of Arabic literature that have theorised the ways in which fiction contests, but may also sustain, a dominant political order. This involves, first, situating literary texts within a specific historical context of colonialism, post-colonialism, and the sundry forms of social, economic, and political oppression that have thrived under former and current authoritarian regimes; it implies an encounter with the fraught relationship that has prevailed, particularly in Egypt, between the 'cultural field' and the 'political field'.[6] In addition, investigating the politics of conspiracy literature entails locating the phenomenon in relation to the modes of 'commitment' that have predominated in Egyptian letters, and reconsidering the oppositional stances or ideological labels that have been attached to famous authors.[7] Perhaps most crucially in this vein, we will assess how, in embracing a radically reductionist model of agency, conspiracist texts have so often fallen short of achieving their critical aims.

But if the Plot is politics, politics is also a plot. That is to say: our interest in reading the assembled texts is not simply to show how literature can be political (this may be assumed of most modern Egyptian literature), but how the presumably 'political' – conspiracy theory – can operate in a literary fashion. This book operates under the premise that literature, and literary criticism, are particularly useful for foregrounding the textual and emotive mechanisms that motivate human speech and action more generally. Accordingly, we turn to literary texts to understand conspiracy theory as deriving from a particular *style* of reading and writing – one that is structured by imminently personal and viscerally felt affects such as panic, paranoia, and pleasure, and that constructs its narratives out of circulating bits of folklore, Arabic and world literature, religious discourses, and old/new media forms. To this end, our investigation unfolds in conversation with studies of American literature and public culture, as well as research in anthropology, psychoanalysis, and literary theory, where the cultural and aesthetic dimensions of paranoia and conspiracism have been and continue to be rigorously debated.

Insofar as this book broaches a hitherto unexamined dimension of modern Arabic literature, our concern shall be less with making definitive pronouncements on the meaning or meanings of a given text, than with recognising problem areas, synthesising previously separate lines of enquiry, and registering the ambivalence and complexity of what are highly controversial cultural forms. We seek to understand and question, rather than diagnose or condemn, conspiracy theory. This can only begin with a clearer definition of our central terms.

Definitions

At its simplest, 'conspiracy theory' may be defined as a narrative that reduces politics and history to the machinations of an omnipotent, transhistoric entity, such as Zionism, Freemasonry, the Knights Templar, or the like. The Arabic term – *naẓariyyat al-muʾāmara* – if an obvious translation from the English, is no longer a foreign expression, having attained widespread use and recognition through its circulation in news media and various domains of public culture. Derived expressions such as *taʾāmurī* and *al-taʾāmuriyya*, correspond respectively to the English 'conspiracist' and 'conspiracism', which we will deploy throughout the present book to denote the practice or 'style' of producing the language, tropes, and narrative structures of conspiracy theory. Put differently, we may say that conspiracism is the *langue*, of which a given conspiracy theory or conspiracy narrative is the *parole*.

While many stories involve conspiracies, not all count as conspiracist. The difference, to return to Richard Hofstadter's seminal study, is that the latter militates against 'a gigantic yet subtle machinery of influence', 'demonic forces of almost transcendental power', a 'free, active, demonic agent [who] wills, indeed … manufactures, the mechanism of history himself, or deflects the normal course of history in an evil way'[8]. The narrative's antagonist, if not omnipotent, overshadows nearly every action and event in the universe. Thus, we may say that conspiracism is reductionist in that it *reduces* history to a single agent or agency, often a secret cabal or organisation. Freemasons, for example, adopt this role in works such as *al-Sirr al-Maṣūn fī Shīʿat al-Farmasūn* (The Hidden Secret of the Freemasons Sect) (1909–11), composed by the Lebanese scholar and priest Louis Cheikho (Lawīs Shaykhū) (1859–1927). This was one of a number of anti-masonic tracts composed in Arabic in the late nineteenth century and early twentieth.[9] Cheikho's book places the group behind centuries of regime change and revolutionary upheaval, drawing directly from European polemics that made identical claims. To further support his assertion of secret Masonic hegemony, Cheikho cites a panegyric in Lebanese colloquial Arabic allegedly composed by one 'Ḥ. M.', a proud member of the group. The following two couplets, loosely translated, are illustrative:

> The world over we own great lots, Our society famously hosts many big
>   shots
> We've got rabbis and priests, women and girls, And princes, hajjis, dukes
>   and earls.

We've got kings, and our purses are packed, And we gain every minute 'til
nothing we lack
We aim to ruin presidents, erase every priest, Then crush the Arab shaykhs,
last not least.[10]

In the Arab World, as elsewhere, Freemasonry is not an imaginary group. Until its abolition by authoritarian regimes in the mid-twentieth century, known members included such luminaries as the littérateur Jūrjī Zīdān (1861–1914), the nationalist leader Saad Zaghloul (Saʿd Zaghlūl) (1859–1927), and the Islamic reformer Jamāl al-Dīn al-Afghānī (1838–97).[11] Undoubtedly, by nature of their secrecy, various masonic lodges may have been involved in intrigue and conspiracy. But to attribute the major events of politics and history to the carefully calculated plots of one small group – and, moreover, to ascribe to Freemasons ideologies of violence and moral depravity – is what distinguishes conspiracism as a mode of criticism and representation.

As distinctive as the *quality* of the agency attributed to the Conspiracy are the various *means* through which this agency is supposed to be exercised. Conspiracist discourse is littered with references to the 'subtle', 'twisted', 'unconventional', or 'new' tactics deployed by the enemy. One hears not only of 'fourth-generation warfare' and top-secret 'geophysical weapons', but of narcotics, anonymous love songs, everyday consumer products, and 'rumours' as vectors of organised and deliberate campaigns for leading astray the masses or manipulating events.[12] In 'al-Tanẓīm al-Sirrī' (The Secret Organisation) (1984), a short story by Naguib Mahfouz (Najīb Maḥfūẓ) (1911–2006), the members of a destructive political cult are ordered to casually recite a seemingly innocent 'new kind of love song' in public places, with the aim of subtly indoctrinating passersby with the general theme and thrust of their ideology.[13] A variation on this theme has been examined by Ted Swedenburg in his brilliant study on the reception of Danna International, the Israeli pop singer, in Egypt.[14] While popular among students in the 1990s, this 'vulgar' music was perceived by at least one detractor as a tool through which the 'Masonic-Jewish conspiracy' seeks to 'penetrate' and 'master' Egyptian youth. This sort of accusation, in Swedenburg's analysis, can be understood in terms of the displacement of political conflicts and anxieties – principally, the looming threat, and history, of Israeli invasion – on to the realm of culture, sexuality, and ethnicity.

For some, the trope of 'unconventional means' has stirred a literary resonance. In the extended introduction to his translation of *The Protocols of the Wise Men of Zion*, Muḥammad Khalīfa al-Tūnisī perceives a resemblance between the book and *Ḥiyal al-Luṣūṣ* (The Tricks of Thieves) of al-Jāḥiẓ (775–868).[15] The transmitter of *The Protocols*, al-Tunisi argues, 'is like al-Jāḥiẓ, who uncovered the tricks (*ḥiyal*) of those thieves and disclosed them to the people, the police, and the government out of a desire to protect lives, honor, and wealth'.[16] Conspiracy theory, it may be said, contains something of the premodern Arabic tradition of trickster literature, or *adab al-muḥtālīn*: the voyeuristic pleasure of uncovering secrets, the apprehension of criminals, the picaresque world of beggars, magicians, and parasites. In a similar vein, the author of *al-Māsūniyya fī al-ʿArāʾ* (Freemasonry in the Open) (1972), a still widely circulated polemic on Freemasons, felt it suitable to depart from the unadorned expository form in which he had composed most of his book and narrate one chapter 'in the style of the *Maqāmāt* of al-Ḥarīrī' – a work full of tricks and tricksters.[17] But these are false comparisons. For the stories of al-Jāḥiẓ and al-Ḥarīrī concerned the *ḥiyal* of impoverished, often hapless types who, if sometimes organised in gangs or guilds, seldom presented an existential threat to society or the dominant political order. Conspiracy theory, by contrast, imagines the dirty tricks of the enemy to have an impact on society that is immediate, wide-ranging, and total – the brainwashing of the masses, the mental enslavement of consumers, the mechanisation of everyday life. If the antagonist of conspiracy theory derives from a literary archetype, it would be the Devil rather than the trickster. It is the conflation of these two types that produces the black-and-white moral universe of the conspiracy theorist.[18]

Quite frequently, narratives of conspiracy overlap with apocalyptic literature, or what in the Arabic Islamic tradition has been known by such terms as *al-fitan*, *al-malāḥim*, and *ashriṭat al-sāʿa*. This is most evident in the trope of eschatological climax, a global catastrophe represented as the Conspiracy's ultimate goal. But the apocalyptic as a genre concerns more than just the end of the world. In his classic study of Christian and Jewish apocalyptic literature, Collins (1979) outlines several other generic features that we may also recognise in conspiracy theories: '*Visions*' and '*Epiphanies*' concerning hidden truths; an '*Otherworldly Journey*', such as a visit to heaven or hell, conducted by the protagonist; a focus on the '*Disposition of the Recipient*' of a secret/sacred revelation, that is, his severe emotional or psychological disturbance; and a recounting of '*Primordial events*, which have a paradigmatic significance for the remainder of history', such as Satan's falling out with God.[19] Conversely, the trope of a grand international Conspiracy has been recognised as a regular feature of modern Muslim apocalyptic texts, as in two recent books on the subject by David Cook and Jean-Pierre Filiu.[20]

The literary texts presented in this monograph, while not 'apocalyptic' as understood in these previous works, often trade in apocalyptic imagery and suspense. The relationship between narratives of apocalypse and conspiracy may be understood as a form of generic overlap, intertexuality, or chronotopic affinity. We may also understand this relationship as deriving from a certain logic: just as the conspiracy theorist perceives himself to be at the centre of the world's attention, so does the apocalyptic visionary imagine himself to occupy a privileged position in human history. The distinction that has sometimes been drawn between the apocalyptic as 'premodern', religious genre and conspiracy theory as a 'modern', secular genre seems to us to be largely overstated, given that the themes, anxieties, and imagery of each almost always interpercolate with those of the other.

One more key feature of conspiracist literature that deserves some elaboration is its seemingly peculiar mode of discovery and interpretation. Anthropologist Kathleen Stewart provides this evocative description:

> Conspiracy theory is a skeptical, paranoid, obsessive practice of scanning for signs and sifting through bits of evidence for the missing link. Enter the world of conspiracy theory (as we all do and must) and you enter the world of global systems with missing details. This is a world of hopelessly arcane, obscurantist systems that are expert at leaving a paper trail that cannot track them. The moment of seduction is the moment when the puzzle is almost solved but there is always something more you need, the missing piece. Conspiracy theory dreams of an end point, an ur-text, a pure and stable past, but it never gets there because it is always pushing the REAL to the outer edge of the horizon – a carrot to struggle toward.[21]

The author or protagonist of conspiracy theory may find evidence virtually everywhere, and for this reason, his journey never quite ends. He will fixate as much on the esoteric – the insignia of secret societies, perverse anagrams, or mathematical puzzles – as he will on the everyday – newspaper headlines, coffee grounds, the casual grin of a suspect lover – in which he detects uncanny patterns, coincidences, and intentions. In this sense, conspiracy theory shares much with the premodern Arabic art of *firāsa* or 'physiognomy' – the divination of interior traits and intentions, as well as future events, through an especially close reading of surfaces, tracks, or trails.

Cast in a different light, the conspiracy theorist's quest for knowledge acquires an uncanny resemblance to the scholar's own line of work. Significant critical attention has been given to the commonalities between the interpretive practices of conspiracism and some of the great hermeneutic projects of modernity (psychoanalysis, critical theory, assorted structuralisms), most remarkably by some of the major protagonists of these very projects. Freud, for example, in his seminal analysis of the 'paranoid' Dr Daniel Schreber, remarked on a 'striking similarity' between Schreber's 'delusions' and his own psychoanalysis.[22] Both, it could be said, proceeded from a radical suspicion in the dark, occult forces that stand behind the illusion of surfaces; both conceived of these occult forces, whether of the unconscious in Freud's case or the conspiracy of deities and cosmic rays with Schreber, as elaborate, irreducible, and totalising structures from whose 'grammar' there was no escape; and both held faith, with airs of a messianic, apocalyptic heroism, that the exposure of these deep or hidden structures would result in the eventual, if not immediate, resolution of worldly problems in a decidedly magical realignment of the order of things.[23] Freud's remarks seem to have been largely ironic, but more recent scholarship has taken these similarities seriously, and drawn divergent conclusions.

One line of argument, represented by Fredric Jameson, evaluates the similarities between conspiracism and critical theory in a positive sense in order to recuperate the former from its long association with pathology or the criminal fringe of society. In an oft-cited passage in his *Postmodernism, Or, The Cultural Logic of Late Capitalism* (1991), Jameson argues that conspiracy theory (and its garish narrative manifestations) must be seen as a degraded attempt – through the figuration of advanced technology – to think the impossible totality of the contemporary world system. It is in terms of that enormous and threatening, yet only dimly perceivable, other reality of economic and social institutions that, in my opinion, the postmodern sublime can alone be adequately theorized.[24]

In other words, conspiracy theory has the advantage of rendering visible – albeit in an exaggerated, figurative, or 'degraded' way – pervasive structures of oppression and control that are all too real. Traditional humanistic scholarship may still be preferable, but it is not of an entirely separate order.

A second line of argument views the overlap between conspiracism and scholarly interpretive practices in decidedly negative terms, and is represented in the works of Umberto Eco, Eve Sedgwick, Rita Felski, and Bruno Latour, among many others. For Eco, what is problematic is what he calls 'overinterpretation', or the attribution of meanings and intentions to a literary text that it cannot possibly bear.[25] Sedgwick and Felski speak more broadly of the humanities and social sciences, whose explanatory powers, they argue, have been severely curtailed by the dominance of an interpretive practice they call, respectively, 'paranoia' and 'suspicion'.[26] These terms are not intended to be pejorative, but are used to call attention to the veritably emotive or affective dimensions of critical practice, which we will explore in more detail below. Latour, writing about the social sciences, draws a distinction between what he calls the 'sociology of the social' and his own 'sociology of associations', also known as Actor-Network-Theory. The former, much like conspiracy theory, too often produces reductionist accounts of human and non-human actors as subservient to some singular, and hidden, system of control. Latour does not deny that human action is 'overtaken' by strange and often elusive forces – this is indeed a central tenet of his sociology. Rather, what he objects to is the '*non sequitur*' that because human action is overtaken by other agencies, these agencies must necessarily be monolithic, immutable, and malicious.[27] The alternative theory he elucidates resonates with a much broader 'post-human' turn in the humanities and social sciences, which seeks to expand, rather than to reduce, the numbers and kinds of agencies we admit to our accounts of history and human action.

It is of course necessary to distinguish between what we may call 'pure' conspiracy theory – extreme, reductive, and grotesque polemics like *The Protocols* – and the nuanced, humanistic, and fact-driven investigations of mainstream social science. But that these represent two points along a common continuum of critical interpretive practices is an insight shared by both sides of the preceding debate. It is an insight, moreover, that will concern us throughout this book, as we investigate critical projects and modes of literary commitment that have not previously been associated with conspiracy theory. Our interest will not be in judging a given text based on its political message, or dismissing as conspiracist what could otherwise be read as a complex literary experiment, but to understand the indebtedness of even the most canonical and 'high-brow' literary and political discourses to common tropological templates and emotive mechanisms.

At last, the preceding points may be combined in order to offer a more complete, if still flexible, definition of conspiracy theory. We will deem as 'conspiracist' a text that exhibits these features:

(1) *A reductionist theory of agency.* This finds expression not only in the central motif of the robustly agentive Conspiracy – and, as an extension, in the uniquely effective 'means' through which the Conspiracy's agenda is executed – but also, as a corollary, in the deprivation of other actors from any degree of autonomy, intentionality, or cognition. Thus, the 'masses', the audience, and sometimes the brow-beaten protagonist himself are perceived as having fallen under the sway of a nefarious puppet-master, a false consciousness, a parasitic infestation, or a demonic possession, and acquire attributes that are markedly, and often grotesquely, animal, robotic, or alien. This gives rise to an array of character types that include the people-as-herd, the consumer-cum-slave, the 'programmed' ideologue, and the zombie.

(2) *Apocalyptic themes.* This may be expressed in a number of images borrowed from eschatological literature, such as the global catastrophe, millenialist panic, primordial events, and the inversion of the ideal social or political order. The apocalyptic also concerns the chronotopicity of the narrative. In terms of place, the conspiracist story nearly always unfolds in an urban setting – invariably in our texts, in Cairo, *maṣr*, 'the Mother

of the World' – and deviates into a social or cosmological 'underground' or 'otherworldly' journey. In terms of time, the story unfolds through the rush of the end times, the confusion of the epistemic rupture, or the ambient sense of things-coming-to-a-head. Even in its putatively secular variants, the conspiracy theory hosts a protagonist, helper, or author imbued with the foresight, acumen, and psychological distress of the prophet or visionary.

(3) *Interpretive hubris.* The author (or hero) is a reader, and everything is a text. More specifically, the author (or hero) is drawn into a practice of reading that may be variously referred to as 'paranoia', 'suspicion', or 'overinterpretation'. As a reader, he fetishises the binaries of manifest (*al-ẓāhir*) and latent (*al-bāṭin*), surface and depth, revealed and hidden. He presupposes, and is driven to find and reveal to a sceptical public, connections between apparently disparate phenomena. In this way, he would appear to be a model reader or analyst, but what he finds is always the same thing: malice, intent, design; the Conspiracy. Revelation, in and of itself, is supposed to work magic: the secret is 'exposed', and the system will collapse, unravel, internally deconstruct.

There are, in addition, a number of ancillary themes that may assert themselves. Quite a few of the narratives we will examine make liberal use of obscene or offensive language. This tactic may ultimately derive from the conspiracist's belief in the magical power of words, although the matter surely warrants more examination than we will be able to afford it here. To the character types listed above, we may add that of the 'double' or 'doppelganger', who makes his appearance felt most forcefully in the texts of Naguib Surur, Gamal al-Ghitani, and Mohammad Rabie (Muḥammad Rabīᶜ, b. 1978), but who may likely be detected in more subdued form in all the works presented in this monograph.[28] Finally and rather curiously, it became apparent to us upon completion of this monograph's first draft that a significant number of the texts in our corpus are examples of what has been called 'gossip literature'.[29] Specifically, works by Ali Ahmad Bakathir, Naguib Surur, Gamal al-Ghitani, and Youssef Rakha were composed, at least in part, as vengeful polemics against particular members of Egypt's literary field, often quite narrowly construed as members of the author's family or workplace. (Even works that do not quite fit this mould, such as Sonallah Ibrahim's *al-Lajna* (1981); *The Committee* (trans. 2001) and the novels of Mohammad Rabie and Ahmed Naji (Aḥmad Nājī) (b. 1985) contain pointed words against predecessors, peers, or trends in the culture industry). At the very least, this aspect of conspiracist literature serves to remind us that although these stories project their dramas on to the sublime realm of the political, or cast themselves quite broadly as conflicts of grand civilisational proportions, their point of departure may be located in the more intimate world of the home, the office, the stage, the barracks, the café, or the salon.

The above criteria may be used as a flexible heuristic for distinguishing conspiracy theory from discourses or narrative practices with which it may otherwise be confused: dystopian fiction such as the work of Franz Kafka or George Orwell; psychological thrillers such as *An Takūn ᶜAbbās al-ᶜAbd* (2003) (*Being Abbas el Abd*) (trans. 2009) by Aḥmad al-ᶜĀyidī (b. 1974); narratives of schizophrenia such as *Awrāq al-Narjis* (2002) (*Leaves of Narcissus*) (trans. 2006) by Sumayya Ramaḍān (b. 1951); tales of small village intrigue and nosey neighbors, as in *Laylat ᶜUrs* (2002) (*Wedding Night*) (trans. 2006) by Yūsuf Abū Rayya (1955–2009). We may also set aside novels centred on palace intrigue, such as *Malik min Shuᶜāᶜ* (*King of Light*) (1945) by ᶜĀdil Kāmil (1916–2005) or *Natāʾij al-Aḥwāl fī al-Aqwāl wa-al-Afᶜāl* (The Results of Circumstances in Words and Deeds) (1887) by ᶜĀʾisha al-Taymūriyya (1840–1902), for the same reason that we dismissed the *Maqāmat* and medieval trickster literature above. although they involve conspiracies, these are quite narrowly conceived as discrete acts of assassination, backbiting, gossip, or betrayal within a limited time frame and with little impact beyond the individual criminals and victims so involved. Although, of course, we shall not insist on these distinctions overmuch, as each of these genres may be engaged to cast light on each of the others at various points in our investigation.

A separate issue concerns the internal diversity of conspiracist narratives. First, it bears pointing out that only a few of the literary texts under consideration exhibit all of the aspects of conspiracy theory in its 'pure' form. Hofstatder reminds us that there are 'highbrow, lowbrow and middlebrow paranoids';[30] to borrow a distinction proposed by Edward Said in his *Orientalism*, we may say that there are 'latent' and 'manifest' forms of conspiracism.[31] Rita Felski makes a useful distinction between four forms of 'suspicion' – 'philosophical', 'literary', 'vernacular', and 'professional' – and traces a history for each, while insisting that they all partake of common logic or mood of interpretation.[32] There are, as we will explore in Chapter 5, 'naive' and 'sentimental' forms of conspiracy theory. Finally, it may be objected that there are, on the one hand, conspiracy theories in politics, and, on the other, conspiracy theories in literature. However, this distinction is not as significant as it may at first seem, given that 'fiction' in Egypt has so often been used as a vehicle for delving into obscured truths of the political field, and that, as we seek to assert through this book, political discourse is shaped according to many of the same motives and mechanisms as literature.

The defining elements of conspiracy theory as listed above may manifest themselves as simple tropes, separated and combined at random by any given author. But most often, they hold together with a consistency that is remarkable enough to warrant investigation into the phenomenon as such. Specifically, we will contend that conspiracism constitutes a coherent and recognisable 'style' of expression, the motives and implications of which we will examine in the next section.

Understanding Conspiracism

> Ṭīfūn: (Turning to the audience) Understand this, O people. It is a conspiracy! It is trickery! Shall we let them conspire against your beloved king? Will you let them connive against your blessed authority? Speak your word! Speak your word!
>
> …
>
> Tūt: Hold on there, Ṭīfūn! Take it easy! Do not rouse people with such words. Conspiracy and connivery have a clear image in your head, because you know them best! It's no wonder, then, that you accuse others of committing them.
>
> Tawfiq al-Hakim, *Īzīs* (Isis), 1995 [1955][33]

How and why does conspiracism emerge? For those who accept the notion of a global, history-hopping conspiracy of men as the driving force in world affairs, conspiracy theory needs no explanation at all: it is simply an exposition of facts. One may also object that, before proceeding with an attempt to elaborate a discourse on conspiracy theory, we should be careful to recognise the extent to which the phenomenon is always already a social construct, the result of an act of epistemological violence that creates or exaggerates a problem that was merely incipient or not previously there.[34] Yet there has been sufficient scholarly interest, in both Arabic and English, in locating the reasons behind conspiracism that the question we pose here is surely not misguided.

Perhaps the most common explanation given for the emergence of conspiracy theory is the appeal to historical and political context. Gray (2010) has shown, for example, how the long history of European and American imperialism in Arab countries – in essence, a history of conspiracies – has made conspiracy theorising a quite reasonable, if not always valid, mode of popular criticism. In Egypt, the increasing involvement of the security services in public and political life since the 1950s has created a situation where even ordinary citizens may become 'suspicious of everything, even the walls and tables', to quote a character in *al-Karnak* (1974), a novel by Naguib Mahfouz that still resonates today.[35] In such a context, conspiracy theory and paranoia may operate as a ubiquitous, even necessary means of self-preservation. In Mohammad Rabie's *ʿĀm al-Tinnīn* (The Year of the Dragon) (2012), a novel we will return to in Chapter 5, an official in Egypt's security establishment complains that it is impossible to brainwash Egyptian intellectuals, because they are already 'chronically paranoid' that someone is trying to brainwash them:

> [The Egyptian intellectual] considers everything to be an attack on him personally, a scheme designed to control him. The opening of a new metro line in al-ʿAbbāsiyya: a conspiracy against old buildings and libraries! The construction of a new building in the area of the Citadel: a conspiracy against Ṣalāḥ al-Dīn! Workers repairing the road: a conspiracy against the flow of traffic, and therefore a conspiracy against the psychological state of all Cairenes! Well, I'll admit that one really is a conspiracy. I admit they sometimes realize the truth of the matter as soon as the evidence presents itself.[36]

The official's observation is obviously humorous, but it illustrates an important point – namely, that the hyper-vigilance of the conspiracy theorist protects him in a city where malicious plots are woven into the fabric of everyday existence. Similarly, Marcus et. al. (1999) have explored how paranoia operates 'within reason' in view of reigning political and social configurations at the turn of the millennium. 'Reason' here does not necessarily mean freedom from delusion, but a mode of thinking that accords with the epistemological and ontological norms of the moment and, sometimes, the available evidence as well.

While the political or historical explanation for conspiracism is certainly valid, it does little to account for the fact that conspiracy theories of a remarkably similar kind can be found in strikingly different contexts. This is evident in the profusion of studies on paranoia and conspiracy in North American and European literatures – discursive realms that surely exhibit considerable differences from those of the Middle East.[37] It is likewise apparent that the proliferation of conspiracy theorising cannot be limited to a single historical period or paradigm. Pagán's *Conspiracy Theory in Latin Literature* (2012) is part of a recent turn against a dominant trend in scholarship that has explained conspiracy theory 'as merely the product of particular conditions unique to the time period and culture under consideration'.[38] This is not to claim that conspiracism is immutable and transhistorical, only that the historical explanation risks becoming parochial and reductionist.

A second manner of explanation is psychological. Hofstadter, although not a psychologist, relies on psychological terms when characterising conspiracism as the 'paranoid style'. Perhaps his most important observation in this respect is that the paranoiac's enemy – the grand Conspiracy – 'seems to be on many counts a *projection* of the self' (1996: 32; my emphasis). Unfortunately, Hofstadter does not pursue this important insight much further, going only so far as to show how some conspiracy theorists have attempted to imitate their enemy in certain aspects, such as the aesthetics of secret rituals, the obsession with evidence, and the use of subversive tactics.

'Projection' plays a much more significant role in Freud's 'Psychoanalytic Notes upon an Autobiographical Account of a Case of Paranoia (*Dementia Paranoides*)' (1996 [1911]), which analyses the published memoirs of the German judge Daniel Paul Schreber, *Denkwürdigkeiten eines Nervenkranken* (1903), and has since become a reference point for subsequent works on paranoia and conspiracism.[39] In speaking of Schreber's fears of conspiracy, Freud proposes what he considers the following 'simple formula':

> It appears that the person to whom the delusion ascribes so much power and influence, in whose hands all the threads of the conspiracy converge,

is either, if he is definitely named, identical with some one who played an equally important part in the patient's emotional life before his illness, or else is easily recognizable as a substitute for him. The intensity of the emotion is *projected outwards* in the shape of external power, while its quality is changed into the opposite. The person who is now hated and feared as a persecutor was at one time loved and honoured. The main purpose of the persecution constructed by the patient's delusion is to serve as a justification for the change in his emotional attitude. (Freud 1996 [1911]: 116; my emphasis)

Dr Schreber, according to Freud, was projecting emotions he felt for his psychiatrist – and at a further remove, for his father – on to the figure of a malicious God bent on his personal destruction. The intensity of his love for his psychiatrist, or father, is distorted into an equally intense fear of a divine conspiracy.

A related argument has been articulated by Timothy Melley (2000) in his study of paranoid 'conspiracy narratives' in post-war North American novels.[40] Authors as diverse as Margaret Atwood, William S. Burroughs, Joseph Heller, and Thomas Pynchon – among countless others – have woven narratives around embattled protagonists who sense that they have lost all control over their lives to nebulous, all-powerful organisations. At the root of all these conspiracy narratives, Melley argues, is a common set of anxieties he calls 'agency panic': 'intense anxiety about an apparent loss of autonomy or self-control – the conviction that one's actions are being controlled by someone else, that one has been "constructed" by powerful external agents' (12). Often, this panic manifests itself in the conviction that other people, even society at large, have become 'brainwashed' or hypnotised hordes, acting out the agenda of some hidden force. This panic about the hollowed-out agency of others, as Melley notes, just as often expresses itself as an individual's fear about the loss of his own self-autonomy.

In this first sense of 'agency panic', the anxieties centre on the loss of agency. Melley adds a 'second sense', in which the organisations responsible for this deprivation are themselves imagined as robustly agentive:

In moments of agency panic, individuals tend to attribute to these systems [or organisations] the qualities of motive, agency, and individuality they

> suspect have been depleted from themselves or others around them. Thus, agency panic not only dramatizes doubt about the efficacy of individual human action, it also induces a *postmodern transference* in which social regulation seems to be the intentional product of a single consciousness or monolithic 'will'. (Melley 2000: 13; italics in the original)

The image of the conspiracy's specific might and muster, in other words, is drawn directly from the detritus of the individual's lost sense of control. Although he speaks In terms of 'attribution' and 'postmodern transference', Melley is here offering a reinterpretation of what Hofstadter and Freud spoke of in terms of 'projection'. Instead of a specific individual or overbearing psychiatrist, however, the object of projection in this case is a deeply cherished, if deeply problematic, ideal of individual agency.

In their focus on projection, Hofstadter, Freud, and Melley are concerned primarily with accounting for the hyperbolic image of power and control that so distinguishes conspiracy theories. But the psychological approach has also been useful in understanding the modes of reading and interpretation that sustain conspiracism. Mark Fenster, for example, characterises conspiracy theory as 'a kind of manic will to seek rather than to know' – an interpretive quest that becomes 'akin to the Lacanian notion of desire which requires that its ultimate fulfillment will be continually deferred'.[41] In this sense, the practice is as much about pleasure as it is paranoia. Eve Sedgwick also appeals to affective processes when commenting on what she terms 'the present paranoid consensus' in the humanities.[42] Drawing on the work of affect theorists Melanie Klein and Silvan Tomkins, Sedgwick describes certain reading practices as 'paranoid' not because they are delusional, but because they are structured according to essentially affective processes like 'anticipation', 'mimesis', and the forestalling of pain. Rita Felski, writing more specifically about literary criticism, prefers to characterise such reading practices as 'suspicion'. A central aim of her recent book, *The Limits of Critique* (2015), is to show how emotions and affects play an important role in the production of literary critical knowledge. In doing so, she demonstrates how modern practices of criticism, far from the neutral and disinterested exercises in reason that they are thought to be, are implicated in some of the same anxieties and suspicions as conspiracy theory.

It is important to note that, although the above scholars employ terms borrowed from clinical psychology or psychoanalysis, they are not, with the exception of Freud, speaking about diseases. Sedgwick theorises paranoia as one among other 'critical *practices*, not as theoretical ideologies (and certainly not as stable personality types of critics), but as changing and heterogeneous relational stances'.[43] Similarly, Felski theorises suspicion as a 'critical mood': 'an overall atmosphere or climate that causes the world to come into view in a certain way'.[44] And although Hofstadter has rightly been criticised for 'pathologizing' conspiracy theory,[45] he made an important qualification in stating that his object of investigation was a '*style* … much as a historian of art might speak of the baroque or the mannerist style'.[46] Hofstadter did not develop this point, but it is crucial. Style, which we understand here as akin to Sedgwick's 'practice' and Felski's 'critical mood', is a concept that draws attention to conspiracism's sometimes intense, sometimes fleeting hold on its practitioner. Style, as we conceive it here, is not an ideology or a pathology into which the author of a conspiracy theory is straight-jacketed; neither is it an opinion that he freely adopts or discards. Rather, like an aesthetic trend or professional practice, it is something he is called into, inhabits, modifies, and is modified by.

'Style' draws our attention back to aesthetics, and can help us elucidate some of the literary structures and functions of conspiracism. As a style, conspiracy theory cuts across genres, both poetry and prose, fiction and nonfiction. As a style, conspiracy theory is extremely contagious, or what in literary terms we would call mimetic or intertextual. Certainly, intertextuality is a feature of all texts, but the conspiracy theorist takes this to an extreme degree, not only to the extent that he rummages through archives and scans every surface for a possible clue, but also inasmuch as he 'styles' himself after other famous conspiracist personas. Thus, Naguib Surur, who we will read in Chapter 2, performs a 'Naguib Surur' that fashions himself in the image of heroic sceptics or paranoiacs like Hamlet, Don Quixote, and Abū al-ᶜAlāʾ al-Maᶜarrī. Finally, style as a critical concept – as, for example, in Dick Hebdige's seminal work on subcultures (2007 [1979]) – foregrounds the thematic 'homologies' that accrue between a performer's language, attitudes, and daily habits. A conspiracy theory, in this sense, is not merely a textual product but constitutes one aspect of an individual's regular rituals of self-presentation.

In the chapters that follow, conspiracy theory appears not only as a style, but as a rhetoric, a set of cliches, a rumour, a theatrical genre, a catechism, a game of seduction, a joke, and more. Conspiracy theory, in short, can take many forms and serve divergent functions, and it is this aesthetic variety, as well as its political ambivalence, that we seek to emphasise. We proceed with an awareness that conspiracism has often seduced a paranoid, alarmist, and reductionist explanation of its motives and effects – in other words, a sort of conspiracy theory of conspiracy theory. Such an approach risks devolving into a manner of evaluative critique that trades humanistic enquiry for policy prescriptions, articulated in a language of 'danger' and 'threat'.[47] This becomes all the more problematic when the object of analysis shifts from individual authors to entire peoples and regions. Instead, we will consider conspiracy theory in/as literature, shifting the analysis to texts – which can be traced, interpreted, contextualised, and even enjoyed – rather than an individual or population to be disciplined.

Scope and Division of Chapters

> For a secret to spread requires an interesting story, an event of importance, a mystery or something abnormal or terrible to have happened … [One] example is the scheming of kings (followed closely by the great and the powerful) against enemies and their closet passions and secret intrigues. The masses, you see, are envious of kings, who loom like a darkening sky above them. Their eyes are raised up to them, their hearts are in thrall to them and their hopes and their fears are directed towards them.
>
> Al-Jāḥiẓ, 'Kitāb Kitmān al-Sirr wa-Ḥifẓ al-Lisān'[48]

Where should a study of conspiracy in Arabic literature begin? Arguably, many of the anxieties, motifs, and practices that constitute conspiracism are of a perennial nature. They may be detected, for example, in these remarks by al-Jāḥiẓ, who provides what we may regard as a psychological explanation for the popularity and persistence of conspiracy stories among 'the masses'. We may observe, too, that some of al-Jāḥiẓ's own writings have the feel of conspiracy theory – not the '*Ḥiyal al-Luṣūṣ*' referenced above, but his polemics against the mysterious group of *agents provocateurs* he called *al-nābita*.[49]

While these are tempting analogies, the relation between these texts and the modern Arabic literature of Egypt is tentative at best. In the event, we have chosen to limit our study to literary texts produced from the mid-twentieth century to the present. This is not to imply that conspiracy theory began, for example, with the Free Officers coup in 1952. Future studies may wish to consider the extent to which the conspiracism we analyse here owes much to the confluence of many styles and discourses, both literary and political, of contiguous time periods in Egypt: the anti-Masonic tracts of the late nineteenth century and early twentieth; the long and storied European Orientalist obsession with Islamic 'heretical' groups;[50] earlier Arabic apocalyptic and heresiographical works; the books and many articles by historian Muḥammad ʿAbd Allāh ʿInān (1898–1986) on 'secret societies' and 'political conspiracies';[51] the occult sciences in both popular and elite manifestations; histories of state as well as vernacular technologies of surveillance; and the fantasies of fetishes cultivated by the unseen officers behind them.[52] While many of these strands of conspiracist practice will warrant some mention in the chapters that follow, it bears pointing out that this book does not pretend to present an exhaustive account of all the significant engagements with conspiracism in modern Egyptian literature. Difficult choices have been made about which works to include.[53] The long and rich histories of Egyptian cinema and political cartoons – two especially significant domains of conspiracist expression – constitute an unfortunate lacuna in our study, to say nothing of the sundry forms of conspiracy theory present in public culture at large. However, narrowing our scope to the handful of authors assembled here will allow us to more accurately trace the connections and commonalities that draw their texts together, and to present a more focused, contextually grounded account of their conspiracist themes.

It will be noted that all of the authors examined in the following chapters, with one notable exception, are men. The omission of women from a study of conspiracy literature is unfortunate; on the other hand, this is no omission, but a consequence of the genre itself: as a discourse on agency and gender, conspiracism nearly always adopts a masculinist, or at least male-centric, view of the world. By this it is meant that the conspiracy theorist perceives agency in essentially gendered terms as coextensive with masculinity or manhood, and vice versa: to be a man is to have agency, to act according to one's own will. On the other end of this equation, women and non-normative genders and sexual orientations are perceived as agency-draining forces, or as icons, indexes, or symbols of the draining of free will and rationality from the individual or society at large. There is certainly much more import to the scarcity of women authors of conspiracy literature, and we will have occasion to discuss the matter further in several of our texts, most especially in Chapter 4. For now, it is sufficient to point out that the exception proves the rule: in the Epilogue, we shall examine a work by Radwa Ashour (Raḍwā ʿĀshūr, 1946–2014) who, although advocating for what she calls 'conspiracy theory', articulates an understanding of the practice that is far removed from what we have outlined above.

And why Egypt? In part, the decision to limit ourselves to one national context – or, yet more specifically, to famous, if not always canonical, male authors involved in the Cairo-centric culture industry – is a methodological one, intended so as to avoid the broad regional generalisations so common in previous approaches to the conspiracy theory. Moreover, it is not our intent to imply that there is something 'peculiar' or 'deviant' about Egyptian conspiracism – as many of the above references indicate, this is a much broader Arab and world phenomenon. Yet there is no use glossing over the specific meanings and functions that conspiracy theory has accumulated in an Egyptian context, at the very least because the texts we consider here are not simply copies or derivatives of conspiracist fiction produced elsewhere. Perhaps, in addition to the texts and histories surveyed above, there is much about the spatial-semiotic dynamics of the city of Cairo itself that compels some of its more imaginative readerly subjects to overinterpret: a disorienting sign-scape of consumerist interpolations, civilisations hailings, and kitsch; sprawling and spontaneous neighbourhoods and architecture; technologies of surveillance new and old; the rot and rumour of the Deep State; secret societies everywhere, or society as a secret. In any event, the persistence, pervasiveness, and variety of literary engagements with conspiracy in Egypt are enough, in our opinion, to warrant the present focus.

Chapter 1 traces the emergence of a conspiracist style in the rhetoric of state actors during the early revolutionary period (1952–6), and the subsequent appropriations of this style in the dramatic works of two playwrights: Ali Ahmad Bakathir (1910–69) and Yusuf Idris (Yūsuf Idrīs) (1927–91). At the same time that politicians like Gamal Abdel Nasser, Anwar Sadat, and Salah Salem expounded in repeated radio addresses and public speeches on the dangers of hidden plots, fifth columns, and malicious rumours, these themes featured prominently in Cairo's theatres, where they found elaboration, support, scepticism and ridicule in varying degrees. We will be concerned to show not merely how conspiracist tropes circulated between the closely intertwined fields of politics and culture, but how modern stage theatre, in its arrangement of actors and audience, accords with the representational structure of conspiracism. Comparing the plays of Bakathir and Idris, we will speculate on the relationship between form and ideology: namely, the extent to which Bakathir's endorsement of reigning conspiracy theories mimicked his commitment to a rigidly classical model of drama, and, conversely, the extent to which Idris's departure from dramatic norms accorded with his departure from the regime's conspiracist rhetoric.

In Chapter 2, we analyse the notorious underground poems of Naguib Surur (1932–78), perhaps the most paradigmatic conspiracist figure in modern Egyptian literature. Surur's *Kuss-ummiyyāt* are a profanity-laced invective against Egypt's cultural establishment, as well as friends and family members, whom he perceived as complicit in a vast Zionist-Masonic plot against him. Although never formally published, these poems remain popular today, with a significance for both the centre and the margins of Egyptian literary life that has yet to be examined. Because of the poems' autobiographical nature, they present a particular challenge for the reader: How can one analyse the conspiracist enthusiasms of the poet without reducing them to the highly publicised tragedy of Surur's mental illness? While locating the *Kuss-ummiyyāt* in relation to their author's personal history, we place greater emphasis on reconstructing the literary intertexts through which they emerged, and the interpretive habits that organised them. In particular, we show how the author 'styled' himself after famous radical sceptics – or, alternatively, paranoiacs – in literature, such as Hamlet, Don Quixote, and Abū al-ʿAlāʾ al-Maʿarrī, while developing a practice of reading premised on a supreme distrust of appearances.

The remaining chapters consider contemporary or recently deceased authors, each writing at a different stage of his career. Chapter 3 performs a critical re-reading of Sonallah Ibrahim's (b. 1937) modern classic, *al-Lajna*

(The Committee). Ibrahim's protagonist has often been celebrated as an intrepid, if tragic, exposer and analyst of the hidden patterns of American economic and political hegemony in Egypt and throughout the world. Complicating this reading, we assess the extent to which the novel's understanding of this hegemony, and the truth claims it presents concerning the plots of ancient Israelites, transnational corporations, and political elites, are implicated in the reductionist logic of conspiracy theory. We will examine the protagonist's adaptation of literary archetypes from detective fiction, as well as his reliance on metaphors of surface and depth, as fundamental in shaping his suspicious view of world politics.

Chapter 4 investigates a *roman à clef* by Gamal al-Ghitani (1945–2015), *Ḥikāyāt al-Khabīʾa* (Tales of the Treasure Trove) (2002), which replays the real-world feud between the author and then-Minister of Culture Farouk Hosni (Fārūq Ḥusnī). The novel dramatises this feud by deploying the usual tropes of the conspiracist style: cryptic signs that elicit interpretive fever; millennialist angst; and an effeminate and feminising conspiracy of international proportions. However, we argue, 'paranoia' here involves more than the usual emotional shades of fear and loathing. Rather, certain characters in the novel are drawn towards their enemy through a game of seduction or *fitna*, where passion and pleasure form the emotional structure of conspiracist fantasy. Refiguring conspiracism as *fitna* will help us understand both the intensity, and sudden reversal, of conflicts and controversies across the spheres of culture and politics.

Finally, Chapter 5 focuses on three novels that ironically appropriate the themes and images of conspiracy theory to varying aesthetic, ethical, and (post-)political ends. The central question we will address is whether irony subverts, or sustains, the conspiracism it targets. We begin with a reading of *Kitāb al-Ṭughrā* (2011) (*The Book of the Sultan's Seal*, trans. 2015), the first novel by Youssef Rakha (b. 1976). The protagonist, Muṣṭafā al-Shurbagī, colourfully displays the most fantastical aspects of the paranoid style, but does so with a measure of ironic distance that suggests parody rather than pathology. In spite of these anti- or post-paranoid gestures, however, Mustafa ultimately aligns himself with some of conspiracism's central reductionisms, attaching himself to the self-redemptive pleasures of the practice while casting away its more extreme expressions as the delusions of irredeemable ideological 'others'. We turn then to a discussion of two more recent novels that attend to conspiracy theory in a playful manner – Mohammad Rabie's *ʿĀm al-Tinnīn* (The Year of the Dragon) (2012) and Ahmed Naji's *Istikhdām al-Ḥayā* (2014) (*Using Life*, trans. 2017) – and assess the aesthetic and political ambivalence of each.

In the book's Epilogue, we turn to the wider field of public culture in Egypt since the fall of Mubarak in 2011 to speculate on the contemporary political relevance of conspiracy literature. The successive waves of revolution and counter-revolution in recent years have been accompanied not only by an explosion of conspiracist voices in mass media (both pro- and anti-regime), but also an array of creative responses by young artists, bloggers, and comedians eager to move beyond what they perceive as the paranoid style of older generations. Our focus, however, will be on a literary work that complicates the presumed division between conspiracist and anti-conspiracist discourses: the two-part autobiography of novelist, academic, and activist Radwa Ashour (1946–2014). In *Athqal min Raḍwā* and *al-Ṣarkha*, Ashour weaves together a narrative of her battle against cancer with observations and commentary on the drama of revolution as it unfolded. A minor but recurrent topic of her remarks is 'conspiracy theory', a practice that the author defends against the criticisms, dismissals, and mockery that it has often provoked on television talk shows. What appears to be a defence, however, is something much subtler. Tying conspiracy theory to *waswasa* or 'demonic whispering', Ashour theorises the practice not only historically but in intimately affective and embodied terms. The image she generates suggests conspiracy theory to be a contingent force that, if sometimes inescapable and even necessary, operates alongside other critical dispositions such as patience, optimism, and hope.

Dramaturgies of Conspiracy:
Bakathir, Idris and the July Regime

In September 1952, a formerly obscure stage actor named Raᵓfat Shalabī took on his last role: mastermind of a vast and sinister conspiracy against the nation. It was not a role he had chosen for himself. Hauled in front of a special military tribunal, Shalabī stood accused of plotting to overthrow Egypt's junta, which had come to power less than two months earlier in what was yet to be officially proclaimed a 'revolution'. The junta's representatives in the media cast numerous aspersions on his character: he suffered from 'megalomania'; he 'intermingled promiscuously with people'; he liked to 'wisecrack' and 'wax elegant'; his 'masculinity was suspect'; and he had previously been accused, but not convicted, of involvement in the murder of a 'sexual deviant'.[1] Most damning, however, was a voice recording of the actor, allegedly intended to be broadcast upon his seizure of power, in which he declared, 'This is Raᵓfat Shalabī, leader of the new movement.'[2]

Shalabī was given a life sentence, later reduced to fifteen years of hard labour. A number of contemporary and subsequent observers deemed him innocent, the trial absurd, and the evidence – if not concocted by the junta's own incipient intelligence services, who proudly admitted to bugging Shalabī's home – no more than the spontaneous performances of a regular clown.[3] To be sure, sundry plots and power plays were being authored and authorised in the clubs, barracks, and smoke-filled rooms of Cairo, as well as the world's other major capitals, both for and against Egypt's new leaders. After all, as a secret society, the Free Officers had themselves prevailed through such means. But the trial of Raᵓfat Shalabī showed that, sometimes, alleged conspiracies against the state were simply a matter of misinterpretation, embellished and exaggerated through carefully staged drama. To the critical observer, what had been so scandalously exposed was not the hidden agenda of a hapless actor, but the innate paranoia of his accusers, their eagerness to find scapegoats for their own missteps and inner squabbles, and their ability, through technologies of surveillance, propaganda, and brute force, to impose their version of events. Perhaps, the case revealed even more than this: the voyeuristic eroticism of intelligence gathering; the construction of notions of national sovereignty and leadership through the violent rejection of non-normative masculinities; a nearly perfect projection, and burlesque parody, of the Free Officers' own pathologies ('megalomania'), crimes ('murder' of a 'sexual deviant'), and aspirations (national hegemony); a taste of things to come.

It was not an isolated incident. In the years that followed, 'conspiracy' – often but not always by foreign entities – would coalesce as a regular trope in the admonitory rhetoric of state actors, in speeches and headlines and trials and treatises. Although this rhetoric could often be a realistic reflection of the anti- and post-colonial struggles, it could also, and often did, depart into the fantastical, not only in its specific and shifting claims but also in its essential premise that political agency was a direct, intentional force either to be possessed in full or not at all. At the same time, the theme of conspiracy would find frequent elaboration in the work of Egypt's most revered playwrights, whose craft would come to enjoy the generous patronage and support of the new regime. This chapter will examine the relationship between these two very intertwined fields of conspiracist expression. Particular attention will be given to two playwrights – Ali Ahmad Bakathir (1910–69) and Yusuf Idris (1927–91) – whose work engaged with the conspiracist discourse of the state, whether through elaboration, adaptation, parody, or critical reflection. More fundamentally, this chapter will examine how a particularly narrow version of theatre, as a genre and medium of representation, both influences and reproduces the conspiracist perspective of politicians, playwrights, and the public. To set the scene for our analysis, it will be necessary to bring into clearer focus the contours and content of the conspiracies that haunted Egypt's leaders from the early 1950s onward.

Conspiracy in the Early Revolutionary Period

One of the first things that the Egyptian public learned about the cadre of military officers that assumed control of the country on 23 July 1952 was that they had powerful enemies. In their first communique to the nation, delivered on the radio by major Anwar Sadat (1918–81), the officers denounced the corruption of the country's political class and assailed the unnamed 'traitors' who had 'conspired against the army'.[4] In a brief radio address the next day, General Mohammed Naguib (Muḥammad Nagīb) (1901–84), who later would be declared President of the Republic, warned his fellow citizens to be vigilant against the 'weak souls' and 'enemies of the nation' who had been spreading 'rumors' about the movement and its intentions.[5] These and other expressions – 'reactionary elements', 'the fifth column', 'hidden hand', 'agents of the colonizer', 'spreading poisons' – congealed, through repeated use, into a dominant language of crisis management and blame that, while not totally new in Egyptian politics, would increasingly come to mediate and define relations between the regime and the national subjects it addressed.

Typical of this language were the speeches delivered at a major rally organised by the junta in al-Jumhūriyya Square on 15 September 1953. One after the other, the junta's most recognisable faces – Mohammed Naguib, Gamal Abdel Nasser, and Salah Salem – reiterated that, contrary to widespread speculation, the revolutionary leadership remained united as one.[6] Naguib characterised such speculation as 'rumors' and 'poisons', transmitted by 'false patriots', 'persons beholden to special interests and reactionary ideas', 'aides to the colonizer', and 'people blinded by lust and egotism'.[7] Salah Salem connected the dots: these rumours were not spontaneous, but were the result of a full-fledged 'conspiracy' of unnamed foreign powers, who were seeking to create a rift between Egyptians and their leaders. As proof, Salem unveiled before the crowd a 'document' allegedly containing details of this conspiracy and the 'organized manner' by which it would spread discord. In addition to the caustic language of the officers, the rally reinforced the gravity of its message through a number of dramatic devices. The audience in al-Jumhūriyya Square, which pro-junta voices in *al-Ahrām* estimated at several hundred thousand, was neatly organised into colour-coordinated squares, divided by ropes, for various professions and segments of society.[8] The speeches were interrupted at regular intervals by choreographed slogans and chants from the crowd. In an obvious display of authority, the officers spoke from the balcony of Abdeen Palace – confiscated from the deposed king a year earlier – and were surrounded by the Grand Imam of al-Azhar, the Coptic Patriarch, the

Patriarch of the Greek Catholic Church, and the Grand Rabbi of Egypt. The rally concluded as the officers held up their interlocked hands, and the band began to play the anthem of the revolution. Everyone, from those on the stage to those in the crowd, and 'all the earth, the heavens, and the air, every being and every thing in the universe' sang along.

The insistence on conspiracy had many motivating factors. Foreign powers – especially those that would later take part in the Tripartite Aggression in 1956 – certainly did 'conspire' against Egypt. Undoubtedly, there were plotters and schemers within the revolutionary leadership itself: the officers' loud denials of infighting, in retrospect, reveal more than they intended. Moreover, while later years would witness the emergence of the apparatuses and appearances of a strong, almost totalitarian regime, the fragility of this mysterious group of new leaders was at this time apparent to both insiders and outsiders.[9] In such circumstances, the language of conspiracy performed important rhetorical work, at once deflecting blame for failures in leadership, justifying the regime's violence against its opponents, creating a pretext for the curtailing of personal liberties, and forging an imagined unity of people and regime against a phantom other. Explanations of this kind, however, overstate the rational and deliberate dimensions of public speech, and can only partially help us make sense of the eagerness and energy that regime actors invested in their increasingly elaborate claims of conspiracy, irrespective of whether these claims had any tangible effect on their audience. Beyond their cynical manipulation of public opinion, what performances like those of Naguib, Nasser, and Salem demonstrate is a particular perspective on human behaviour, structured in a way that may be described as reductionist, ostentatiously symbolic, and, indeed, theatrical.

The rally in al-Jumhūriyya Square was merely the induction for what was to follow: a series of show trials, known as the 'Court of the Revolution' (*maḥkamat al-thawra*), that would begin later that month and continue into the following year. It was the second of three exceptional grand tribunals established by the junta, not including the numerous other cases, such as that of Raʾfat Shalabī and the workers at Kafr El Dawar, brought before military courts. Like its predecessor, the 'Court of Treason' (*maḥkamat al-ghadr*), the Court of the Revolution tried figures associated with the *ancien régime* for crimes committed both before and since the July coup. The charges brought against the defendants – 'treason', 'contacting foreign powers', 'acts against the foundation of the revolution', 'rumourmongering'[10] – reflected, once again, the junta's determination to expose and combat sundry plots that were as vague as they were dangerous and grandiose.[11]

What distinguished this new tribunal was not only its ability to hand out real prison terms, as well as the death penalty, but the more carefully coordinated drama of its proceedings, extended parts of which were broadcast on the radio and covered extensively in the press.[12] A further creative innovation was that the full transcripts for the cases of all thirty defendants – with the exception of several sessions held in secret – were published in six slim paperback volumes by the Ministry of National Guidance, the precursor to the Ministry of Culture.[13] Each book in the series reads very much like a collection of plays, with dialogue rendered in a somewhat elevated form of colloquial Arabic, and each of the 'characters' presented in the opening pages through caricatural illustrations, photographs, and brief descriptions of their personalities, appearances, and speaking styles. For example, the introduction to the first volume features a thin face sketch of 'Major (*bikbāshī*) Anwar Sadat' – one of the tribunal's three judges, all of whom were members of the junta – which rests above a bullet-point list of details such as the following: 'Member of the Revolutionary Command Council'; 'Appeared often on the national stage (*al-masraḥ al-waṭanī*) prior to the 23rd of July, 1952'; 'A calm operator, talks slowly as though thinking before he speaks, his strong gaze shines at you to reveal the depths of his calm psyche and enthusiastic soul'; 'Blood rises to his cheeks when he receives a compliment'.[14] Further illustrations and photographs, portraying some of the trials' most dramatic moments, intersperse the text, and bring to mind the simple black-and-white illustrations that commonly accompanied novels and plays printed in Egypt during this period. Brief but evocative descriptions of the courtroom itself – 'the word "silence" (*sukūn*) written in the color of blood' hangs above the entrance[15] – as well as occasional indications of the gestures and movements of those in attendance, may easily be compared to stage directions.

Taken together, the speeches, rallies, and trials directed by the junta indicate a strong aesthetic element in their fight against conspiracy; more than this, it may be argued that this conspiracism was aesthetic to the core. This is not to say that Egypt's military leaders, equipped with an extraordinary creative faculty, were merely conjuring non-existent demons out of thin air. Rather, their presentation and representation of serious political problems was structured in a way that privileged and exaggerated certain kinds of threats, erased others, and dramatically simplified human historical agency to a set of discrete, individual actors onstage and dangerous, inscrutable forces offstage. In other words, the conspiracist *Weltanschauung* can be viewed as depending on many of the same representational devices as traditional stage theatre. In both arrangements, words and whispers have immediate effects, action is the monopoly of a dozen or so 'key players' – except, of course, to the extent that they are perceived as mere 'puppets' of a 'hidden director' – and the public audience remains largely silent, while their attention and support are anxiously coveted, lest they be seduced by some more powerful competitor. To place conspiracism next to stage theatre may also help us understand the officers' frequent complaints about 'rumour' as 'poisons' – a trope that held a special place in Shakespearean theatre.[16] One of the most interesting cases of the Court of the Revolution, not coincidentally, produced in the flesh three individuals, dubbed the 'Trinity of Rumours', who were accused of having authored nearly all the gossip and innuendo that plagued the officers during their first year in power.[17]

Litvin's brilliant study of the Arab 'Hamlets' has revealed many of the ways in which theatre and theatrical metaphors shaped the Free Officers' view of themselves and their role in history.[18] Beyond the regime's financial and moral support for the dramatic arts, many of its most prominent members, including Nasser, had themselves performed in adaptations of Shakespearean drama in their youth, and retained some of its tones, figurations, and even specific lines when later they pursued the art of government. We may expand on Litvin's insights by connecting the 'dramatic imagination' of state actors to their penchant for conspiracist discourse and performance, not only as regards their conscious or unconscious adaptation of specific embattled personas like Hamlet or Julius Caesar, but also in their dependence on the theatrical world view as such, with its peculiar rendering of action between individuals and words. This is not to say that watching, performing, and sponsoring theatre 'caused' the conspiracist bent of these actors – or, conversely, that a primordial conspiracism turned them into theatre aficionados. Rather, the two phenomena hold together in what modern social theorists would call a homology: each possesses a structure that resonates with that of the other, as the two are drawn together through repeated use and association. Neither phenomenon is originary; both derive from a common set of mental habits or embodied practices.[19]

We should be careful not to assume, as 'effects'-centred studies of culture often do, that the performances so far described could successfully 'brainwash' a putatively gullible public, instantly converting them into strict conspiracy theorists.[20] On the contrary, the junta's claims of conspiracy would be met by scepticism, and even radical critique, by a number of prominent authors and intellectuals from the 1950s onward. Among the critical voices was Ihsan Abdel Quddous (Iḥsān ʿAbd al-Quddūs) (1919–90), who is today often remembered for his prolific authorship of popular romance novels and short stories, but who at the time was a rising star in journalism and a well-known liberal opponent of the military's intervention in politics. In an article entitled 'The Secret Society that Governs Egypt', published on 22 March 1954, Abdel Quddous effectively turns the junta's conspiracist rhetoric on its head.[21] The 'secret society' of the title is the 'real' revolutionary leadership, who Abdel Quddous accuses of hiding behind front men like President Mohammed Naguib. Salah Salem, for example, 'never appears', and Gamal Abdel Nasser, a true *éminence grise*, would always be photographed 'sitting in the third or fourth row'. According to Abdel Quddous, people in Egypt had become more and more unsettled by the constant surprise decisions announced by the leadership, and the contradictory statements they make. Indeed, he says, people 'do not trust the leaders when they say that they are combatting reactionary elements and the supporters of colonialism, because they do not understand the meaning of the words "reactionary elements" and "supporters of colonialism"'. The article certainly struck a nerve, as its author was sent to prison almost as soon as it hit the press.

Liberal voices in the press – and, presumably, private conversations – were not the only places that conspiracism met with a critical reception. Nor were courtrooms and rallies the only places it was produced. Naturally, the tropes of anti-regime plots, backroom schemers, poisonous rumours, and passive publics would feature in numerous plays performed and published during the early years of the junta, and throughout the 1950s and 1960s.[22] Examining some of these works in relation to the reigning conspiracism of the times will allow us to offer new understandings of the politics of Egyptian theatre, beyond the allegorical lens through which they have often been viewed.

Ali Ahmad Bakathir

In a private letter addressed to 'Major (*bikbāshī*) Anwar Sadat, Member of the Revolutionary Command Council' and dated 20 February 1953, the playwright Ali Ahmad Bakathir appealed for help.[23] *Imbarāṭūriyya fī al-Mazād* (Empire for Auction), a satirical play he recently composed, had been accepted for production by the Modern Theater Troupe, but was then 'postponed' several times by the censorship board. This, despite his growing renown as a major dramatist, as evidenced in the recent successes of plays like *Sirr al-Ḥākim bi-Amr Allāh* (The Secret of the Caliph al-Hakim) (performed in 1948) and *Mismār Juḥā* (Goha's Nail) (performed in 1951). Bakathir began the letter with a brief plot synopsis: after an electoral victory by the Conservative Party in Great Britain, the increased brutality of the British empire provokes a 'bloc of Asian and African countries' to hold a conference in Delhi, from whence they successfully plot to overthrow the worldwide imperial regime and install a new order of peace and justice for all. (He did not mention that the drama, as such, does not kick off until the end of the second act, after which the audience's patience would likely have been spent on a series of rather uninteresting parlour-room dialogues – a more probable reason, at least in part, for the censor's ultimate disapproval). Bakathir then concluded:

> I see no reason for the censor to object to this nationalistic, patriotic play, which deals with the ills of colonialism in the form of a satirical comedy – especially in this new age, the age of the Blessed Revolution. I hereby submit the work for your consideration, confident that you will allow it to perform its nationalistic message under the auspices of this new age, the age of freedom, honor, and dignity.[24]

It is not known whether the playwright received a reply. Yet the letter reveals, more than a personal intimacy with one of the junta's most prominent members, an assumption of shared interests regarding the role of politics in theatre, and theatre in politics. The value of a play was less in its aesthetic ingenuity or philosophical depth than in its ability to carry a 'message' deemed 'patriotic' and 'nationalistic'. Additionally, the significance of a given dramatic work was bound to a rather narrow temporal frame, and any 'postponing' by the censor would be tantamount to a formal rejection. Although it is not stated explicitly in the letter, Sadat and Bakathir agreed on more than this. While the latter remained for the better part of his life associated informally with the Muslim Brotherhood, the relationship between the Islamist group and the Free Officers was at this time still amicable, and indeed rumours continued to circulate that the two were in league with each other.[25] Beyond any ostensible ideology, what the officer and the playwright shared was a dramatic perspective, a particular narrowness of vision that split the world into persecuted, misunderstood heroes and an ever-growing list of enemies, with the volatile, easily swayed masses in between.

More to the point: if militant, Manichean conspiracism had a spokesperson in mid-century Egyptian theatre, it was Ali Ahmad Bakathir. So committed was the playwright to this style of expression that a number of his plays may be indistinguishable from the angriest conspiracy tracts of the day, with only the barest traces of artistic adaptation beyond the use of dialogue and stage cues. A brief look at one work in particular – *Ilāh Isrāʾīl* (The God of Israel), written in about 1957 but never performed on stage – allows us to view conspiracy theory in its 'pure' form.[26]

In his introduction, Bakathir begins with a pseudo-scholastic gesture typical of the true believer, saying that he has 'derived the facts [of the play] from the three holy books – the Torah, the Gospels, and the Qurʾan – as well as from the Talmud and other books written by or about the Jews over the ages' (5). The author thus invests his text – a historical drama, in three acts, about the 'Jewish people' and their dealings with Satan – with the epistemological status of divinely inspired, eternal truths. Conspicuously absent from the introduction, as well as the play itself, is any reference to more immediate and locally tangible traumas, such as Israel's participation in the Tripartite Aggression against Egypt in 1956, or the exposure of Operation Susannah in 1954, that may have provoked Bakathir to write such a work. Instead, *Ilāh Isrāʾīl* connects disparate scenes from Moses's prophethood in Egypt (Act I), the trials of Jesus (Act II), and the First Zionist Congress in 1897 (Act III) into a transhistoric metanarrative that trades in the crudest anti-Semitic stereotypes and other assorted essentialisms of race, religion, and gender. The grand conspirator appears at first to be Satan (*Iblīs*), who turns the Israelites against Moses, leaves a magically disguised Judas to be crucified instead of Jesus, and whispers in the ears of Theodor Herzl. But in the end, Satan himself is driven to repentance and a reconciliation with God after 'the Jews' have usurped his role and committed unfathomable atrocities. Throughout, the play deploys the perennial tropes of the 'paranoid style': misogyny, as when Moses curses women as 'obstinate mules' and threatens to pull them by the braids of their hair (23); the hegemony of secret societies, as when a rapt Theodor Herzl praises 'freemasonry' and 'all the other general humanistic organizations founded by our forefathers' (121); and an excess of apocalyptic kitsch, as when the back wall is draped over with a map of the world being devoured by a gigantic 'yellow serpent', which proceeds to engage Satan in dance amidst a stage full of demons who screech and throw off their clothes (109).

We will return to similar images in subsequent chapters to examine the affective and psychological mechanisms that structure conspiracist literature. Suffice it to say here that they do not testify to any aesthetic originality on Bakathir's part, nor was *Ilāh Isrāʾīl* in any way an anomaly in his massive literary, mostly dramatic oeuvre. Anti-Israeli, often anti-Semitic animosities defined most of his plays that may be considered conspiracist,[27] even if the principle object of ridicule and blame was not necessarily Jewish. Such was the case with *Libas al-ʿIffa* (Chastity Suit) (written 1966), which deserves mention at least for the fact that it was never formally published, let alone performed, and thus has hitherto escaped critical attention.[28] The play is an open polemic on Tunisian President Habib Bourguiba (al-Ḥabīb Būrqība) (r. 1957–87), whose call in 1965 for Arabs to accept a two-state solution with Israel was deemed by Arab nationalists to be a betrayal, and one that Bakathir seems to have taken rather personally.

The first of four acts opens with Bourguiba prancing about naked through the streets of Tel Aviv. Rachel (Rāshīl), his Jewish lover, along with his son ('Bourgiba, Jr') and a financial consultant named Eliyahu (Ilyāhū), await his return to his hotel suite, where he has been residing in debauched luxury after escaping a revolution against him in Tunisia. Once the clearly deranged ex-president has been clothed and relatively sedated, he enters into a boisterous argument with a team of American filmmakers commissioned to make him a glowing biopic. After much back and forth, Bourguiba is persuaded to accept a final product that would seem far from his original intentions: instead of himself, the ex-president is to play a clown (*bahlawān*) who falls in love with a girl from a respected family. The girl's disapproving father is to be played by Bourguiba, Jr. Through subsequent scenes, Bourguiba is reduced to penury, his wealth frittered away by expensive concubines, a son with ambitions, and his 'hosts' in the Israeli government. Ultimately, his life unravels through a web of interconnected conspiracies: the American film is a flop; Bourguiba, Jr. is executed after attempting to seize power in Tunisia; and the ex-president himself is handed over by the Israelis to revolutionaries in his home country. He is set 'free' to wander the streets of Tunis as he pleases, on the condition that he lock himself in a full-body suit of aluminum – the 'chastity suit' of the title – so that he does not expose himself to innocent passersby.

On balance, *Libās al-ʿIffa* contains some genuinely hilarious moments, as when the ex-president is bound and gagged by his son, and aides attempt to discern his wishes by interpreting the movements of a muzzled dog. As a hyperbolic satire of a contemporary head of state, the work even anticipates the popular political thrillers and dictator novels of the Mubarak years (1981–2011), most strikingly Ibrāhīm ʿĪsā's *Maqtal al-Rajul al-Kabīr* (The Murder of the Big Man) (1999).[29] Yet the play succumbs, like Bakathir's other political dramas, to a heavy-handed moralism and untempered condemnation of the usual suspects. On several occasions, the play almost seems to mock its own over-baked suspicions – Bourguiba is portrayed, after all, as a raving lunatic who shouts 'conspiracy' (*muʾāmara*) at someone in nearly every scene. Yet in every single instance, the further unfolding of the drama proves that his fears were in no way exaggerated: all the hidden agendas and intrigues turn out to be true. Similarly, the playwright's brief flirtation with meta-theatrical commentary – the failed biopic – serves only to reinforce the drama's essential conspiracism: quite simply, Burgiba is a 'clown' propped up by the Americans and seduced by the Israelis.

It should come as no surprise that a playwright so committed to exposing the totalising grip of demonic cults and international secret societies on the Arab World should find an explanation for his own artistic and personal infelicities in these same terms. Such is the thematic core of what was perhaps Bakathir's most controversial play, *Ḥabl al-Ghasīl* (The Laundry Line) (1965), a scathing attack on the perceived hegemony of 'atheists' and 'communists' on Egypt's culture industry. The scale of the conspiracy is summarised by Mīrghanī, a director betrayed by members of the sinister clique, in a rant that continues for several pages:

> MĪRGHANĪ: I didn't want to have to say this, but it seems time to confront you with the painful truth. Those who wrote these articles [against my play] are not just hired pens. They're something much more vile than that.
>
> ABŪ AL-DUYŪK: What are you saying?
>
> MĪRGHANĪ: I'm saying these people take not money, but orders from a particular group with a special point of view. This group operates in a conspiratorial fashion to impose its viewpoint by all means possible. It combats its adversaries through intrigue, subterfuge, and intellectual terrorism. It battles them in the press, or else punishes them with silence and neglect.
>
> ALL: What on earth are you talking about?
>
> MĪRGHANĪ: Let me finish what I'm saying. This dangerous group has penetrated sensitive areas through organized means. They've taken to the press, and are mobilizing to control other media as well.[30]

After a few pages, he continues:

> MĪRGHANĪ: [What matters is] this strange situation we find ourselves in. It would appear to me that the press has been penetrated by a group of people who've organized themselves as a kind of unofficial, illicit party – this, in a country where we should have no parties or warring factions. In the press, they pursue their agenda under the banner of socialism, while in reality their principles are far from it. They stand against Arab socialism and all its cultural and spiritual values!
>
> ṢALṢĀL: And where exactly is this group? They exist only in your sick imagination.
>
> MĪRGHANĪ: Hold on a minute, don't interrupt me until I've finished speaking! In the artistic sphere, by means of the press, they wage a secret crusade on every writer or artist who does not belong to their party. If such an artist produces a book or artistic work, they purposely ignore it, even if it is a genuine masterpiece. But if one of their own produces a work – even

if it is utter trash – they laud it in glowing terms and celebrate it in every newspaper and magazine![31]

Mīrghanī here is speaking for Bakathir himself, who viewed the rejection of a number of his plays as a deliberate and sustained campaign against him since Free Officer Aḥmad Ḥamrūsh and other alleged leftists or communists gained appointment to several state newspapers and cultural organs, including the National Theater (al-masraḥ al-qawmī), beginning in the late 1950s. In a sensitive and richly documented book, ʿAbū Salāma (2013) has effectively debunked the notion that Bakathir was the victim of any organised conspiracy, even if his allegations about the prevalence of Marxist or quasi-Marxist ideologues in the culture industry contained some measure of truth. The number of Bakathir's plays approved for the stage after the alleged communist takeover of Egyptian theatre, as Salāma notes, were equivalent to the number of plays approved before.[32] *Ḥabl al-Ghasīl* itself was performed on stage in the same year Bakathir submitted it, even though it had been refused by the Modern Theater's review committee and was severely attacked in the press.

A more likely reason for the poor reception of Bakathir's work from the late 1950s on would seem to be his abandonment of aesthetic inventiveness in favour of direct political commentary. As is evident in the excerpts above, and throughout *Ḥabl al-Ghasīl*, there is little that separates the 'dialogue' from monological polemic apart from the obviously contrived objections of almost randomly placed secondary characters. Lest we view this inelegance of form merely in terms of artistic failure or success, however, it is important to appreciate Bakathir's nearly life-long commitment to a singular model of theatre as tightly bound up with his broader conspiracist worldview. In spite of his prolific literary output, the playwright rarely if ever experimented beyond the boundaries of stage drama as traditionally conceived. For Bakathir, actors had fixed roles, and the fourth wall was rarely broken, except to reinforce the chains that bound actors to their creators and words to their authors. This rigidity of genre and form finds its analogy in conspiracism's reductionist view of human agency: all the world's a stage, and all the action is confined to a restricted circle of players. It was a view, as suggested above, that he shared with many influential state actors, and indeed it is with styles and discourses of the political field, more than the vibrant and increasingly experimental field of Egyptian theatre in the 1960s, that his scripts for the stage resonated the most. Plays like *Ilāh Isrāʾīl*, *Libās al-ʿIffa*, and *Ḥabl al-Ghasīl* not only mirrored the basic structure of the junta's mass rallies and show trials. They also aimed for a similar rhetorical function, encouraging audiences to cultivate fear and suspicion, and inspiring in them a particular image of the enemy, in a tone of exasperated urgency that had no patience for even meek petitions for clarity along the lines of 'What are you saying?' or 'What on Earth are you talking about?' The similarities between Bakathir's dramas and those of the junta extended also to the level of language. In *Ḥabl al-Ghasīl*, much of Mīrghanī's and other characters' declamations on 'secrets groups' and 'subterfuge' seem as though they were copied straight from the headlines of the state-controlled press. In particular, Mīrghanī's reference to 'a group of people who've organised themselves as a kind of unofficial, illicit party' directly invokes warnings that President Nasser had recently made about 'an organized, reactionary group that is (like) an unofficial party'. The president's reference seems to have been to alleged 'remnants' of colonialism and feudalism, although it was vague enough that Bakathir could offer his own interpretation of the hidden enemy.[33]

Taken as a whole, Bakathir's drama was nothing if not consistent, as one can find little if any significant change in tone, form, or message between one of his first prose plays, *Shaylūk al-Jadīd* (The New Shylock) (1945), and one of his very last, *al-Tawrā al-Ḍāʾiʿa* (The Lost Torah) (1967). The dates of these two plays are significant, as they roughly correspond to the period encompassing the founding of the first Free Officers cells, their rise to power, and the climax of ʿAbd al-Nasir's presidency. Bakathir knew both Anwar Sadat and Mohammed Naguib before the July coup; despite claims of a professional 'crisis' beginning in the mid-1950s, he undoubtedly reaped many rewards from his proximity to the July regime.[34] The year after drafting the appeal to Sadat cited above, he was appointed manager of the Popular Theater (*al-masraḥ al-shaʿbī*), and later gained appointment to the censorship board for artistic works at the Ministry of Culture and National Guidance, where he remained until obtaining a grant to write an epic work of Islamic history in 1962. A novel of his, *Sīrat Shujāʿ* (The Sira of Shujaʿ) (1954), was apparently written at the behest of the minister of education, and was dedicated to 'Gamal and his fellow heroes'.[35] Still, these facts should not lead us to assume that Bakathir's aesthetic style can be attributed solely to the putative influence of regime figures – he was not the only author, after all, to maintain personal connections of this kind. Indeed, his political works went considerably beyond, in detail and intensity, the tropic nationalist rhetoric of the regime's representatives.

Neither should it be assumed that Bakathir's dramatic disposition, however extreme, set him completely apart from other artists and intellectuals. This much is evident in the discourse of Bakathir's fiercest critics, whose responses to *Ḥabl al-Ghasīl* came heavily laced with the same tropes of organised plots and hidden agendas he had used to criticise them.[36] The controversy that the play provoked would appear to have been about the ideological colours of the grand conspiracy, rather than its existence as such. This should not be surprising, given the politicised and highly toxic atmosphere of Egypt's cultural establishment, especially since the passing of laws regulating the media in 1961, and the increasing penetration of nearly all levels of society by security agents and informers. The anxieties of national as well as bodily autonomy and possession that inspired Bakathir's work were very real, even if, in his particular case, these were to be misdirected into grotesque depictions of cultural, political, and religious others.

Yusuf Idris

Egyptian theatre produced other reactions to the climate of fear and suspicion that resulted from the tightening of the state's grip – or, perhaps more accurately, the grips of competing and contradictory state entities – on cultural production in the 1960s. A perspective very different from that of Ali Ahmad Bakathir was articulated by a renowned author who, not coincidentally, spent most of his literary career outside of stage drama. Yusuf Idris is best known for his short stories and novellas, although he composed what are considered some major contributions to theatre as well, such as his 1964 play *Farāfīr* (Flipflaps), in which he experimented with notions of audience participation and attempted to recreate a kind of Egyptian dramatic authenticity. At least two of his plays directly confronted contemporary fears of conspiracy, not only in their daringly explicit dialogue but in their experimentation with the form of stage theatre itself.

The first of these, *al-Mukhaṭṭaṭīn* (The Striped Ones) (1969), is a dark and eccentric political drama that is difficult to comprehend in one sitting. The play opens as the curiously named Ahu Kalām ('just talk, nonsense') attempts to climb a pile of rubble in order to summon the rest of the characters, who he assumes are either asleep or impertinently delayed. Ahu Kalām is the Shakespearean Rumour that sets the scene, the primordial noise necessary for the birth of a new symbolic order; his confusion, at once discursive and sartorial, is a warning for the pandemonium of names, shapes, tricks, and mutations that are soon to crowd the stage. He is interrupted by the 'somewhat elegantly dressed' Farkit Kaᶜb ('A stone's throw', literally 'a rubbing of the heel'), who alerts him to two facts to which he is oblivious: that they are in a theatre, and that his body is covered in sewage (6). Before Ahu Kalām is able to fully absorb the situation, the two are joined on stage by a giant walking and talking Egyptian one-pound note who, after identifying himself as one Dr ᶜAbd al-Wāḥid ᶜar-Rīᵓ ('Dr. Abd al-Wahid "on an empty stomach"'), decides to transform into an investment certificate from the National Bank of Egypt. But the carnival is not yet complete. Next to enter are a rickety public bus named 56 Gharbiyya, and Ṭaᶜmiyya, a woman who crawls out of a manhole and speaks only in proverbs. These five characters anticipate the arrival of 'Brother', their leader who soon descends on to the stage from a helicopter and commands them to return to their regular human forms. With the subsequent arrival of Almāẓ ('Diamond'), a famed actress, the group is complete, and the stage is set for the unveiling of their grand design. So ends Act I.

For such a ramshackle group, their ultimate goal is remarkably ambitious: the literal striping, or painting over in stripes, of the entire world (whence the 'Striped Ones' of the title). The actors themselves wear costumes with vertical black-and-white stripes. The first phase of their plan is implemented in Act II. On stage we see the headquarters of The Foundation of the Greatest Happiness, which is also the name of a play, 'adapted with liberties from French folklore', that the Striped Ones intend to invade and take over (30). From their positions among the audience, the members cunningly install themselves as employees in the foundation, displacing the general manager and re-branding it as The Foundation of True Happiness. Act III opens with a film showing how the entire world has been painted over in stripes, including 'even children's balloons, the airplanes and birds in the sky, and the fish in the sea' (75). A loudspeaker broadcasts what is clearly a parody of contemporary Egyptian regime-speak, with recognisably religious accents:

> And thus did the whole world become covered in stripes. The faith that was born in the heart of a single individual was soon embraced by a group of devout believers, who fought and struggled and endured persecution. But through faith they prevailed, and misery was wiped from face of the earth. Where once there was chaos, there now were stripes/lines … We gather here today to celebrate the first anniversary of our mission's completion, and stand with our hearts and souls devoted to our leader, the leader of those who have striped the earth, the man who believed, and prevailed, and through whom we too have prevailed: to our Big Brother, our Leader, our Teacher, the Creator and Master Striper of the whole world. (75–6)

In spite of it all, Brother is not wholly content. He is not convinced that the striping of the world has made people 'truly' happier – the original conceit behind the 'Foundation of True Happiness'. Yet so robust is the ideology he founded that he is unable to persuade his original circle of devotees to begin to reconsider things. They turn against him. Distraught, Brother disappears into the streets; he is later discovered sitting at a café dressed in red, and is apprehended and brought back to his office. From there, he runs out to the balcony, with the intention of delivering a speech renouncing the ideology of stripes and calling for a revolution against the order he founded. His words are quickly drowned out, however, by loudspeakers blasting an entirely opposite message. And so the play comes to an end, with the black-and-white dichotomies that Brother-*cum*-Father has imposed ultimately rendering his own speech outside of signification, incomprehensible.

Most critics have been tempted to see in the *Striped Ones* a thinly veiled assault on the authoritarianism and corruption of the Nasser regime, which had been scandalously exposed in the *naksa* of 1967 – just two years before the play was first published in the Egyptian theatre magazine *al-Masrah* (*Theater*).[37] Indeed there is much to suggest such a reading, beyond the obvious similarities between the 'Striped Ones' and the Free Officers – both secret societies that successfully plotted to overthrow one order and install another. In his ultimately unsuccessful attempt to convince his followers to reconsider the regime they had created, Brother begins by saying, 'My task tonight is difficult, and I would like all of you to help me see it through' (87). His words directly echo those of Gamal Abdel Nasser in his famous resignation speech – ultimately rescinded – which he delivered to the nation on 9 July 1967 following Egypt's devastating defeat by Israel. A subtler dig at Nasser is embedded in the play's intertextual gestures to Luigi Pirandello's *Six Characters in Search of an Author*, which the president famously cited in his *Philosophy of the Revolution* (1955) as a metaphor for Egypt's need for a strong leader.[38] As author of *al-Mukhaṭṭaṭīn*, Idris has effectively wrested this script away from Nasser and made a mockery of it and, by extension, the entire political and symbolic basis for his legitimacy. It is not surprising, then, that the play was banned on its opening night, and was not performed on stage until 1985.

Such a directly allegorical reading, however, falls far short of appreciating the full range of meanings generated by this disorienting assemblage of signs. One access point to the play's complexity is in the semantic play set in motion, and never fully resolved, by the title. *Al-mukhaṭṭaṭīn* (or in the colloquial, *il-mikhaṭṭaṭīn*) are agents of *takhṭīṭ* – understood in the play as literal 'striping' or 'drawing lines', but in the context of 1960s Egypt, much more commonly as 'planning' or 'regulation'. The term loomed large not only in the economy, in which the state, since the agrarian reforms pushed by the Free Officers in the beginning months of their rule, became increasingly involved. It also featured as a key word in discourses on society and culture, and indeed in theatre itself, where debates on the relative merits of direct state 'regulation' continued throughout the 1950s and 1960s.[39] More fundamentally, as historian Roel Meijer has argued, 'planning [*takhṭīṭ*] grew to become the main, formative element of the ideology of authoritarian modernism that legitimized the regime' in the late 1950s. 'As a discourse of power,' Meijer continues, 'planning [*takhṭīṭ*] created the image of a "modern", rationalizing regime. It was the main principle behind the destruction of civil society, and the regulation of economic society.'[40] The discourse of planning, as well as near synonymous terms like *tarshīd* ('guidance') and *tawjīh* ('directing'), materialised in numerous state-sponsored projects, institutions, and media spectacles, and even attained a certain 'magic' of its own, wielded with 'exhilaration and boundless optimism' by an expanding class of mid-range intellectuals, bureaucratic rhetors, and 'experts'.[41] Beyond the immediate context of the mid-twentieth century, we may also understand *takhṭīṭ* as the central organising principle of the 'techno-politics', or rationalised forms of governance, control, and human–object relations, that Timothy Mitchell has examined in the context of colonial and post-colonial Egypt.[42] At a further degree of abstraction, *takhṭīṭ* forms part of a grammar of agency that positions free and willing subjects over passive, governable objects. This much is implicit in the word's morphology, the 'form II' verbal pattern in Arabic, which moreover has structured much of the vocabulary of educational, social, and political modernisation projects in Egypt and other Arab states. It is the linguistic and ideological fetish of both conspirators and conspiracy theorists.

There is considerably more to *al-Mukhaṭṭaṭīn* than simply a critique of Nasserism, or even totalitarian regimes in general. In its satirical portrayal of the machinations of a secret society, it also continues the Egyptian theatrical engagement with themes of conspiracy and conspiracism. Read against the fear-mongering of the regime and its rhetors, the play redirects the suspicions of the audience through a farcical exposure of the 'real' conspiracy: that perpetrated by the Egyptian leaders themselves. The 'Striped Ones' are not only perpetrators of a 'plot' (*mukhaṭṭaṭ*), they are literally forcing people to wear it (*labsīn mikhaṭṭaṭ, bīlabbasu il-nās mikhaṭṭaṭ*) – a colloquial expression that can also be interpreted as 'pulling a trick' or 'framing' someone for a crime. The play contains many other commonplaces of conspiracist drama. In Act III, after the entire globe has been striped, the organisation Brother controls is called The Board of Directors of the World (maglis idārat al-ᶜālam) – an eerie foreshadowing of The Supreme Council of the World (al-maglis al-aᶜlā li l-ᶜālam) that would surface in conspiracy theories decades later.[43] Also familiar is the paranoid imperative of *cherchez la femme* implicit in the role given to the actress, Almāẓ. She is the last member to join the core group of conspirators, but is described by Brother as 'the most important thing' in the plot; later, she is the closest to Brother and the first to attempt to dissuade him from renouncing his ideology. Finally, despite their outward commitment to rationality and order, the Striped Ones find it necessary to employ a 'diviner of sand and shells to see the future and tell our fortunes' (63). Here we have a likely shot at Egyptian and other authoritarian regimes in history that have been rumoured to rely in their decision making on fortune tellers and magicians.[44] This is more fundamentally a jab at the rationalistic pretences of authoritarian modernity and European Enlightenment, which have been famously critiqued for their reliance on the 'magic' of spectacle, as well as their internal inconsistencies, inequalities, and ideologies, despite their ostensible embrace of pure reason. The trope of fortune telling also emerges through yet another spin of the play's central pun: 'to draw lines (with shells)' (*yikhaṭṭaṭ bi-l-wadaʿ*) is an Egyptian folk practice for telling the future.

In addition, the popular tendency to view modern Egyptian drama through a strictly allegorical lens has stood in the way of letting critics recognise what would otherwise be an obvious fact: *al-Mukhaṭṭaṭīn* applies its critical edge to the world of theatre itself. In other words, we are dealing here not only with the conspiracies of officers and autocrats, but with those of the actors, directors, and playwrights with which Yusuf Idris was intimately familiar. With this in mind, it is more than probable that the play emerged from the same set of critical concerns that inspired Bakathir, who died the year it was published, to write *Ḥabl al-Ghasīl* just four years earlier. Just as Bakathir railed against the machinations of Marxist culture workers, so *al-Mukhaṭṭaṭīn* mocks the authors of 'lines' (*khuṭūṭ*) who begin their quest for full-spectrum dominance by literally taking over a play. Idris's play is of course much more abstract than Bakathir's, and the object of his critique may thus be understood more broadly as all those who advocate 'planning' in the dramatic arts, or whose artistic vision is limited by strict black-and-white dichotomies. Given the timing of its publication, as well as its similar title, *al-Mukhaṭṭaṭīn* may have been conceived in part as a response to *Ḥabl al-Ghasīl* and its narrow vision of politics and culture.

Whatever we suppose to be the primary target of Idris's play, it is apparent that the general contours of the critique have much in common with conspiracist discourses that circulated at the time. To what extent, then, does *al-Mukhaṭṭaṭīn* depart from the structures of domination, be they political or aesthetic or both, against which it has hitherto seemed so fit to oppose? The answer depends on how much latitude we allow ourselves in interpreting the agency of each of the characters in relation to their world, their audience, and one another. If we expect this play to offer nothing but a bleak vision of a totalitarian future – and thus, as has often been done, draw comparisons with Orwell's *Nineteen Eighty-Four* – then it becomes simple to argue that we have here yet another conspiracist staging of power and politics, albeit with the conspiracist gaze of the audience redirected at the erstwhile conspiracists themselves.

While there is much to recommend this expectation, the audience has, in the sundry signs that crowd the stage, considerably more to contemplate than the black-and-white dichotomies of domination and defeat, or the sort of stripped-down ideological diatribes that fill much of Bakathir's drama. Here again we may turn to word play for a fuller appreciation of the play's politics. Oddly, previous critics have been nearly unanimous in transliterating the title, following the Standard Arabic vocalisation, as *al-mukhaṭṭaṭīn* (or *al-mukhaṭṭaṭūn*) – a reading that yields, in Badawi's version, the passive participles 'planned' or 'programmed', and reinforces the notion that the drama's actors are mere tools of the grand conspiracy. Yet the title, like the entire play, is quite clearly written in the colloquial, and as such should more properly be vocalised as *il-mikhaṭṭaṭīn*. This reading introduces a significant degree of ambiguity that is not present in the Standard Arabic pronunciation, since the colloquial *mikhaṭṭaṭ* serves as both active *and* passive participle, that is to say both subject and object of *al-takhṭīṭ*. The linguistic and semantic ambiguity is a cue for us to hesitate before too quickly assigning roles to the actors, and to remain curious about where power is located, who wields it, and how it may be shared, amassed, hidden, or channelled complexly. In spite of their apparent stupidity and craven indolence, the motley crew of conspirators on stage cannot easily be dismissed as one-dimensional dupes, nor can their leader be credited with all of the play's action. The Striped Ones are constantly in motion. They spin, sprint, and change shapes; they affect and are affected. The playwright has devoted much detail to the descriptions of his characters, their expressions, and their gestures: Ahu Kalām is elaborately dishevelled (5); Farkit Kaᶜb is given a distinctive smile (6); the general manager of The Foundation of the Greatest Happiness does yoga in his office (33); and the language of the characters constitutes a full range of styles, accents, registers, and secret codes. Brother himself is as much moved as he is moving, and displays – apart from his stern arrogance – considerable degrees of irritation, delight, and, as we have seen at the end, exasperation that devolves into lunacy. In addition, at the beginning of Act II, the Striped Ones take up positions among the audience, from which they interrupt and comment on the play they are about to invade. While the playwright has not left open any roles for potential audience members themselves, the positioning of the actors as spectators and critics is a significant breach of the dichotomy of onstage and offstage forces – in other words, agency is distributed less rigidly than in the typical conspiracist worldview.

The total effect of all of this on the audience must be quite disorienting, and thus rather than a clear delineation of active subjects and passive objects, we are confronted with a performance of morphological, sartorial, and political confusion. While the climax and conclusion of the play – that is, the 'striping' of the entire globe and the silencing of a repentant Brother – would seem to militate against this confusion, even here the open-minded interpreter may find more than a dystopian closure of signs. The extent of the striping is patently absurd, and thus as a dramatic device is more effective as a mocking satire of the conspiracy's plan than an Orwellian warning against it. Indeed, this is a major difference between *al-Mukhaṭṭaṭīn* and *Nineteen Eighty-Four* (or other 'paranoid' narratives): while the former is suffused with a streak of slap-stick, if occasionally grim humour, the latter is dominated by dark seriousness. Significantly, the humour is directed not only against the buffoonery of the powerful – as one often encounters, for example, in Bakathirian drama – but against the very pretence of their control. It is as if, despite the apparent victory of the ideology of stripes at the play's end, the utter impossibility of a world so thoroughly 'striped' intervenes to prevent a pessimistic conspiracism from dominating the audience's imagination.

The playful ambiguity of *al-Mukhaṭṭaṭīn* can be compared with the more explicitly polemical stance of another play by Yusuf Idris that engages with the fears and phobias that suffused political and cultural life in late-1960s Egypt. *Shillat al-Ghad* (The Tomorrow Gang) was allegedly written in 1974 and never published in full.[45] Yet what can be gleamed of its content, based on a highly abridged version published in the magazine *Ruz al-Yusuf* in 1997, suggests that the author has crafted a radical, if partially flawed, critique of the voyeurism and interpretive mania of the Egyptian security services. The play opens with a musical score heralding the beginning of the academic year at Cairo University, together with a dance routine that is meant to 'give the atmosphere of student life prior to the 6th of October' – in other words, we are transported back to the anxious state of 'no war and no peace' that prevailed between the 1967 *naksa* and the war of 1973, during which many students clamoured at once for a regime change at home, and a settling of scores with Israel. In the penumbra of the early morning hours, we glimpse 'the ghosts of boys and girls' scribbling something over the walls. When the stage reaches full light, we see the walls covered in the words *shurum burum,* an almost nonsensical phrase that means something like 'chaos' or 'mess', and is sometimes used in magical incantations. The second scene takes place in 'the office of some important person, such as, for example, the president of the country', and contains a humorous dialogue between the Official and his Assistant, in which the two speculate about the meaning of the phrase *shurum burum.*

> THE OFFICIAL: How bizarre indeed! I've lived and travelled and seen all sorts of things, but I've never seen anything like this. What on earth is '*shurum burum*'? There isn't a wall in all of Cairo or Giza or the suburbs that isn't covered in '*shurum burum*'.
>
> THE ASSISTANT: Things have truly come to a pretty pass, sir. We've never seen anything like this.

As we have come to expect from Yusuf Idris, these lines contain some clever punning that sets the mood for the remainder of the play. The 'walls' are all '*shurum burum*' – in other words, we can look forward to some serious deconstruction of the divisions between the stage and the audience, or theatre and society – and 'things have truly come to a pretty pass' (*iḥna ẓ-ẓāhir fi ᵓākhir iz-zaman*) – that is to say, we are in the 'end times', and a battle between good and evil is looming in the distance. Significantly, too, it is the youth who have magically pronounced a curse upon the walls, rather than an all-powerful director or playwright.

Caught in this moment of interpretive panic, the Official and his Assistant have nothing to rely upon but the tropes and figures of the police imaginary. Behind the graffiti campaign, they surmise, is a 'wicked gang', or perhaps a 'secret organisation', that seeks to spread unpatriotic propaganda. Correctly, as it later turns out, the Official guesses that the perpetrators are university students. He soon produces a file containing a report on the so-called 'Tomorrow Gang', whose name he feels has 'a hint of communism about it', and assigns an informer to report back to him – personally and on a daily basis – everything he can learn about the troublesome group. With the opening of the third scene, a group of students are practising a performance of Dumas's *The Lady of the Camellias*, and thus we learn that the 'Tomorrow Gang' is nothing more, and nothing less, than a university theatre group! The informer enters the auditorium in the middle of the performance and asks to join. The director, Professor ʿAwīs, begrudgingly accepts his request without asking more than a few questions. No sooner does the practice commence, however, than a philosophical dispute erupts between the director and the actors over truth, aesthetic realism, and the function of theatre in society. While the director argues that theatrical performance is a hyperbolic and pleasurable 'lie' told in order to reveal a fundamental truth, his students insist that theatre should function as a direct and unadorned 'truth' amidst a world founded on lies. The dispute ends with Professor ʿAwīs ejected from the theatre, allowing the students to put on a play of their own design, entitled *Shurum Burum*.

It would seem logical that the next scene, which is comprised of five separate amorous dialogues between different members of the group, should be understood as the spontaneous performance of the new play, however this is not stated explicitly. What is important is the sense of metatheatrical confusion, during which neither the audience, nor the informer, is able to draw an easy distinction between the acting and the 'real' thoughts and feelings of the students. At the end of each dialogue, we see the informer taking notes, lasciviously smacking his lips, and clearly enjoying himself even while much of what goes on is probably lost on him.

Act II takes us back to the office of the Official, who is receiving the report of the informer. His suspicions heightened, he orders a team of security officers to reserve seats for the opening night of the students' play. This is, indeed, the eagerly anticipated *Shurum Burum*, which begins with an argument between university students about love and the ideal behaviour of men and women. It is possible that many of the details here are elaborations of the amorous dialogues witnessed in Act I between the various actors, but again, this is not stated explicitly, and the text's editor has left this section highly abridged. *Shurum Burum* reaches an aborted climax when a female student, about to announce her candidacy for president of the student union, instead departs from the play's script to deliver a fiery denunciation of the country's lassitude and inaction in the face of the continued Israeli siege. There is much that one may read into this scene, beyond the explicit call to arms: a challenge to the censors and/or security officers in the audience; an abandonment of pre-1967 social reform and progressivism (that is, the preceding debate on love) in favour of a narrow militant nationalism; a belittling dismissal of the students' experiment in aesthetic innovation and democracy in favour of a return to political commitment; or, conversely, an exposure of the formal similarities between the performance of a student play and the 'performance' of nationalist political rhetoric. In the event, Act II comes to an end amidst the sound of rockets: 'and the October War has begun'. Act III commences with scenes from the war, with a lengthy commentary by the playwright that seems to 'depart from the genre of theater in favor of an opinion piece'.[46] A missing scene is then followed by a rather traditional denouement in which the informer reveals his identity and two of the star students celebrate their marriage.

Although it would be unfair to draw too many conclusions about the message of a work left unfinished, these fragments of *Shillat al-Ghad*, when placed in the historical context of their production and their author's larger work, constitute a potentially scathing rebuke to dominant interpretive practices in the political field. A likely backdrop for the play, written in 1974, was the worker and student demonstrations in early and late 1968. Act I of *Shillat al-Ghadd* seems crafted as if it were a direct response to accusations levelled by regime spokespeople in the press that the students were part of a foreign 'plot'. In their scandalous inability to understand *shurum burum* – or, more precisely, in their distorted 'overstanding' – Egypt's security services are exposed as incompetent readers of scripts and scenarios. It may be admitted that the student actors are not entirely innocent of forming a 'wicked gang', at least as the regime defines the term – after all, as we have seen, the second and third acts bristle with open political polemic. But what matters is that the Tomorrow Gang is shown to embody the antithesis of the Official's expectations. Rather than an organised conspiracy of militant fanatics, the students form a rather loose association of emotionally volatile, yet independent-minded individuals who not only argue with their director about philosophy and aesthetics, but manage to remove him from the scene and put on a play of their own making. Yet even in this latter endeavor they turn out to lack discipline and a unified agenda, as the female student representative's departure from the script reveals. Thus, the actors of the Tomorrow Gang fall far short of the hegemonic ambitions of the Striped Ones, to the extent that we may surmise that they represent the author's attempt to present a model of theatrical and political agency directly opposed to that of his previous play. Indeed, placing these two plays side by side reveals that the playwright could entertain more than one conception of group formation, quite unlike the impoverished imagination of rival authors and interpreters.

Yusuf Idris was not unaware that his tampering with the conventions of modern Egyptian theatre had implications far beyond the stage; he was outspoken and insistent on such implications. His oft-cited 'Towards an Egyptian Theater', a series of articles published in 1964, is not so much a manifesto as a scattered collection of thoughts marshalled to support a shifting and elusive thesis about the existence, or non-existence, of an authentically Egyptian theatre.[47] Like all searches for cultural or artistic authenticity, Idris's is an essentially circular pursuit based on broad generalisations and questionable or only superficially described historical data. His central concept of *al-tamasruh* – 'theatricising' or perhaps 'theatricity', used to denote an autonomous Egyptian form of theatre – would seem to be essentially flawed, given its derivation from *al-masrah* ('theatre'), a practice for which he posits a foreign origin.

Yet the real significance of 'Towards an Egyptian Theater' is not Idris's insistence on authenticity – many if not most of his contemporaries in the theatre world shared such concerns – but the aesthetic values he associated with this ideal dramatic form. In fact, Idris's entire argument may be less objectionable if we gloss 'authentically Egyptian' as, instead, 'radically local'. In his view, audience participation was essential. He did not use the word 'democratic', but he made it clear that theatre was at its best when 'spontaneous' (*tilqāʾiyya*), 'collective' (*jamāʿiyya*), and opposed to the 'official form' (*al-shakl al-rasmī*) sanctioned by a ruler or a religion (69). He found these values embodied in the Egyptian village *sāmir* – an evening gathering that featured spontaneous performances of jokes and simple dramatic skits – and in the trickster-like figure of the *farfūr* that was often the centre of attention at such performances. An additional and not unrelated notion forwarded by Idris concerned the agency of the hero in folk tragedies. He suggests, not without some equivocation, that 'Eastern' folk heroes differ essentially from their 'Western' counterparts in that the former possess free will, whereas the latter are beholden to fate or predetermination – a suggestion that would certainly confound the traditional Orientalist. He even goes so far as to claim that the entire debate about whether man is 'free willed' (*mukhayyar*) or 'of predetermined fate' (*musayyar*), together with its underlying concerns about human agency (*fāʿiliyya*), is alien to the Egyptian or Arab cultural matrix, having been imported wholesale from classical Greece (91).

Critics have been divided over whether Idris's theatrical productions ever managed to attain the ideals he set forth in his famous essay.[48] To be sure, his published texts leave little room for spontaneity or any real 'collective' participation, beyond the placing of scripted actors among the audience. Yet if we take the ideals of *al-tamasruh* seriously, then the dictates of Yusuf Idris, as codified in the texts of his plays, are largely beside the point, since what matters is the performance itself, where the potential remains for the 'free will' of future actors and audience members to assert itself. Moreover, the limited gestures towards spontaneity within the lines set down by Idris are quite substantial when compared to the rigid dramatic structures endorsed by those authors and directors, in theatre and politics, which may be deemed 'conspiracist'. In plays like *al-Mukhaṭṭaṭīn* and *Shillat al-Ghad*, the core 'gang' of characters is far from an organised and intentional cabal of pure evil, and their leader or director, when he manages to lead or direct, does so temporarily and after much verbal sparring. Likewise, the Idrisian *farfūr*, if only an unrealised ideal, is no grand conspirator. He is a comic fool whose actions are not entirely his own, and whose primary function is to bring everyone down to size, to disrupt any grand claims to hegemony that may arise among his peers.

And, thus, we are brought back to the hapless Raʾfat Shalabī, the true and original *farfūr*. Reviewed against the drama and dramaturgical notions associated with Yusuf Idris, his trial gains new meaning as a case of a foreign or 'official' theatrical model imposed on an authentically Egyptian, spontaneous, and comical performance. Put another way, Nasser and his security officers, steeped in rigidly dichotomous (or 'striped') concepts of action and authority, were unable to appreciate the ambiguity and jest implicit in Shalabī's role, and thus mistook and miscast the trickster as the devil. Through this mismatch of director and actor, or critic and performance, the

Egypt envisioned by these new rulers was founded on what was at once an aesthetic travesty and a political and ethical crime.

Conclusion

This chapter has attempted to draw connecting lines between the conspiracist performances of state actors, and texts and concepts current in Egyptian theatres in the 1950s and 1960s. The narrow suspicions and scapegoating rituals of the junta leaders, it was argued, can be understood in part as a corollary to the impoverished dramatic figures and frameworks that dominated their imagination. Similarly, the formally static and rigidly constructed dramas of Ali Ahmad Bakathir could be understood as homologous to the conspiracist politics he expressed both through the monologues of his characters and his own broader view of society. Conversely, the comparatively experimental dramatic practices of Yusuf Idris – in particular, his concern for audience participation, endorsement of 'spontaneity' in acting over rigidly scripted roles, unsettling of the authority of the director and playwright, and cultivation of ethical, affective, sartorial, and semantic ambiguity – could be understood as homologous to the critique of political paranoia expressed in the content of his plays. Thus, far from being separate and autonomous phenomena, politics and aesthetic practice may be perceived to be closely intertwined, performed along similar lines.

The same idea may be detected in an exchange of dialogue that occurs in the second act of Idris's *al-Mukhaṭṭaṭīn*, as Almaz, the actress, leads the takeover of the play/organisation called The Foundation of Greater Happiness. The foundation's general manager is enamoured, but suspicious of this dazzling woman who has appeared out of the blue to offer her opinions on how the place should be run. He is particularly bewildered by the fact that Almāẓ, just like the other new employees she begins installing in sensitive positions, is dressed from head to toe in vertical black-and-white stripes. 'I'd like to know, at the very least, why it is you've made yourself up like this?' he asks. Her reply, the first of several equivocations, is simple: 'So I've got on stripes, big deal. It's the latest fashion (*mōda*). Haven't you heard of the Striped Ones?' (48). Ideological affiliation has become a matter of style; art and politics are one.

Although Almāẓ is just being glib, it is worth taking her words seriously. To think of *takhṭīṭ* – the dichotomies and reductions of conspiracism – as a fashion, a style, a *mōda* that one wears or is made to wear, has significant implications for how we perceive the agents it envelopes. A *mōda* isn't exactly the deliberate choice of its follower, nor is it a straight-jacket into which the individual is forced, and from which there is no escape. It is somewhere in between these two extremes. Put another way, the conspiracist model of drama we have scrutinised above is neither consciously and freely crafted discourse, nor is it pure and unconscious ideology, but a style that one catches and is caught by, an aesthetic trend that one gets the feel for, uses to express oneself, becomes infatuated with, grows weary of, is consumed by, and may or may not ultimately abandon (as does Brother at the end of Idris's play).

The question posed by the general manager – 'Why have you made yourself (up) like this?' (*inti ᶜamla fi nafsik kida lēh*) – addresses only part of the issue. As an executive, perhaps it is only natural that he perceives style in terms of actor intentionality. But the text is not a deliberate 'plan' (*mukhaṭṭaṭ*) controlled by a single, free-willed 'master planner' (*mukhaṭṭiṭ*). In their dramas and performances, the Free Officers were no more free agents than their contemporary playwrights were autonomous and unprecedented – or, indeed, 'authentic' – creators of form. Nor would it be accurate to assert, in spite of the focus of this chapter, that dramaturgical structures and concepts alone dictated roles, positions, and performances of playwrights and politicians. As the coming chapters will explore, affect, emotion, critical practice, and play are also crucial frameworks through which to understand the scripts and styles of conspiracy.

2

Naguib Surur:
The Poetics and Politics of *Niyāka*

Mansura, a provincial capital in the Nile Delta, is too small to harbour the ambitions of the would-be singer and entertainer il-Ḥilwa ʿAzīza (lit. 'Pretty Aziza' or 'Pretty Darling'). Encouraged by her good looks, her indomitable *baladī* sass, and a constant entourage of admirers, she sets off for the lights and glamour of Cairo without a doubt in her mind that fame and fortune will be soon to follow. Her dreams are shattered, however, when on a return visit to her hometown, a local suitor she once rejected surprises her at the train station and hurls a bottle of acid in her face. 'Pretty ʿAzīza!' he shouts in the manner demanded by B-grade drama, 'You won't be pretty any more!' The man and his accomplice are tackled by passersby, but the deed is done, and ʿAzīza, her face now horribly disfigured, finds work as a nightclub manager while she plots her revenge.

This rather conventional tale of city-bound, recalcitrant femininity and provincial, take-it-or-leave-it masculine pride – dramatised in the 1969 film *il-Ḥilwa ʿAzīza* (dir. Ḥasan al-Imām) – would be unremarkable, were it not for the names behind the roles: playing ʿAzīza, the famed diva and star of the silver screen Hind Rustum (1931–2011), and, as her assailant, the poet and playwright Naguib Surur (1932–78). While the role was a familiar one for Rustum, it was for Surur his sole cameo appearance in film, and a performance that would soon be forgotten amidst his many and mighty contributions to modern Egyptian literature. That is not to say that he was acting out of character. After graduating from the Higher Institute for Dramatic Arts in Cairo in 1956, Surur would begin to draw attention to himself as an uncompromising son of Egypt (in particular, his native village of Akhṭāb), who was capable of answering his critics and oppressors through unique, if not unprecedented in the history of Arabic literature, expressions of vengeance and spite. This was a persona that Surur fashioned for himself both in poetry – as in his debut ode 'al-Ḥidhā'' ('The Shoe') (1956), which tells of a violent encounter between a villager (Surur's father) and a local landowner[1] – and in public, as when he delivered a fiery speech against the Egyptian and Syrian 'dictatorships' while a student in Moscow in 1959.

Among younger generations, Surur is remembered not through performances like these, nor through the dramas he based loosely on folk legends,[2] but through a collection of profanity-laced poems he would begin to compose shortly after leaving the set of *il-Ḥilwa ʿAzīza*. These *Kuss-ummiyyāt* ('[Quatrains] of Your Mother's Cunt' or perhaps 'Mother-Cunt-ets') are the versified rantings and ravings of a man who refuses to be 'fucked' (*mitnāk*) by the sundry oversexed hypocrites and thieves who he believes have overrun art, politics, Egypt in its entirety, and, indeed, the world as a whole. In addition to vengeful shots of misogyny fired at actresses and movie stars – the verbal equivalent of the author's putatively make-believe 'acid' attack on Hind Rustum – the poems contain allusions and accusations regarding an age-old, global conspiracy of 'Jews', 'Zionists', and 'Freemasons' that stands behind everything from modern colonialism, Egypt's police state, and bad literature to the poet's own personal traumas of divorce, professional failure, exile, psychological collapse, imprisonment, torture, homelessness, impotence, and imminent death.

Although the mavens of taste and custodians of value would surely dispute it,[3] the *Kuss-ummiyyāt* may be counted among Surur's most important literary works. This is not only because, in the opinion of at least one observer, the poems have been secretly consumed in some form by 'most, if not all' of Egypt's intelligentsia since their composition in the early 1970s.[4] It is clear that Surur himself valued the *Kuss-ummiyyāt* as a rare 'historical document' that he wished to see 'spread by any means' for the sake of posterity – despite claims by friends and critics like Rajā' al-Naqqāsh (1934–2008) and Safinaz Kazem (Ṣāfī Nāz Kāẓim) (b. 1937) that the poet expressed regret about their composition.[5] In addition to their enduring popularity and undiminished ability to shock, the poems are notable for their uncanny vitality, their success at seeming spontaneous and even 'authentic', their unapologetic rending asunder of literary and linguistic norms, and the frankness and scope of their political critique that, in the context of a particularly dark period in Egypt's modern history, was almost without parallel. Certainly when considering the literary elite with whom Surur mingled and who, while far from complacent, generally preferred the protections afforded by allegory, absurdism, or abstraction, his indictment of the powers-that-be was unmatched. In comparison to much of the rest of his work, too, the *Kuss-ummiyyāt* stand out not only for their vulgarity, but for their aesthetic inventiveness. At the same time, they are not, despite sustained attempts to whitewash Surur's legacy[6] – a total anomaly in his literary oeuvre, but rather channel, concentrate, and refine the themes expressed in numerous previous and subsequent poems, plays, and critical essays.

While the anxieties about national sovereignty, political oppression, and artistic authenticity that found expression in Surur's larger oeuvre were shared by many, if not most, of his fellow artists and intellectuals in Cairo and beyond, the invective delivered in the *Kuss-ummiyyāt*, as well as his subsequent critical, dramatic, and poetic work, was so flagrant and over the top that both contemporary and subsequent critics deemed him out of his mind. When, in the late 1960s and early 1970s, Surur was on several occasions admitted – forcibly, in his own account – into various mental asylums, and moreover when rumours and reports circulated that he was stomping about barefoot and delirious on the streets of Cairo, friends and foes alike found mental illness the easiest way to make sense of the man, and a good justification for disparaging or ignoring his creative work. Thus, both the caustically critical Fārūq ʿAbd al-Qādir, and the generally sympathetic Rajāʾ al-Naqqāsh, could agree that the *Kuss-ummiyyāt*, if not other works by the author, were the product of a severely disturbed mind, and therefore did not warrant any serious attention.[7] In reaction to this view, recent attempts have been made to absolve Surur of the accusation of madness by showing that in his most extreme performances, such as the poems under consideration, he was in fact playing the well-rehearsed role of clown or buffoon, aiming for jest but ending up tragically misunderstood.[8] A third view, not entirely separate from the previous, is that Surur, if not actually the victim of a global Zionist conspiracy as he claimed, nonetheless spoke important fundamental truths about the powers-that-be, and therefore could not be considered genuinely mad. At various times, whether wittingly or unwittingly, Surur himself seemed to encourage all of these interpretations, with frequent allusions to madness and the pretend role of the author/actor in nearly all of his works.

Rather than adjudicate on what is an easily misleading choice between authorial intentionality and psychosis – that is, the question, 'Was Surur really mad?' – this chapter aims instead to gather up some of the many pieces of the author's conspiracist style, and attempt to discern the principal aesthetic patterns and processes that fit them together, or don't. Our methods for pursuing this task, like the *Kuss-ummiyyāt* themselves, may appear deceptively unconventional in some respects, while at base they rely on conventions that are quite established and familiar in literature and literary criticism. For the sake of clarity, let us list them here:

(1) Historical and Biographical Data
(2) Translation of Selected Verses
(3) Synopsis and Exegesis

In the first section, we attempt to make sense of the *Kuss-ummiyyāt* in terms of events, texts, and performances in the author's life that preceded and coincided with their composition. While some of the sources we assemble here have existed in the relative obscurity of personal collections, critical anthologies, and nearly inaccessible editions of periodicals, many enjoyed wide circulation in Egypt, and would frame, if not wholly determine, the poems' subsequent reception. In the second section, we present a translation of those portions of the poems that are most relevant to our discussion of conspiracy and conspiracism. Thus, while we hope to present a fair sampling of the poems' overall style and content, the more humbling task of a full English edition is left to future scholars. In the third section, we divide the poems into a total of fourteen thematic 'parts'. Of these, conspiracist themes are especially salient in seven (1–5, 7, 14), which we privilege with closer reading, to the exclusion of the other parts. The goal in this section is not to marshal all of our observations into the service of a single argument (or diagnosis), but to open up various routes for interpretation, allow ambiguities and contradictions to rise to the surface, acknowledge the resistance of certain verses to analysis, and, ultimately, to appreciate the complexity of the poems as both aesthetically and psychologically significant works of literature. Although piecemeal and often digressive, the critical work done in this section is, we believe, that most suited to the object itself. In this, we set aside critical anxieties about being 'contaminated' by conspiracism, and open ourselves to being moved, affected, manipulated, enchanted, and repelled by the text all at once.

Historical and Biographical Data

The relationship between a given literary text and the life of its historical author is often, when not dismissed as either theoretically or ethically out of bounds for criticism, subject to intense conjecture. Yet with much of his work, Naguib Surur was eager to close the gap between his biographical self and the performative 'I'. This is especially the case with the *Kuss-ummiyyāt*, which are not only accompanied by their author's own explanatory and autobiographical footnotes, but can be placed alongside a number of key documents and testimonies that illuminate the pretexts and contexts of their composition. In what follows, our main concern is not the veracity of this paratextual material – or, as has been the case with the bulk of the poems' critical reception, to deploy tragic biographical data in an effort to 'absolve' the author for the supposed 'guilt' of their composition – but its ability to provide a meaningful departure point for our reading of the poems.

Although the *Kuss-ummiyyāt* are usually dated to the period from 1969 – when Surur was forced into the ʿAbbāsiyya Hospital for Psychological Illnesses, Egypt's most notorious mental asylum – to 1975 – when the poet was discharged from the country's second-most notorious mental asylum, the al-Nabawī al-Muhandis Hospital in al-Maʿmūra, Alexandria – the events it recalls began well before this.[9] In addition to the 1967 *naksa* – a moment of collective trauma that for many Egyptian authors signalled the end of a fantasy of national progress, and for some even an end to meaningful literary output – the crisis that gave rise to these poems was the result of years of exile, rejection, illness, and loss.

In 1959, Surur travelled to Moscow after winning an Egyptian government scholarship to study theatre. It was to be a transformative experience. While in the Soviet Union, he met and married his first wife, Sasha Korsakova, with whom he would have two children (a section of the *Kuss-ummiyyāt* would later be dedicated to his son Shuhdī, b. 1962). Also while there, he publicly embraced communism, an ideology that he would later renounce; had his Egyptian citizenship revoked after denouncing Nasser at an event for solidarity with Cuba at Moscow State University and refusing an order to return to Egypt; became an alcoholic; and was beaten and arrested by Soviet police after a quarrel at a restaurant.[10] It was also in Moscow that Surur's anti-Zionist conspiracy theories seem to have been first articulated to a public audience. In his account of the poet's time abroad, Surur's fellow student Abū Bakr Yūsuf describes how, in about 1963, Surur started to complain about what he perceived as 'Zionist influence' in the Soviet Union, to which his friends responded with scepticism.[11]

During 1963 and 1964, Surur took refuge, at the invitation of an Egyptian exile, in Budapest, where he worked for the Arabic department of state radio. Thus began his painful seven-year separation from his Russian wife and his son, Shuhdī, which would also feature as a major theme in the *Kuss-ummiyyāt*. It was also during his time in Budapest that the distinct nature of his emotional and physical crisis began to be known to a wide audience back home in Egypt. This was largely due to an article published by the famous journalist and literary critic Rajā᾽ al-Naqqāsh in the newspaper *al-Jumhūriyya* – an organ founded by the Free Officers as the voice of their regime soon after coming to power – in which he appealed to the Minister of Culture and fellow intellectuals to help Surur regain his Egyptian citizenship and thus be allowed to return to the country. Al-Naqqāsh gives a general impression of what he refers to alternately as the artist's 'internal torment', his 'unrelenting anxiety', 'diseases of the soul', and 'crisis', writing that, from his own memories of encountering Surur back in Egypt,

> he [Surur] was not the only victim of his acutely painful psychological nature. All those around him suffered from it as well. For his psychological torment was quite often mixed with a great suspicion and mistrust in people and life in general. He often imagined that people were not being true, and that they did not hold him in proper esteem or admiration. In fact he believed that they had nothing but intense hate for him.[12]

Al-Naqqāsh insinuates that Surur's personal torment had, in Budapest, erupted into something of a nervous breakdown. As evidence of Surur's desperate state, he quotes directly from a letter that the artist had recently written to his father. 'Dear father', al-Naqqāsh's transcription of the letter reads,

> Without getting into details, which my time does not permit me to recount, I write to you urging that you keep calm [lit., 'take control of your nerves'] until this storm I am passing through goes by. If anything happens to me, anything at all, know that it is not suicide but murder, and that those responsible are Zionist agents in Hungary as well as anti-Soviet forces, seeing that my wife herself is a Soviet. I thus urge you to insist on an autopsy – an autopsy of my corpse, if what I suspect does indeed happen – and that this be carried out by Egyptian doctors – only Egyptians – and that I be buried in Egypt, only Egypt, the homeland. However, should I manage to escape this time, as I hope and you hope, then I and you will be relieved of these troubles forever. The coming days will be decisive. I will call you on the telephone as soon as the storm passes. If it does not pass, then I bid you all farewell, my dear loved ones. Farewell, and until we meet again, O native soil, Egypt. Your son, Naguib.[13]

Given what we know from Surur's own polemics about the competitiveness, backstabbing, and vitriol that infused cultural politics in Egypt in the 1960s and 1970s – to say nothing of more recent times[14] – al-Naqqāsh's article is remarkably sympathetic and forgiving. He even goes so far as to plead with his readers to overlook Surur's ostensible malice and not take his 'behaviour' and 'positions' personally, given his tremendous talents and great potential. Although he has referred to what he called the artist's 'acutely painful psychological nature (*ṭabīᶜatihi*)', he goes on to say that he is not 'evil and ill-intentioned by nature (*bi-ṭabᶜihi*)' but rather afflicted by 'a great crisis of the soul, perhaps due to circumstances in his private life that no one knows about'.[15] While absolving Surur of personal culpability for his eccentricities, al-Naqqāsh thus also refuses to speculate overmuch on their possible etiology, preferring instead to leave them unknown and, perhaps unintentionally, contributing an attractive aura of mystery to the poet's public persona.

It is worth noting, before moving on, that although both Abū Bakr Yūsuf and Rajāʾ al-Naqqāsh dismissed Surur's dark suspicions about those around him as pathological, they nonetheless shared some of his notions about the nature of the forces that ruled the world. Thus, Yūsuf, although he states that

Surur's claims about 'Zionist influence' in the Soviet Union were frowned upon by colleagues, indicates that their objections concerned not the existence of a worldwide Zionist conspiracy as such, but the idea that the Soviet Union, held in such high esteem both ideologically and in terms of its defiance of the United States, could possibly be tainted by the forces of evil.[16] Similarly, al-Naqqāsh vouches for Surur's patriotism and good intentions by noting that the artist 'refused to sell himself to the Devil and work against his country, [to cooperate] with the many forces that conspire against us and try to exploit any means and every opportunity to harm us and to tarnish our reputation and that of our Revolution'.[17] In one sense, given that he was writing an appeal to Egyptian state authorities, al-Naqqāsh probably had no choice but to invoke conspiracy theory: by this time in the mid-1960s, the tropic language of 'conspiracy' and of enemy forces 'tarnishing Egypt's reputation' had become something of a catechism by which to measure a writer's loyalty to the regime. Whatever the case, these testimonies indicate that the central images of Surur's 'crisis of the soul', while given particularly dramatic expression, were not his own creation but were part of a circulating set of tropes and themes in Egyptian public discourse and perhaps in the Arab World more broadly.

The next chapter in Naguib Surur's journey began with his successful repatriation. It seems his re-aggregation into Egypt's cultural field, evident in his appointment as professor at the Higher Institute for Dramatic Arts and his directing of a number of plays, was initially felicitous. In an interview with the magazine *al-Jīl* ('Generation') upon his return to Egypt, Surur sounds remarkably optimistic. Asked to comment on his plans for directing and the future of Egyptian theatre, he refers, among others, to a playwright (Khalīl al-Raḥīmi) who had withdrawn from the world of Egyptian theatre due to what he perceived as its 'corruption and phoniness'. Fortunately, Surur observes, after returning from abroad he has found that Egyptian theatre had 'indeed rid itself of the atmosphere of phoniness and falsity, and become a serious art with real advocates and patrons'; al-Raḥīmi had thus promised him he would return to writing.[18] Even if one may detect a hint of sarcasm in Surur's remarks, they contrast sharply with the very direct and unrestrained style of criticism for which he was known.

Yet whatever optimism he may have entertained in this interview was incredibly short-lived. The very next year, he announced that he was retiring from directing, complaining in an interview with *al-Jumhūriyya* that low wages had forced him to choose between being either a 'suicidal warrior' (*fidāʾī*) or an 'opportunist', and that the few plays he had managed to direct were the target of an organised assault by familiar forces against him personally.[19] Thus began Surur's second, and more devastating, departure into the wilderness, from which he would only manage to return for a few brief periods of calm before his death in 1978. It was during this period, especially following the 1967 *naksa*, that his personal agony again made news. In a letter published in the cultural magazine *al-Kawākib* in 1968, Surur lists his consecutive tragedies: he had been suffering from 'crushing' unemployment, had been made homeless, had been dismissed from his teaching position after only two years, and had divorced his Egyptian wife.[20] This was a reference to the actress Samīra Muḥsin (b. 1945), whom he had married shortly after his return to Egypt while remaining wed to his Russian spouse, and who would soon feature as a central target of his highly sexualised polemic in the *Kuss-ummiyyāt*. It is thus all the more remarkable that Surur was able to appear alongside (or rather, in the path of) Hind Rustum in *il-Ḥilwa ʿAzīza*, which was released in theatres the very next year. In the film, despite his violent 'act', he appears relatively healthy, far from the emaciated build and worn features he would display in later years. Sometime in 1969, amidst obscure circumstances, Surur is alleged to have been abducted by the Egyptian security services and held against his will at the ʿAbbāsiyya Hospital for Psychological Illnesses.[21] On this experience, we may quote the poet himself. In a letter he wrote, but never managed to get delivered, to Yusuf Idris, Surur calls out the revered author for failing to engage with the true extent of the suffering endured by generations of Egyptian writers and patriots.[22] To drive home the point, he recounts his own suffering in detail, and relates the disturbing stories of his fellow inmates. It is worth quoting his words at some length, not only as a testimony to his plight, but also in order to preserve the anxious and elliptical style of his prose:

> They[23] caught me as soon as I returned [to Egypt] from Damascus and sent me … but wait, not to one of the well known and overcrowded government prisons, but to the insane asylums, the Hospital of Psychological Illnesses at al-ʿAbbāsiyya!! There they have a secret department – Department One

– where they applied to me the latest methods and techniques in torture! There with me were university students, high school freshmen, textile factory workers, university professors, engineers, *fallāhīn*, and atomic scientists. Among the latter was Dr. Imām, professor of atomic science at Alexandria University [Egypt]. I don't know why he trusted me and felt able to warm up to me, especially since he distrusted even himself. He told me that, while in the United States, he refused to accept huge, unimaginable sums and diabolical [lit., 'hellish'] offers, and returned to his homeland, because he loved his country and wanted to put his knowledge and expertise at her service. [He refused] because these were Zionist offers, and because his nation was in danger, our enemy was strong and multi-tentacled [lit. 'octopus-like'], and because matters were reversed or upside-down: it wasn't America that controls Zionism, but Zionism that controls America and the West in general. [He refused] because of our weakness, because 'What was taken by force can be retrieved only by force', because what was desired for the people of Palestine and for the Arab Umma as a whole was that they should end up just like the Red Indians [that is, the Native Americans], save for the mercy of God and our own might! He begged me to stay awake next to him so that he could have an hour of sleep, for the dark angels [*al-zabāniya*] could come for him at any moment, and do to him at night what they had done to him during the day. He often insinuated that the Zionists had tried to kill him in America, and all around the Arab World. He asserted that ᶜAlī Muṣṭafā Musharrafa, the colleague and equal to Einstein, had been killed by poison, just like the great archaeologist Dr. Salīm Ḥasan – this being the fate of any great talent or genius in Egypt especially, and in the Arab World more broadly, from the Nile to the Euphrates.[24]

Surur goes on to cite Dr Imām's favourite quotations from *The Protocols of the Wise Men of Zion*, as well as from famous speeches by Gamal Abdel Nasser, on the essential 'evil' of both Jews and Zionists. He resumes:

Dr. Imām would say: How long will we remain generous, tolerant, accepting? For how long will we forget and forgive?! Such is real suicide, such is madness! Then he would insinuate with much embarrassment that they had violated him in the manner of 'al-ᶜAskarī al-Aswad' [The Black Soldier, 1962] and had forced him repeatedly to write reports on his students, colleagues, etc. And he would always say: The Jews never left Egypt. They are here, inside us, at all levels of society, in every profession, sect, and religion, in every political party and organization from the far right to the far left, and from the left of the right to the right and the center-left and what have you. They are there in all the nationalities, all shapes and sizes, all colors and dyes and makeup. They are that wondrous mix of hybrids and mixed-raced people, or as you put it in *al-Mukhaṭṭaṭīn* [The Striped Ones].[25]

Unfortunately, the following quote from Idris's play is deemed 'illegible' by the editor of Surur's manuscript. This last section of the poet's testimony is nonetheless of great significance, in that it reveals his interest in articulating personal and political events in specific literary terms. This is part of a larger strategy – or, if we are to avoid privileging authorial intentionality, let us call it a habit or style – that we will encounter in our analysis of the *Kuss-ummiyyāt*, and evident in Surur's other works, in which famous literary and cultural figures, motifs, scripts, and theories are channelled into his representations of self and other.

What we have here is not simply the case of a sensitive individual falling under the 'influence' of dangerous imaginings. Although the poet's indebtedness to major touchstones of (conspi)racist literature – notably the *Protocols* and Egyptian regime discourse – is evident, there are at least three points we may raise to complicate any direct and unmediated model of textual causality. First, the reality of the torture suffered by Surur and many uncounted other 'undesirables' in Egyptian state hospitals and prisons is not to be disputed – it is rather the interpretation of these traumas in conspiracist terms that warrants further critical reflection. Second, not all of Surur's anxieties and accusations are borrowed wholesale and uninspected from other texts. Quite the contrary – in many cases, we see he has significantly repackaged, shaken up, or altered the contents or meaning of a particular text, sometimes beyond recognition. In the testimony above, we see this in his insinuations about Idris's play, *al-Mukhaṭṭaṭīn*, the message of which he seems to have completely reversed. Whereas Surur sees the play as a warning against what he calls 'that wondrous mix of hybrids and mixed-raced people' who take on 'all shapes and sizes, all colors and dyes and makeup', we will recall from the previous chapter that it is not colour, but black-and-white dichotomies that the play presents as dangerous. This is in one sense a grotesque misinterpretation; in another sense, it is likely that Surur has rather identified with the earlier ideological version of 'Brother', and has placed the blame for his downfall not on the ideology of black and white, but on the wily and opportunistic phonies that surround him. (Although Surur does not explicitly state it, he appears to imply that these 'Striped Ones' are also Jewish – thus interpolating the play into traditional anti-Semitic conspiracy theory.) Third, the conspiracy theories expounded in the excerpts above are not directly spoken by Surur himself, but are attributed to a mysterious 'Dr. Imām'. It is possible that this figure, or his discourse, is in essence a projection of Surur's own opinions, either because he wished to create a certain distance between himself and notions about which he harboured some doubt, or because he felt they would be deemed more credible coming from a man who was at once a doctor, an 'imam', and a nuclear scientist. 'My imam' is also how Surur often referred to Abū al-ʿAlāʾ al-Maʿarrī, the tenth-century poet and philosopher who would also whisper assorted plots to him.[26] Whatever the case, the existence of this other figure imposes a dialogic dimension on the conspiracism, and wraps its origins in the inscrutable ambiguity of minds that doubt even themselves.

Surur's release from al-ʿAbbāsiyya is as obscure as his admission, although it is clear that by 1970 he was out on the street again. In May of that year, the poet and critic Aḥmad ʿAbd al-Muʿṭī Ḥijāzī (b. 1935) pulished an open letter in the magazine *Rūz al-Yūsuf*.[27] 'The dramatist, poet, and author Nagib Surur faces an imminent catastrophe', the letter, entitled 'Anqidhū Najīib Surūr' ('Save Naguib Surur'), begins. 'He has been seen in the streets and public places of Cairo in a pitiful state: disheveled, confused, and in deteriorating health.' Ḥijāzī concludes the letter with an appeal:

> Surely one of these bodies [the Ministry of Culture, the Egyptian Radio and Television Union, the Actors' Syndicate, and other cultural institutions and personalities of influence] would be able to pay for his treatment at some sanitarium. No doubt his family, friends, and colleagues will contribute emotionally to his completion of this necessary treatment, before taking care of any other problem he faces, most especially that of employment!

Ḥijāzī seems unaware that Surur had already received 'treatment' at a 'sanitarium', and that it had not only exacerbated whatever illness he suffered previously, but compounded it with many new traumas.

It is often assumed that the *Kuss-ummiyyāt* emerged from the agony and otherworldliness of al-ʿAbbāsiyya.[28] There is indeed a poetic truth to this belief, which we will explore in more detail below. It deserves noting, however, that other equally plausible and significant origins have been suggested. The author Shawqī Fahīm, a friend of Surur, states that the poet began writing the *Kuss-ummiyyāt* in 1968 – in other words, immediately after his divorce from his Egyptian wife, but before entering al-ʿAbbāsiyya.[29] Curiously, Fahīm does not even mention al-ʿAbbāsiyya in his account, only the asylum at al-Maʿmūra in Alexandria, which Surur first entered in 1973, and seems to have been a much less traumatic experience.[30] It is at al-Maʿmūra, too, that the author of the *Kuss-ummiyyāt* says in a postscript he finished composing them – however, in the manuscript we discuss here, this postscript is followed by additional poems, presumably written at some later date.

For obvious reasons, the *Kuss-ummiyyāt* were not published during Surur's lifetime. Rather, they circulated underground in informally jotted-down copies, by word of mouth, and on scratchy cassette recordings of the poet himself reciting them in public to the intermittent laughter and weeping of his audience. The novelist ʿAbdū Jubayr describes one such performance in 1977:

> No sooner did I enter [Café Riche] than I witnessed Naguib Surur acting out a piece of the *Ummiyyāt*. He stood in the middle of the place and expressed himself with his hands, his face, his voice, and his captivating presence – that is to say, with his entire body. Instead of laughing – for in the *Ummiyyāt* there is much humor – the audience became teary-eyed. Then he turned to gesture with his hand at the cafe's owner, who was displeased with the offensive expressions, saying 'Alright, just a couple more words'. And I heard the owner mutter: 'What he's saying is alright, but it ain't alright saying out in public'. Then Naguib sat back down, still shaking.[31]

The setting of Café Riche is highly significant, as this was perhaps the most famous watering ground for Cairo's literati and intellectuals for several decades. Naguib Mahfouz, Amal Dunqul, Aḥmad Fuʾād Nijm, Khayrī Shalabī, and other stars of the literary scene were regular customers, and a number of them were either parodied, insulted, or otherwise mentioned in the *Kuss-ummiyyāt*. Thus, while the poems have been censored, gone underground, and been met with the scorn of orthodox critics, they were performed and indeed flourished at, or within hearing distance of, the very centre of the Egyptian cultural field, rather than on its margins as may be presumed.

The poems existed in an ephemeral state until 1998, when the poet's son Shuhdī (b. 1962), to which a portion of the *Kuss-ummiyyāt* were addressed as a sort of last will and testament, published them online. It took at least a year for the Egyptian authorities to take notice, and Shuhdī was subsequently sentenced to time in prison for breaking laws on 'public morality'; he fled abroad before the sentence could be implemented. Today, the version Shuhdī published is readily available on many websites, as are portions of the audio recordings made of Naguib Surur sometime in the 1970s.

Translation

What follows is a translation of select verses, based on the version of the *Kuss-ummiyyāt* published online by Shuhdī Surūr (S1).[32] The few, but significant, differences that exist between this written version and the available audio recordings (S2, S3) will be discussed in later sections.[33] It bears keeping in mind that the *Kuss-ummiyyāt* present the translator with numerous, perhaps insurmountable, difficulties, quite apart from the expected challenges of rhyme, rhythm, and linguistic register (in this case, coarse Egyptian colloquial and slang). To do these poems justice, the translator must take into account not just the literal meaning of the words, but the web of images and associations they conjure for the listener, the sense of appropriateness and humour that accompany their use, and the larger discourses, genres, and literary and linguistic ideologies with which they conflict, interact, and conspire. The body of the performer – his affects and emotions, coughs and verbal slips – should also be read as integral to the text, as should the reactions of the audience, such as those described by ꜥAbdū Jubayr. Future studies and translations may wish to consider not just the 'signal' of the poems, but also the 'noise': the quality of the recording, the sirens and car horns in the background, the cacophony of the café. Ultimately, however, I have opted for a mostly plain and literal translation of the *Kuss-ummiyyāt*, given that our interest is more in the content of the poems (that is, their tropes, imagery, symbols, and intertextual references) than in their prosody.[34] Although the idiomatic nature of the text has required in many instances a departure from the letter of the Arabic, attention has been given as much as possible to reproducing the intended meaning.

Selections from 'The Mother-Cunt-ets of Nagib Surur' (*Kuss-ummiyyāt Nagīb Surūr*)

[1] The first one goes 'Oh'
[2] The second one's 'Pfui'
[3] The third one's a 'Hee-haw!'

[4] O fuck, O fuck, O night!
[5] O fuck, O fuck, O eye!

[6] Where can I find people to recite/reach the meanings of my words,
[7] Who, like a horny man, would fuck a faggot when they see one?

[8] It's a wondrous time when a faggot's a director,
[9] And a manager, too, O twisted scales of time!

[10] When a kiss-ass bastard rules over a team of artists,
[11] Working for a bigger kiss-ass, and controls our theatre
[12] You can bid farewell to art, dear gents,
[13] And make way for corruption, shenanigans, and kiss-assing,
[14] (And jobbery, mobbery, mulberry and strawberry!)

[15] Get over it, man! Tell me something useful
[16] Swallow your mother-fucking pride, do yourself a favour
[17] Art's a racket [lit., 'a stock market'], you take and you pay
[18] Bend over so I can fuck you, and pray for He Who intercedes

[19] We said we'd clean up our act, they said don't bother
[20] We've only had one *naksa*, we'll have a hundred others

[21] It's a country of fuckers, everyone's given her a fuck
[22] Just take a look at the map, she's got her legs spread apart
[23] God's made her that way, what are you gonna do about it?

[24] O fuck, O fuck, O night!
[25] O fuck, O fuck, O eye!

…

[80] I take a look at the people in the 'studio' and say, 'What Wonder!'
[81] Who's bent over, and who hasn't bent over yet
[82] Out of despair, I put my hand on my cock
[83] And tell him to bend over too, he tells me to watch my language

[84] Art's a real bitch, but I got no spare change
[85] I'm lost to lust, and it's no help I got talent
[86] The testy bitch's all made up with giggles and groans
[87] If only I were a bitch and smoked Kent, you bastards!

…

[118] My luck's all rotten, even with the dames
[119] I once knew a whore and thought she'd go clean
[120] But her cunt's diseased, you'd sooner cure cancer
[121] Her cunt's got 'adultery' written all over it!

[122] She's a riddle, this wicked girl, she'd even go for a fuck in China
[123] And manage to get fucked on the same day in Qalyūb!
[124] She's a Phantom [fighter jet], man has she got wings
[125] What can I do but hurl rocks at her?

…

[170] Tharwat ʿUkāsha's a fag, take it from me
[171] A minister, and he still out-mans me – when I'm already down, of course
[172] He fucks my wife, I swear, just ask al-Ṣāwī
[173] What's a poor fellow to do when nothing's any use

[174] Directors, actors, managers – even the minister's fucked her
[175] Even that 'Naguib' fellow I've written so much about
[176] See how's she's got 'adultery' stamped on her thighs
[177] Say it after me: 'Naguib's' returned the favour to 'Naguib'

...

[192] I pushed on like a camel, and they threw me in the slammer
[193] Said it's an 'asylum' – that means 'whack pow bam'
[194] Which is to say they'll beat the living daylights out of you
[195] 'You wanna play tough guy with me, you little pansy?!'

[196] 'You can bet your mother's cunt,' I replied, 'Hang me and I'll die a man.'
[197] They called my bluff and strung me up by a towel
[198] They hung me twice in one day, and I looked up to heaven
[199] 'Take me, O Lord, I'm no son of a whore'

[200] I'm a son of Egypt, which has known hangings and cholera
[201] Since the age of Khufu, Khafra, and the Door-Knocker[35]
[202] If the Jews hang me in the secret, what would happen?
[203] They'd say he's crazy, he hung himself, and *I'm* the liar

[204] Hang him up, but give him an injection before his pulse stops
[205] He'll come to, then hang him again, then give him another shot so he comes to
[206] That day I said, 'O Lord, let us die'
[207] But the injection replied, 'Your mother's cunt! Take *that*!'

...

[216] Why does every Egyptian have snipers watching him like eagles
[217] Watching him sleep, one behind the door and another through the window
[218] Say, why are our talents snatched away one after the other
[219] Of course so we go backwards, meaning so we get fucked

[220] O Sayyid, O Darwish, you brilliant mind: Why were you poisoned
[221] While the people were distracted with Saʿd's return from exile
[222] Died on the Day of Resurrection, who would mourn
[223] The deceased, when everyone's got smacked on the back of the neck?

[224] O Egypt: It's all the work of the Jews in the dark
[225] These wolves who've been hunting your children for years

[226] Snakes in the pigeon coop while the country's been sleeping
[227] It's no wonder we've been disgraced and defeated!

[228] They made me go thirsty for three days in the hot sun
[229] Until I went blind, then they led me out to the tanks
[230] I groped around 'til I found me a pump
[231] Turned out it's not water, but gas! Help me out here, my friends

[232] Where be the fountain (*sabīl*) when the fountain is poisoned and I'm thirsty
[233] Pray assist me, O Mighty Ḥusayn! Look upon me, O generation of gas!
[234] My privates are ruined, looks like it could be cancer
[235] How delightful to see hippies dancing to jazz

[236] They brought in children like my own son and fucked them right in front of me
[237] So that there's your children's future for you
[238] It ain't any use, they'll just throw your children away
[239] To get fucked and gassed, just like your forefathers

[240] Why I swear by my own mother's elbow:
[241] It's you faggots who'll drink your gas and go get fucked for the rest of us
[242] And if you escape this time, then fuck me
[243] And fuck he who writes the *Kuss-ummiyyāt*!

[244] Well I suppose they could have fucked me when I was sleeping
[245] I don't mean natural sleep, I mean doping
[246] They might have filmed the whole thing for all I know
[247] They'd even deny those they fuck the pleasure to groan

…

[254] They asked me what's all this about fucking
[255] Why'd you quit talking about politicking?
[256] Don't you know, you fuckers, that politics means fucking
[257] And fucking means politics? And her guardian is her robber!

[258] Those hook-up flats aren't just for a having a good time,

[259] For cocktails and cocks in tails

[260] The trouble's not with fucking – a cock in a cunt,

[261] That's simple – but behind the fucking there's espionage!

...

[278] Why everywhere I go I catch whiff of fucking

[279] Like I've been getting fucked for thousands of years

[280] Well what can I say when there's fucking all around me

[281] All I've got left are these *kuss-ummiyyāt*

[282] There's nothing wrong with saying *kuss-ummiyyāt* when my brain's gone burst

[283] There's no shame or blame or bull in it

[284] While Egypt's got her cunt torn up right in front of me

[285] Full of ulcers from all the fucking, and there's nothing you can do about it

...

[458] In the restroom I find they've banned all rest

[459] The investigations squad comes in right behind me

[460] Watching me left–right and all around

[461] Pardon the intrusion, we'll have a sample of that urine

[462] After analysis they find it's type E for 'emergency'

[463] So they can put me in a category, even if it's 'Shiite'

[464] It makes no difference, as long as they can get their Q&A

[465] When it matters they can make 'Shiite' read 'communist'

[466] I'm no communist, no Shiite, no nothing

[467] But there's still a long list to go, all colour-coded categories

[468] A blind interrogator and stupid wolf stabbing

[469] In the dark, and I say pity the poor sheep

[470] He's sitting in front of me staring and recording

[471] Asking who I just signalled to, who I laughed at, why did I cough

[472] The other guy's got his eye fixed on my sandals
[473] Thinking maybe I'm sending a code to someone in the room

[474] Just toying with me, he says, it's tit for tat
[475] We already know, we've got smarts too and can't be duped
[476] Really? So how did Moshe fuck us inside and out
[477] When you're so smart? Have you no shame?

[478] Why don't you go find the Jews and spy on them
[479] Quit spying on us poor fellows even in the lavatories
[480] O you tails of the Jews, however much you protect them
[481] Soon you'll be made women and like women have your period

[482] Winking and nodding and secret codes are their specialty
[483] They're a people who can only be beat through trickery and cheating
[484] Now that we've understood you, and found out your game
[485] Let's go play and let the smart guy take all

[486] It's in the restroom where I find words with balls
[487] That's the real 'Frankness', my fellow men
[488] So long as they're shovelling shit in the papers
[489] The lavatories will be the oppressed man's gazette

[490] Honest to God, I'm no communist or Brother
[491] Shuhdi's killer is Sayyid Quṭb's executioner too
[492] Death has many categories, colour-coded with malice
[493] It's a slaughterhouse, and we're the sheep hung up from our heels

…

[546] I finish these words of fuckery with fuck on top of fuck
[547] An' let fuck go fuck the fuckery and the fuckery the fuck
[548] Even fucking the fuckery is, in the end, just fuck
[549] Multiply, divide, and subtract – it's a table for fuck

[550] O fuck, O fuck, O night!
[551] O fuck, O fuck, O eye!
[552] Where can I find people to recite/reach the meanings of my words,
[553] Who, like a horny man, would fuck a faggot when they see one?

After the final line, the poet has written the following postscript:

'The *Kuss-ummiyyāt* will be followed by more, if we live any longer'
Naguib Surur
Doctor al-Nabawī al-Muhandis Hospital – al-Maʿmūra – Alexandria

This is followed by a section titled 'Sequels to the 'Mother-Cunt-ets'' (*Mutatābiʿāt ʿalā l-Kuss-ummiyyāt*), of which the following verses will concern us:

[622] And Gamal, O people of Gamal! What sorrow! What shame!
[623] The scoundrels got to him, too! Abducted him from El Alamein!

[624] They handed him over to the Jews, Whose masks were those of Germans
[625] From the whey comes the worm, And the worm overcame our man

[626] They replaced him with a scoundrel, Just like him, a carbon copy
[627] And gave him the throne, A throne full of holes!

[628] Such is the game of Freemasons, since time before time
[629] In the words of Sitt al-Kull, 'Be to them like Pharaoh'

Synopsis and Exegesis

Typed in Arabic, the poems run to some thirty-three pages in length. They contain elements of narrative – mostly intimations of the author's biography, which he assiduously points out in the endnotes – yet their thematic structure is loose and even rhizomatic, with direct insults interwoven with anecdotes, and entertaining rumours patched together with scenes of extreme physical and psychological torture. There are, in addition, frequent unmarked shifts in perspective, with the poet's speech juxtaposed with that of his sceptics and interrogators. While a measure of order is imposed by the poet's general adherence to the form of the quatrain in the *Kuss-ummiyyāt* proper, the occurrence of the refrain is ungoverned by the number of verses and is therefore somewhat unpredictable. The following divisions have been chosen based on what we perceive to be thematic shifts, and are meant only to assist in the reading. Parts selected for closer reading are marked in bold.

'The Mother-Cunt-ets of Naguib Surur'

1 (lines 1–7): Parodic introduction and refrain
2 (lines 8–117): Invective against culture industry
3 (lines 118–191): Invective against second wife
4 (lines 192–253): The 'Asylum'
5 (lines 254–386): Assorted themes
6 (387–457): *Waṣiyya* ('testament, advice') to Shuhdī
7 (458–517): Assorted themes
8 (518–41): *Waṣiyya* to posterity
9 (542–53): Conclusion to the first collection of *kuss-ummiyyāt*

'Sequels to the 'Mother-Cunt-ets''

1 (1–90): 'Risāla ilā Dufᶜa' ('Letter to a Private')
2 (91–226): Parody of Sayyid Darwīsh's 'Iqraᵓ yā Shaykh Fuqqāᶜ' (Read, O Shaykh Bubble!)
3 (227–317): Parody of Amal Dunqul's 'Sifr al-Khurūj/al-Kaᶜka al-Ḥajari- yya' (The Book of Exodus/The Stone Cake)
4 (318–619): Assorted themes
5 (620–715): Assorted themes

Part 1: Lines 1–7

The poems share with the *shaᶜbī* or 'popular' poetic genre called the *mawwāl* a formulaic introduction, a vernacular linguistic register, a shifting rhyme, and certain tropes. Lines 4 and 5 constitute the refrain, in which the poet has inserted the profanity *nīk* ('fuck') alongside the conventional elegiac ejacu- lations 'O night' and 'O eye'. A more colloquial rendering of the refrain, together with the following two lines, may go something like the following:

[4] Fuckety fuckety-fuck
[5] Fuck fuck fuckety-doo

[6] Get me some gents who get what I mean,
[7] Hard up howlers who would bugger a queen

In lines 6 and 7, the poet has parodied the opening of a particular *mawwāl*, that of *Adham al-Sharqāwī*, which Margaret Larkin has translated as follows:

> Where am I to find people to recite the meanings/ideas of my speech
> [They are] like al-m[M]u'ayyid when they memorize the sciences and recite it[36]

Pierre Cachia understands the first 'recite' (*yitlūh*) in the original to be an intentional distortion of the verb 'reach' (*yiṭūlūh*), following a convention for punning that is characteristic of the genre.[37] Paronomastic distortions of this kind, deployed in order to challenge the audience's comprehension, are an essential part of the traditional Egyptian *mawwāl*;[38] the *Kuss-ummiyyāt*, while teeming with regular puns, seem not to use this device at all. As Cachia has noted in regard to Surur's other work, the poet avoided this and other phonetic devices common in popular poetry because he held them to be distortions wrought by 'Zionists' and 'Jews' as part of a larger plot to control Egypt.[39] As we will see later on, Surur was in general suspicious of linguistic ambiguity, although this misreading of what are established features of a local art form is particularly remarkable, coming from a poet who so often expressed his concern for Egyptian cultural authenticity. Despite his frequent valorisation of life and lore in his native village of Akhṭāb, Surur appears in this case to be oddly divorced from the texts and traditions of the place. This is not so much a contradiction, as it is the partly expected condition of the culturally alienated intellectual who received higher education abroad, as well as in Cairo at a time when 'folk' traditions had yet to establish themselves comfortably in university curricula.

Still, the poet's invocation of *Mawwāl Adham al-Sharqāwī* is not entirely superficial. As we move further along with the streams and strands of Surur's poetic narrative, a few general similarities emerge that link the tortured and oppressed anti-hero to the figure of Adham al-Sharqāwī – a real historical individual later mythologised in his *mawwāl*, which tells of his defiance of the law in order to avenge his uncle's murder and uphold local ideologies of honour and masculinity. Surur has no uncle to avenge, but his honour and manhood are no less at stake; like Adham, too, he spends time in a 'prison' where he mingles with or memorialises folk heroes of the past.[40]

Some extended comments are in order on line 7, which has the following variants:

(S1) Who, like a **horny man**, would fuck a **faggot** when they see one?

(S2) Who, like a **horny man**, would fuck a **Jew** when they see one?

In S3, the performer includes three variants. The first, (a), is identical to the variant in S1. The next two are as follows:

(b) Who, like a **Jew**, would fuck a **Jew** when they see one?

(c) Who, like a **Freemason**, would fuck a **Freemason** when they see one?

Taking into account Surur's larger oeuvre, as well as the rest of the *Kuss-ummiyyāt*, we should note that these three figures – the 'faggot' (*khawal*) or homosexual, the 'Jew' (*yahūdī*), and the 'Freemason' (*māsūnī*) – featured regularly as targets of his conspiracist polemics. That they occur here as variants of the same verse suggests that there is more than a casual relationship that binds them together in the poet's symbolic order. That is to say, they perform some common function for the poet, beyond eliciting his general scorn. As the following verses reveal, these figures are all 'on top', both politically and sexually, and thus feature as those demonic agency-draining forces that rule the world through conspiracy.

There is something more that these figures have in common other than agency in a strictly political sense, and that is interpretive authority. Returning them to the context of lines 6 and 7, we see how they appear in conjunction with the poet's call for people to understanding the 'meanings' of his words. The people's understanding is likened to their ability to 'fuck' the *khawal-yahūdī-māsūnī*. It is tempting to see here the re-emergence of what Jaroslav Stetkevych has called the 'liminal herm': the mediator of the sacred text, the seductive go-between who smuggles meaning between the divine and the worldly.[41] As Suzanne Stetkevych has shown in her reading of the imagery of wine and immortality in al-Maʿarrī's *Risālat al-Ghufrān* (Epistle of Forgiveness), the ancient Greek and Arabic traditions commonly portrayed this figure as not only possessing immortality and prophecy, but also youthful and even effeminate beauty – thus Dionysus, Ganymede, Yūsuf, the *sāqī*.[42] Surur's thrice-damned, thrice-desired *khawal-yahūdī-māsūnī* slips easily into this role. More than just a homophobic, anti-Semitic call to arms, these verses articulate a cry for interpretation of meanings so seductively, and so frustratingly, withheld. The world is not just a mysterious place for Surur, it is unjustly so. 'Catch the queer', the poet seems to be saying, and you'll gain his secret knowledge, the keys to salvation, an immediate path to get back 'on top'. In these lines, the hermeneutic of conspiracism – the anxious, wide-eyed search for hidden meanings behind beautiful and deceptive exteriors – finds its perfect poetic expression. It is, quite appropriately, the desire that introduces and sets him on his quest.

Part 2: Lines 8–117

After the parodic introduction and refrain, the poet launches into an invective on Egypt's culture industry, which he faults for literal as well as figurative prostitution. The key figures of this polemic include the *khawal* ('faggot' or 'cocksucker', pl. *khawalāt*), the *maʿarraṣ* ('ass-kisser', lit. 'pimp'; pl. *maʿarrasīn*), the *miḥarraʾ* ('horny' or 'hard up'; cf. the Standard Arabic *muḥarraq*, 'hot' or 'on fire'), the *sharmūṭa* ('whore', pl. *sharāmīṭ*), and *labwa* ('testy bitch', lit. 'lioness'). These characters, who at this point in the poem are still anonymous, are complicit in a zero-sum game of *nēk* or *niyāka* (both 'fucking' or 'fucking over') where the *manāyik* or *mitnākīn* ('fucked ones') trade their 'honour' for the ability to 'direct' or perform 'roles' in films and plays.[43] This *niyāka* happens, on the one hand, everywhere, and on the other, is confined to specific, symbolically charged *topoi* such as the *garsunyērāt* ('hook-up flats', that is, apartments for sexual rendezvous) (34), 'offices' (61, 96), and 'the studio' (80). It is worth noting, by the by, that the poems' principal obscenities – with the notable exception of *miḥarraʾ* – still form the core of the average Egyptian Arabic speaker's stock of insults, and while for certain communities, both online and 'in the street', their lustre has dimmed or refracted through irony and overuse, their ability to shock and offend has remained intact.[44]

The poet's footnotes appended to this section are mainly meant to clarify that, by words such as 'director', 'script', 'testy bitch', and 'office', the poet is speaking generally about all directors, all texts, all women, and all workplaces in Egypt. In a note to line 80, he declares, 'Egypt in its entirety is nothing but a great big "studio" for collective fucking on a global scale.' In addition, we get a foretaste of the poet's penchant for perverse, and indeed paranoid, etymologies in a note to line 87, in which he ponders whether it is 'just a coincidence' that the letters of the word 'Kent' (*kint*) may be rearranged to spell 'you/I fucked' (*nikt*) and '(that) you/she (may) fuck(s)' (*tanik*).

Part 3: Lines 118–91

The language and tropes of *niyāka* pervade the entire *Kussummiyyāt*. After warming up with his take on Egyptian cultural politics in general, the poet then moves on to specific targets and themes. The first of these is an unnamed actress and *sharmuṭa*, about whom further details are provided in the author's note to line 119:

> It must be remembered during my lifetime, or after my death – especially after the campaign of slander [against me] in the press – that the author of the *Kuss-ummiyyāt* married an actress after his Russian wife and their son were prevented from coming to Egypt. Mind you, there is a difference between an 'actor' (*mumassila*) and an 'act-whore' (*mūmassila*).[45] It later became known that the actress was that niece of the former head of the secret police (back in the days of the monarchy), and later became General Director of Passports and Naturalization!!

Later, in the footnote to line 141, it is claimed that this actress's uncle is the 'head of the intelligence services and Office for Combatting Communism', and that his niece had been planted by his office in order to spy on the poet. Sandwiched in between these two accusations is a general account of the actress's moral depravity, in which she is described as a 'Phantom' fighter jet because of her ability to have intercourse in China and Qalyūb (an Egyptian provincial city) in the same day. This is not a metaphor: the poet does not say the actress is 'like' a fighter jet; he says she *is* a fighter jet: in his moral and semantic universe, private sexual humiliation and collective military aggression are functional equivalents. The invective quickly flares up into an attack on women in general, and is followed by a lament on the poet's poverty and his commitment to notions of honour and manhood (lines 142–61).

The poet departs briefly from wife bashing to level accusations of corruption and sexual deviance at those who have denied him employment (lines 162–73), a thematic detour that culminates in a sudden *ad hominem* attack on the Minister of Culture Tharwat ʿUkāsha (1958–62, 1966–70), who is accused of being a *khawal* in line 170. As the author asserts in a note, the predicament dramatised here is Surur's inability to find steady employment after his return from Russia, and indeed for the rest of his life.

Swiftly then returning to his wife, the poet accuses her of having been 'fucked' by nearly everyone in Egypt's culture industry, including a certain 'Naguib'. A note to line 175 reveals this to be none other than the would-be Nobel laureate Naguib Mahfouz (1911–2006). The accusation is incredible, for although Mahfouz was a prolific author on quite a variety of themes, his fiction on gender and sexuality generally gives the impression of a simple and untroubled innocence; moreover, his personal life, in particular as regards his relationships with women, has not attracted the same sort of interest experienced by other literary giants such as ʿAbbās Maḥmūd al-ʿAqqād, Tawfīq al-Ḥakīm, or even Yusuf Idris. It is clear that Surur had a particular dislike for Mahfouz, a fact that is evident in the letter he wrote to Yusuf Idris. Contrasting Mahfouz with his addressee, Surur describes the former as inhabiting 'a world forever confined to the borders of the middle class'; as 'always ready to serve any authority, to go along with any authority in any age under any regime'; as pretending to be 'neutral, gray, and apathetic' while in reality 'belonging, in the depths of his soul, to the powers that be'; and, 'finally', as 'a prime example of the cursed routine and bureaucratic Egyptian civil servant'.[46] Things were not always this way: from 1959 through 1963, Surur wrote a book-length study of Mahfouz's famous 'Cairo Trilogy', entitled *Riḥla fī Thulāthiyyat Najīb Maḥfūẓ* (A Journey through Naguib Mahfouz's Trilogy).[47] The work is remarkable not only for the generally positive critical attitude that Surur adopts throughout, but also for the rather plain and sober nature of his claims – in other words, there is barely a trace of the conspiracist hermeneutic style that would characterise almost all of his subsequent creative and critical work.

Beginning with line 180, the poet repeats his accusations regarding his wife, her paternal uncle, and their work for the security services. It bears pointing out that there is a certain confusion surrounding the uncle's exact position. In the note to line 119, he is formerly 'the head of the secret police' (*raʾīs al-qalam al-makhṣūṣ*) and currently 'General Manager of Passports and Naturalization' (*mudīr ʿāmm al-gawāzāt wa l-ginsiyya*), while in the note to line 141 he has become 'the head of the intelligence services and the Office of Combatting Communism' (*ra'īs al-mukhābarāt wa qalam mukāfaḥat al-shuyū'iyya*). Finally, in line 181, he is simply 'the head of the secret police' (*ra'īs al-maktab al-makhṣūṣ*). Whatever factual inaccuracies or inconsistencies we may notice here, they are in harmony with the poems' broader conception of time, which often telescopes events of the present into the distant past (for example, the poet's remarks on Freemasonry, discussed below), and projects events of the past into the present or the future. Thus, it is possible, within the temporal universe of the *Kuss-ummiyyāt*, that the uncle is both formerly and presently the head of the secret police, and the offices and power structures of feudalism, colonialism, and the monarchy have remained unchanged into the present.[48] In literary terms, we may recognise these leaps and returns as characteristic of the genre of prophetic revelation, or as among the features of the 'temporal axis' of the apocalyptic that Collins has identified in his seminal study.[49] It will not be surprising, then, that the poet aligns himself later in the poem with prophetic figures of history and legend.

Part 4: Lines 192–253

With these lines, the poet swiftly transitions to what is perhaps the most moving, and most disturbing, section of the *Kuss-ummiyyāt*: the time he spent in an 'asylum', identified as the al-ʿAbbāsiyya Hospital in a note (line 192). It is here, too, that we encounter the entirety of the poems in a single line:

> [196] 'You can bet your mother's cunt,' I replied, 'Hang me and I'll die a man.'

More loosely translated, the line may read as follows:

> [196] 'Go fuck yourself,' I said. 'And you can "choke" me on that.'

The first part of the line contains the curse word *kuss-ummukum* ('your mother's cunt'), from which the title is derived; it performs much the same function as 'fuck you' or 'go fuck yourself' in English. Used here as a reply to those who have 'institutionalised' him, the phrase mimics the larger performative aims of the poems, which were composed as an obscene 'response' to the poet's enemies in politics and culture.

The 'hospital' wardens take him up on the offer, and a gruesome torture session commences. The poet describes how he would be hung with a towel, and then be given an injection to return to consciousness and be hung again, and then given another injection, and so on. The sudden joltings in and out of consciousness are mimicked by the disorienting shifts in perspective between first, second, and third persons, in addition to shifts between tenses and times, within the space of just a few lines. A note to line 197 specifies that these hangings were carried out the first time with a towel, and the second time with a rope, and directly connects this incident to the former wife and her uncle's work for the security services. A thematic detour connects the poet's personal torture to the injustices suffered by the nation as a whole (lines 208–27). The poet takes this opportunity to invoke several historical martyrs: the nationalist army officer Aḥmad ʿUrābī (1841–1911), who led a reform movement that was quashed by the British occupation of Egypt (line 209); the nationalist prime minister Saʿd Zaghlūl (1859–1927); and the popular singer and composer Sayed Darwish (Sayyid Darwīsh) (1892–1923), who he claims was poisoned. The defeat of all these figures, and the defeat of the poet, are attributed to 'the Jews'. Although it merits only a passing reference in the poem, the assassination of Darwish was an idea about which Surur was especially adamant in other writings. The full theory is expounded in an article he wrote sometime towards the end of his own life, entitled 'Perplexing Question Marks surrounding the Death of Sayed Darwish', in which he alleges that it is no coincidence that the artist died on the same day that Saʿd Zaghlūl returned from exile.[50]

Line 228 takes us back to the asylum with an account of a second torture method. This time, the poet is deprived of water for three days, and then forced to drink 'gas' (that is, kerosine). Instead of praying for divine intervention as in the previous instance, he now appeals for the intercession of Husayn, grandson of the Prophet Muhammad, and to his contemporaries, the 'generation of gas(oline)' – the latter presumably a reference to the corrupting influence of petro-dollars and predatory Arabian Gulf princes, who appear elsewhere in the poems. With each appeal, the poet moves further away from orthodox religion – or, alternatively, away from the authoritative, eternal, familiar text of the Father to the base materialism and foreignness of his brothers – a shift that marks, apart from increasing desperation, the author's own literary vagabondage. The appeal to Husayn would appear to be consonant with the previous line, where the phrase 'Where be the fountain, when the fountain …' has the flavour of a popular Egyptian religious incantation. That both lines also may sound somewhat 'Shiite' to a non-Egyptian audience is significant, in light of the poet's later refusal to be labelled as such by his interrogators (lines 465–6).

In line 235, 'hippies' (*khanāfis*, lit. 'beetles', originally in reference to The Beatles) appear as yet another sign of moral depravity, and may be understood as nearly synonymous with *khawalāt*. The rhyme between *jāz* ('jazz') and its homograph *gāz* ('gas, kerosene') two lines earlier establishes a metonymic link between two 'substances' the poet has been forced to consume. Both substances are in a sense 'false', in that they are contrasted, whether explicitly or implicitly, to 'genuine' or 'authentic' substances: water and poetry. Both substances are also equally 'poisonous', causing him extreme physical as well as psychological pain, and leaving deep and lasting wounds. We should note here that the association of certain musical or poetic genres with poisonous fluids, noxious substances, and physical torture may be found elsewhere in Surur's writings. In a polemic against the popular musician Aḥmad ʿAdawiyya, Surur describes his voice as a 'whip' (*kirbāg*) that 'violates your sleep, ruins your nerves, and makes you feel that you are living in a hell of noise, a hell of meaninglessness, of irrationality, of incomprehensibility, of nonsense and the unknown'.[51] In the same article, he even accuses such revered musical stars as Umm Kulthūm, ʿAbd al-Ḥalīm Ḥāfiẓ, and Muḥammad ʿAbd al-Wahhāb as constituting the same 'chorus of whips', and compares the cacophony they create to the torture methods of 'the Hitlerian, Nazi, fascist Gestapo'.[52] Given this strong association between bad music and physical torture, it is perhaps no coincidence that Surur, in a rambling paragraph on the silencing and assassination of talented artists in Egypt, casually alludes to his own experience in al-ʿAbbāsiya:

> [A]ssassination in the middle of the night, assassination in broad daylight, assassination through sundry methods: starvation, displacement, expulsion, exile, and secret detention in mental hospitals, [followed by] hanging, then an injection before the pulse stops, then hanging, then an injection before the pulse stops as long as the hyoid bone doesn't break.[53]

Although Surur does not identify himself as the victim of the methods he describes in this paragraph, the language is nearly identical to that that appears in lines 204–5 of the *Kuss-ummiyyāt*. The two traumas – torture in the asylum, noise in the street – are so closely linked that it is difficult to determine which one is meant as a metaphor for the other,[54] or, indeed, whether the poet makes any distinction between them at all. Both have the same effect, and what is more, both are attributed to the same prime mover: the Zionist-Masonic conspiracy.

Taking into account the practical, if not material, equivalence of decadent music and physical torture/assassination (in particular by poison), the conspiracy theory about Sayed Darwish (lines 220–3) would seem less mysterious. The particular method of Darwish's murder is not random, but makes sense in terms of Surur's symbolic universe. The 'poisoning' of the musician, who Surur held in great esteem, may be understood as the projection, or perhaps 'corporealisation', of anxieties about the corrupting influence of new musical genres and their displacement of older, genuine art forms.

More scenes of torture in al-ʿAbbāsiyya follow. A deeply disturbing account of the rape of children, presumably other prisoners, passes with surprisingly little elaboration: unlike the other traumas that the poet experiences both before and after, there is no endnote here to specify the identity of the perpetrators or victims, or to add any contextual details (lines 236–9). Apart from channelling the terror of the experience, this scene serves to bring the pessimism of the poems to a climax, as it is suggested that even future generations will be unable to escape the violence and oppression of the powers-that-be. The fourth and final torture technique is hypothetical: the poet submits that he, too, may have been 'fucked'. Surur's sense of humour, however dark, returns here to make light of the situation, as in a note to line 244 he muses that the pain of being 'fucked' would probably be no more than a 'pin prick'. He adds that, even if he were to derive pleasure from the experience, he was denied this too, as the hypothetical rape would have occurred while he was anaesthetised.

Taken as a whole, the poet's descent into the hell of al-ʿAbbāsiyya constitutes one of the longest and most distinct narrative units of the *Kuss-ummiyyāt*. The potency of its verses, however, derives not just from the gruesomeness of the crimes they expose – these details are presented elsewhere in Surur's work – but in their linking of the poet's plight to more widely resonating literary and cultural motifs. As noted above, the poet's detention in the asylum shares certain similarities with the imprisonment of Adham al-Sharqāwī: as the latter consorts with famous brigands and criminals, so does the former evoke the memory of political and cultural heroes such as Sayed Darwish, Saad Zaghloul, and Aḥmad ʿUrābī. The incidents in al-ʿAbbāsiyya also resonate with another text that had particular significance for the poet: *Risālat al-Ghufrān* (The Epistle of Forgiveness) by Abū al-ʿAlāʾ al-Maʿarrī, who appears in nearly all of Surur's work, including several of the endnotes of the current poems.[55] The similarities here relate not to the content of the two narratives – al-Maʿarrī's protagonist travelled to various levels of heaven and hell, and did not endure torture – but to the function or outcome of the journey, at least as Nagib Surur perceived it. In his *Taḥt ʿAbāʾ at Abī al-ʿAlāʾ* (Under the Auspices of Abū al-ʿAlāʾ) – a book-length study of the eleventh-century author, published posthumously – Surur sees in al-Maʿarrī's otherworldly journey an elaborate pretext for the communication of certain occult truths about the authenticity of ancient Arabic poetry, the necessity of imitating one's enemies, and, rather expectedly, the existence of a worldwide, age-old conspiracy of Zionists and Freemasons.[56] Al-Maʿarrī's protagonist encounters deceased poets, as well as their inspiring jinn – 'Jews' in Surur's reading – whose verses contain these messages in 'code'.[57] For the poet of the *Kuss-ummiyyāt*, the descent into an otherworldly realm is similarly illuminating, as through his communing with the spirits of iconic martyrs and verbal sparrings with demonic beings he articulates special knowledge of the hidden (Zionist) order of things.

A more local intertextual resonance with Surur's entry into and return from al-ʿAbbāsiyya may be found in a folktale about a parallel universe, or 'utopia', recounted by folklorist Hasan El-Shamy.[58] Wandering aimless and depressed one day, a man stumbles upon a cave where he finds a group of men slapping themselves in the face and shouting, 'It serves me right!' He attempts to join the group, but they reject him, and cast him deeper down into the cave. There he finds himself in an ideal world where every man knows his place and all his basic needs are provided for; the man is welcomed to join this society, on the condition that he not 'inquire about things which [are] not his concern'. Tragically, he is unable to hold to this condition, and is ejected from the ideal world to join the men in the cave who shout, 'It serves me right!' El-Shamy notes that this story has been told in many rural locations across Egypt to explain the 'severe emotional disturbance' of a member of the community who 'dressed in rags … continuously roams the streets of his town in total bewilderment'. Typically, such an individual – described as a 'Sufi (mystic)', carries 'a small rock in his hand with which he beats on his chest shouting, "It serves me right! It serves me right."' Again, the connection to Surur's story is not in the precise content – al-ʿAbbāsiyya for him is the opposite of the ideal community – but in the structure and outcome. The poet descends into a netherworld where his curiosity is strictly forbidden, yet repeatedly seduced; he emerges later in the poems, as well as in real life, dressed in rags and ranting and raving around the streets of Cairo about his experience.

Part 5: Lines 254–386

In this section, the poet, still reeling from the memory of his torture, catapults into a dizzying array of topics. He begins, in lines 254–77, by musing on the intertwined nature of *nēk/niyāka* and politics. On the one hand, in keeping with the equivalence he has established previously between sexual profligacy and political exploitation, he states that 'politics means fucking' and 'fucking means politics'. On the other hand, in lines 260–1, he seems to suggest that the political crime is worse than the sexual sin. These statements may be compared to other instances in the poems, such as during his torture, or in his denigration of women and effeminate men, in which this assessment is reversed.

Next, in lines 278–85, the poet offers a justification for the obscenity of his verses in terms of the obscenity of present reality: the world is decadent, violent, and corrupt, so why shouldn't poetry be as well? This sort of argument recalls that of other, contemporary Egyptian authors who were also faced with the charge of writing obscene literature.[59] In Surur's case, it is one of many instances in which he advocated a manner of extremism or violence as a tactical imitation of the enemy, in art as well as in politics.[60] Indeed there are striking similarities between Surur's verses, both in form and content, and the methods and traits that he associates with his enemies. His invective and vitriol have their match in the 'poisons' and 'gas' of his critics and literary competitors; his obsession with occult themes and elliptical and allusive language mimic the secret 'codes' and 'ciphers' he would find in the language of 'Jews' and Egyptian intellectuals; his parodying of folk motifs and genres, his low-register language, and his jarring repetition of key words and verses are precisely those elements he found blameworthy in the poetry and songs of fellow artists; and the secret, underground production and circulation of the *Kuss-ummiyyāt* mirror the hidden plots and secret societies he detected everywhere.

These similarities are numerous enough to suggest that conscious, tactical imitation of the 'other' is only part of the equation. For one, the poet seems to be aware of some of them, such as obscenity and violence, yet painfully unaware of others, such as his linguistic solecisms, repetitions, and unfaithful rendering of folk themes. Thus, it is arguable that, as is the case with Hofstadter's archetypical conspiracy theorist, many of these deplorable traits and practices originate with the poet himself, who first suppresses them, and then deploys them in his literature to construct an image of the enemy. When these traits and practices then come back to the poet, he rationalises the uncanny similarities between self and other by claiming them as products of his conscious will. In other words, rather than tactical imitation, what characterises the relationship between the poet and his enemies is a process of projection, followed by partial recognition and rationalisation.

Part 7: Lines 458–517

After concluding a 'testament' to his son Shuhdī, the poet transitions to an interrogation scene with a clever pun. He seeks the privacy and comfort of *bayt al-adab* – the 'restroom', but also literally the 'house of etiquette/literature' – but finds that *adab* (etiquette/literature) has been banned. Just as he is about to urinate, the *mabāḥith* (the notorious investigations division of the Egyptian police) barge in and demand a sample. Yet it is not drugs or disease they are looking for, but ideological affiliation: they find it is 'type E' for 'emergency', and give him the label 'Shiite' or 'communist'.[61] He denies the accusation, and urges them instead to 'spy on' the 'Jews', who he considers the real threat.

The single scene contains a number of paradoxes that, more closely examined, reveal much about the poet's symbolic universe and interpretive style. First, there is the issue of the sample taken in the restroom. While the liquid is identified as 'urine' (*bōl*) in line 461, in the next line it is described as having a 'type' (*faṣīla*), which would rather indicate blood. On the one hand, this confusion further testifies to the interpretive incompetence of the police: they cannot tell the difference between the two liquids, and seem not to realise that political affiliation doesn't run in the blood. On the other hand, the inflated significance given to urine/blood fits well with the poet's broader preoccupation with liquids of various kinds as potent means for making, and unmaking, the self. We have already seen the destructive force, both figurative and literal, of 'gas' as opposed to the life-sustaining force of water. Elsewhere in the poems, 'blood' (*damm*) occurs as a substance which makes or breaks character. Note the following lines:

[126] Turn the pot over, you'll find she's her mother's daughter

[127] Like mother, like daughter: the bitchiness (*labwana*) is from the mother

[128] The serpent laid an egg and hatched a serpent like her

[129] What can the doctor do when the fuckery (*manyaka*) is in the blood?

And:

[152] For me to be a kiss-ass, you'd have to give me someone else's blood

[153] My lot/luck (*ḥaẓẓ*) is my blood, and by blood is also my lot/luck

In the former selection, the poet's second wife carries her negative personal traits in her blood; in the latter, the poet's own blood is, following many popular idioms to this effect, the depository of character. There is 'light' blood (good), 'heavy' blood (bad), and 'poison' blood (very bad); there is just plain blood, which, unadulterated, stands for (manly) honour and courage.

A second paradox that arises in this scene is the poet's condemnation of his interrogators' paranoia about hidden agendas and secret codes. He pointedly denies the accusation of belonging to a dangerous group, and mocks the insinuation that he may be passing coded signals to someone in the room. Yet he immediately proceeds to authorise this same paranoia against those he perceives as genuine conspirators, calling on the police to 'go find the Jews and spy on them' (line 478), since the latter are specialists in 'winking and nodding and secret codes' (line 482). This apparent hypocrisy may be understood, first, as consonant with the poet's explicit call for imitation of the enemy. This, indeed, is how he rationalises it in the following lines:

> [483] They're a people who can only be beat through trickery and cheating
> [484] Now that we've understood you, and found out your game
> [485] Let's go play and let the smart guy take all

As in our discussion above on the similarities between the poet and his adversaries, we may wonder here whether this is a case of 'tactical imitation', or rationalised 'projection'. Yet unlike the previous instance, the poet is not alone with his enemies. He is joined by the police, who are always already interpreters of conspiracy, indeed conspiracy theorists, by nature of their training. Thus, we can understand the poet's strange suspicions not simply in terms of some internal process of suppression and projection, but in terms of his relationship with those who wield paranoia as a regular instrument of interpretation and control. In the interrogation chamber, that violent crucible of subject formation, the poet is forcibly made to internalise the mental habits and discourses of the police. The process of suggestion, interpolation, and internalisation of paranoia appears more clearly in an earlier quatrain, which immediately follows the poet's torture in al-ᶜAbbāsiyya. In response to an accusation that he is a Zionist, the poet cries:

> [212] Why would they say such a thing, if the Zionists are out there, not in here?
> [213] Well, Mr. President, that means the Zionists are in here, not out there
> [214] 'Til when will our Egypt remain a bitch in heat (*labwa*)
> [215] A dumb donkey, waiting to be wed to a horse

In these verses we hear paranoia, in the voice of his interrogators, calling out the poet, who rejects the call, before suddenly accepting its basic claim: the Zionists are not just outside (in Israel), but in here (Egypt). It is through torture – hanging, injections, gasoline, and rape – that the suspicious world view of Egypt's repressive apparatus is injected into the poet, who is refashioned as a model theorist of conspiracy.[62]

'Sequels', Part 5: Lines 620–715

This final part of the *Kuss-ummiyyāt* presents several of the poet's conspiracy theories in more elaborate detail, and thus provides an appropriate opportunity for synthesis and conclusion. In lines 622–9, we hear about 'Gamal', who, given the context, is certainly Abdel Nasser. Summarised in prose, the story may go something like this: Gamal was stationed at El Alamein (line 623), west of Alexandria, presumably sometime during the Second World War. During the famous battle at that location, Gamal was abducted by 'Germans', who turned out to be 'Jews' in disguise (lines 624). That this act of treachery was an inside job is implied by the modified proverb in line 625. The authentic Gamal was then replaced by a fake one, a 'scoundrel' that looked 'just like him' (626); this second Gamal was the one to later become president of Egypt (line 627). Thus, it is implied, the tragedies that would befall his country over the next several decades, climaxing in the 1967 *naksa*, were the work of some other man, a puppet installed by Jews. In line 628, the Jews become 'Freemasons' (*al-māsūn*), who are explained by the poet in an endnote:

> Freemasonry is the secret religion, or secret organization, or secret government of the Jews since the time of the Babylonian Captivity. It is behind all the governments of the world without exception, and its regimes are, without exception, based on this game of abduction and impersonation.

Much removed from their original literary and political milieu, these lines may certainly appear aberrant, pathological, even incomprehensible. Yet they do not come from nowhere. We may consider, first, the scripts, scenarios, images, and motifs that likely buzzed and ricocheted around the poet as he composed the poems. As regards the vapid anti-Semitic conspiracism that appears here and throughout the *Kuss-ummiyyāt*, it is quite easy to trace how Nagib Surur received his inspiration. We know that he was a close follower of the cultural journal *al-Risāla* from a letter he wrote to its editor while still a high-school student in early 1951.[63] It was this journal that first published Muḥammad Khalīfa al-Tūnisī's Arabic translation of *The Protocols of the Wise Men of Zion* in 1949.[64] Just as significant was Surur's relationship with Ali Ahmad Bakathir, who was an instructor of his at the Higher Institute for Dramatic Arts. In 1958, Surur directed Bakathir's *Shaᶜb Allāh al-Mukhtār* (God's Chosen People), a play that, apart from trading in the playwright's regular conspiracist themes, fantasies the destruction of the state of Israel.[65]

The peculiar vision of regime change depicted in these verses, however, cannot be reduced to a simple matter of intertextual borrowing. The conspiracies recounted are carried out through a 'game of abduction and impersonation' (*liᶜbit il-khaṭf wi-l-tashbīh*): thus, Gamal is not Gamal. Nor, for that matter, is any head of state really himself: 'Yasser', 'Hussein', 'Faysal', 'Nixon', 'Hitler', and 'Harun al-Rashid', among others, are all in reality 'Cohen' (line 644). The poet goes further to allege that 'every nation (*shaᶜb*) has bent up inside it another nation' (line 654): one 'authentic and pitiful' and the other the product of 'hybridization' (line 656). This conception of humankind resonates with the notion of 'fleeting-improvised-men' a term coined by the German judge Daniel Paul Schreber in his famous *Memoirs of My Nervous Illness*.[66] Schreber, who would become Freud's paradigmatic case of *dementia paranoïdes*, perceived as 'fleeting-improvised' individuals who were not genuine, but who had been produced through 'miracle' and could take on various forms, and just as easily 'dissolve' into nothingness. On one occasion, taken out of his asylum, Schreber described having the related impression that streets he passed through, and the people he encountered in them, were no more than 'theater props'.[67]

If the poet's perception of false doubles and duplicates bears a resemblance to this famous case of psychosis, it may be understood in aesthetic terms as a reflection of his preoccupation with playing a 'role'. Surur is indeed hyper-aware of the gap between his 'authentic', private self and his carefully contrived, and not always felicitous, poetic persona. There are, in addition to the performative 'I' of 'Naguib Surur', the numerous other personalities he adopted in the *Kuss-ummiyyāt* and other works: Adham al-Sharqāwī, Abū al-ᶜAlāʾ al-Maᶜarrī, Guḥā, Agamemnon, Ṣalāḥ al-Dīn al-Ayyūbī, Hamlet, Don Quixote, Jesus Christ, the madman of Cairo. From his own experience in acting, he would become attentive to, even obsessed with, the artifice of appearances more generally, not only as regards human 'actors' and 'agents' but also with respect to language, physical substances, poetry, and race/ethnicity. Thus, casual phrases and expressions are revealed to contain puns and secret meanings, what appears to be water is actually gasoline, and the much-vaunted authenticity of folk songs is nothing but a screen for Zionist propaganda. Such is the perspective of paranoid conspiracy theory; such is also the perspective of poetry unable to forgive itself for the lies it tells.

The sources and functions of the 'Naguib Surur's' conspiracist poetics are multiple and intertangled. We may return many of his plots and polemics to an intertextual network of plays, poems, folktales, and histories, not in an effort to explain or 'debunk' them by tracing them to their putative origin, but to register their debt to, adaptation of, and departure from potent and appealing cultural forms. We may also seek to align certain patterns in the poet's texts with conditions and mechanisms recognised in the literature of psychoanalysis. This is not to pronounce a diagnosis of Nagib Surur, the man and historical individual, but to provide an account of his poetry that does not fetishise the conscious decisions and deliberations of the author as solely responsible for every sign he produces. In the final analysis, aesthetic and psychological processes mimic and rhyme with one another, intermingle promiscuously, and conspire to produce visions in verse that resist any totalising mechanism of comprehension or control.

3

Sonallah Ibrahim's *al-Lajna*: Between Critical Theory and Conspiracy Theory

On 14 August 2013, a month after the toppling of President Muḥammad Mūrsī, the Egyptian military and police killed in the region of 1,000 people during the dispersal of pro-Muslim Brotherhood sit-ins in Cairo.[1] Ten days later, the novelist Sonallah Ibrahim (b. 1937) was interviewed by the sensationalist daily *al-Yawm al-Sābiᶜ* to assess the country's state of affairs. Long celebrated in Egypt and around the world as a pioneering voice in modern Arabic literature, Ibrahim is best known for his starkly minimalist and documentary style in prose, his ascetic personal life, and, above all, his fierce and sustained political committedness. His early career paralleled in certain ways that of Naguib Surur: the same years the latter spent in exile (1959–64), the former spent in prison; both were, during this period, members of a communist group; like many of Surur's own works, Ibrahim's debut novel, *Tilka al-Rāᵓiḥa* (1966) (*The Smell of It*, trans. 1971) was rejected by the censor for its alleged obscenities. In 2003, having established himself as a consistent opponent of the Sadat and Mubarak regimes, he famously rejected an award from the Ministry of Culture in a stirring speech delivered in front of the minister himself. It therefore came as a shock to many of his readers, particularly those in the West, when in this latest interview he not only expressed admiration for ᶜAbd al-Fattāḥ al-Sīsī, Egypt's new military leader, but seemed to give his endorsement to the regime's repressive techniques, including its self-declared 'war on terrorism', the reinstatement of the notorious Mubarak-era Emergency Laws, and the massacre that had occurred just days earlier.[2]

At this moment in recent history, Ibrahim was not alone among Egypt's 'liberal' or 'leftist' writers and intellectuals, many of whom offered statements in support of al-Sīsī's government that scandalously contrasted with their own histories of dissent. Novelists like Gamal al-Ghitani, Bahaa Taher (Bahāʾ Ṭāhir) (b. 1935), Alaa Al Aswany (ʿAlāʾ al-Aswānī) (b. 1957), and Ibrahim Eissa (Ibrāhīm ʿĪsā) (b. 1965) – all known for having been targets of past authoritarian regimes, and all but Eissa having spent time in prison – seemed to have changed overnight from radical defenders of freedom and social justice to apologists for the military and police state. Critics are still attempting to make sense of what has been called the 'authoritarian turn' of some Egyptian littérateurs.[3] Several leading scholars have made calls for a critical re-reading of the literary work of these authors and a re-assessment of their politics, and a few preliminary but significant investigations have recently been conducted along these lines.[4] What these calls imply is not only the need for a 'new' look at 'old' works, but for the academic discipline of Arabic literature to reflect on its own interpretive practices, and attempt to understand why the authors we privilege in our classrooms have surprised, disappointed, or confounded us so dramatically. Is it possible, perhaps, that we have received certain authors too uncritically?

This is not the place to resolve all of these issues. Nor is it our intention to indict an entire generation of novelists as complicit in the same political project, or to imply that their literature is somehow less valuable because of it. In this chapter, we concern ourselves much more narrowly with one novel by Sonallah Ibrahim, and attempt to re-assess what most readers have interpreted as its oppositional stance towards, and essential difference from, political authority. *Al-Lajna* (1981) (*The Committee*, trans. 2001), a Kafkaesque tale of a man interrogated and condemned by an obscure body for obscure reasons, is one of Ibrahim's most brilliant works.[5] Like many of his novels, it contains a scathing, richly documented critique of the capitalist world order, United States imperialism, and the resultant decay and corruption of Egyptian social and political life. While previous readings of *al-Lajna* have focused on the positive aspects of the critical quest undertaken by its protagonist, this chapter asks whether we may, in addition, read the novel as a cautionary tale about the perils and pitfalls of a particular mode of hermeneutic suspicion that has much in common with what we have been calling conspiracism.

Here, our aim is not to put the novel or its author back in the courtroom on political charges, but to understand how the protagonist becomes, as he puts it, a victim of his own 'quixotic search for knowledge'.[6] Indeed, the translators' choice of 'quixotic' for *mahwūs* ('maniacal' or 'obsessed') is quite appropriate, for, as we will see, the investigative journey in question is not only haunted by literary predecessors but, like Quixote himself, derives from a cultural milieu that is as 'Western' as it is 'Arab'. Thus, our re-reading of Ibrahim's modern classic will implicate critical practices that are just as European and American as they are locally Egyptian. With *al-Lajna* as our focal point, we follow the 'post-critical' turn in the broader humanities and social sciences to ask: what are the limits of suspicion, and what are the alternatives?[7]

Motives and Metaphors of Suspicion

A middle-aged man appears one day at the headquarters of a group known only as 'the Committee'. He has not been explicitly forced to come, nor does it seem he is there of his own free will. He enters a room, and stands before the seated members of the Committee. They ask him to dance, to take off his clothes, to answer vague questions. Where was he during '"that" year?' (13). Why did he fail to have sex with a certain woman? (15). 'By which momentous event among the wars, revolutions, or inventions will our century be remembered in the future?' (16). And what does he know about the Great Pyramid? (24). He is sent home; he waits. He is asked to produce a report on the person he considers 'the greatest contemporary Arab luminary' (31). He complies, and despite numerous difficulties and injustices that include official secrecy, surveillance, censorship, dilapidated public transportation, and, finally, a man in his bed with a gun, he is able to piece together an increasingly coherent and sophisticated picture not just of the requested 'luminary' figure, but of the grander forces of empire and commerce that rule the world. It is not enough to save him. Frustrated with the Committee's restrictions and its invasion of his private space, he murders one of its members. As punishment, he is condemned, but never explicitly ordered, to literally eat himself.

Critical reception of *al-Lajna* has been nearly unanimous in its appraisal of the protagonist as model of committed political critique. While the accusations he levels are not usually endorsed in all their particulars, it is his methodology for exposing painful truths that merits approval and even emulation. It has been argued, for example, that the 'documentary record' assembled by the novel's protagonist is 'a type of defiance' that

works to create identity, to elevate an empty life to a new one of purpose
and discovery. Its difference from colonial or post-colonial identifications
lies in its discovery, through research engagement, of global capital and its
native middlemen. This intellectual pursuit, the one that we trace in writings by a great number of scholars, poets, critics, novelists, and journalists
like Robert Fisk and Seymour Hirsch, should draw attention to it as a
minority discourse of great potential.[8]

Thus, the novel's critical project may be justified not only in terms of its
difference from, and defiance of, hegemonic structures, but in terms of the
positive emotional effects it has on its hero. It is implied that *The Committee*
invites readers to follow his example.

Part of the appeal of the novel's critical project lies in its subtlety, and
in its apparent commitment to universal principles like truth, justice, and
freedom over passion or partisanship. The protagonist is simply a man down
on his luck, drawn into a confrontation with powers beyond his control.
Virtually no information on his history or personal background is provided to
the reader: he is uninteresting, and thus disinterested. He does not explicitly
adopt a particular ideology – when 'ideological' issues come up, he is careful
to avoid them (17, 36). He is for the most part calm – indeed comically so, as
he barely protests even when he is asked to strip naked and has a digit inserted
in his behind. Although the conclusions he draws may sometimes seem far
fetched, they are based on painstakingly thorough research and an irrepress-
ible desire to get to the bottom of things. His investigation is methodical,
empirical, and clear-sighted. His enemies are, for the most part, the right ones.

By all appearances, then, the protagonist of Sonallah Ibrahim's novel is a
model intellectual, doing only what intellectuals do best: thinking, reasoning,
critiquing, and suffering the incomprehension of self-appointed bureaucrats
and the public at large. But what if Ibrahim's protagonist is not just a model,
but also a warning? May we understand his ultimate demise – that famous
final scene of auto-cannibalism – not just as an indictment of an unjust
political order, but as an indication that his own strategy of 'defiance' has
ultimately failed him? It may be easier to consider this possibility if we first
recognise that the protagonist's quest is not the impartial, objective, innovative, and purely intellectual pursuit it appears to be, but rather relies on a

particular and historically contingent conglomeration of affects, attitudes, narratives, and generic structures. Specifically, this section will explore how the hero of Ibrahim's novel is drawn into what Rita Felski has called 'suspicion': a critical mood that relies on an assumption of guilt, on metaphors of surface and depth, and on the scripts and motifs of detective fiction, among other genres and intellectual histories. The hero is not just practising critique pure and simple, but becomes engrossed in one particular mode/mood of critique that has both advantages and disadvantages.

To understand what is at stake, let us consider more closely two theories expounded by the protagonist early in the novel. These are responses to questions posed to him during his first appearance before the Committee. In the first, he is asked to identify the most 'momentous event' of the twentieth century. After rejecting wars, revolutions, and movie stars, he hones in on the following names: 'Phillips, Gillette, Michelin, Shell, Kodak, Westinghouse, Ford, Nestle, and Marlboro' (18). Their significance, he explains, derives not only from the fact that 'the whole world uses these brand-name products', but from the fact that 'the giant corporations producing them, in turn, use the world, transforming the workers into machines, the consumers into numbers, and countries into markets' (18). Among all the brand-name products of the world, he chooses Coca-Cola as that that will define the current century for future generations. In justifying his response, he connects Coca-Cola to a string of events and symbols that include: the Statue of Liberty, the Klu Klux Klan, the Spanish–American War, the beginnings of modern advertising, movie stars, The Beatles, the Marshall Plan, the wars in Korea and Vietnam, American masculinity, and, perhaps most importantly, the Trilateral Commission and its secret plot to install Jimmy Carter as President of the United States (19–23). He concludes his demonstration by saying,

> Actually, we are justified in believing what is said about this [seemingly innocent][9] bottle and how it played a decisive role in the choice of our mode of life, the inclinations of our tastes, the presidents and kings of our countries, the wars we participated in, and the treaties we entered into. (23)

In his response, the protagonist has expressed the significance of his object (the Coca-Cola beverage/bottle/corporation) not only in terms of its coincidental association with various events, but its direct and deliberate influence on them. This significance, in addition, is contrasted to the product's external 'innocence'; implicitly, the protagonist is contrasting his ingenious discovery with the naivete and complicity of consumers-*cum*-numbers.

The Committee's next question concerns the Great Pyramid of Cheops (Khufu), and is open-ended. The protagonist decides to focus his response on the issue of its construction. Observing that the Ancient Egyptians possessed only the most primitive building technologies, and quite limited powers of creativity and innovation, he surmises that it is likely that they had benefited from 'Israelite technical expertise' (27). In fact, because he deems it unlikely that such a tremendous structure could have been built through coercion alone, he surmises that its builders must have shared a strong religious faith in the divinity of their king. Thus, in a declaration that recalls Naguib Surur's theory of a Zionist Abdel Nasser, he prefers 'the theory that Cheops was the secret king of the Israelites' (27).

In both of these answers, the protagonist shows his extraordinary investigative abilities. If we take political committedness and critical practice as our frame for analysing this novel, it may seem easier to highlight the first answer (on Coca-Cola) and ignore the second (on the Great Pyramid). The first seems to align with critiques of consumerism and globalisation that activists around the world may identify with, while the other seems to be the stuff of fringe conspiracy theory. Yet both theories are expounded, one right after the other, by the same person. This alone should give us pause before assuming that, as exercises in knowledge production, each is totally distinct and separable from the other. What, then, could they possibly have in common?

Part of the beauty and sophistication of *al-Lajna* is that, contrary to what conservative critics may see as its commitment to politics at the expense of narrative, a significant portion of the novel is dedicated to the narrator-protagonist's rich and detailed introspection into his own thought processes. Thus, in order to understand how both of the above theories come together, we need only to keep reading.

We are aware that the protagonist has spent an entire year studying in preparation for his first interview with the Committee, a process that assisted him in articulating his Coke and Pyramid theories. Considerably more detail is given about the research he conducts in response to a telegram sent by the Committee, several months after this first interview, asking him to produce a 'study' on 'the greatest contemporary Arab luminary' (31). Not much time passes before he latches on to a certain figure referred to only as 'the Doctor' – an *éminence grise* who crosses between, and exerts an unparalleled influence on, the intertwined worlds of politics, economy, and culture. Despite the Doctor's fame and significance, good information on him is decidedly hard to come by. The protagonist finds that more research is required. He delves into the archives of several newspapers and magazines, only to find that the issues he has requested are either unavailable, or that particular articles have been cut out of their pages. He attributes these mysterious lacunae to what he calls a 'secret razor' (47; *al-mūsā al-khafī*, 40), which may be read as a clever pun on the central image of conspiracist discourse, *al-yad al-khafiyya* ('the hidden hand'), or perhaps the more ethnically inflected 'hidden Moses (*Mūsā*)'. Undeterred, he turns to the archives of an obscure women's magazine, and to the library of the American embassy. At these locations he finds luck is on his side, and with the new information he gathers, he finds himself drawn to a process of penetrating deceptive surfaces to uncover secret links and connections.

'The incessant work I had recently undertaken stimulated my mind,' he says. 'I began to delve deeply [*al-taghalghul fi al-aᶜmāq*] into what came my way, trying to deduce underlying motives and relationships' (53–4). His interests 'gradually and unintentionally expanded to include some general matters', and he becomes more and more aware of 'diverse interconnections' (55). It is not long before the protagonist realises that he has developed a sort of methodology. Here he distinguishes between 'the traditional approach, which entails compiling a biography of a person' and his own alternative 'method', which works by 'drawing on a number of studies in various scholarly disciplines' (72). He states with confidence to the Committee that this method has made him 'aware of a number of hidden relationships and connections among a collection of strange and diverse phenomena' (75) and that he is on the verge of 'lifting the veil'[10] off a number puzzles and riddles. Later, alone with the member named 'Stubby', he again asserts that he is 'on the brink of understanding the relationships between a number of miscellaneous phenomena' (94–5).

Thus, throughout his quest, the protagonist speaks of his discoveries in terms of 'phenomena' (*zawāhir*) (that is, that that is apparent), penetrating 'depths', hidden 'connections', and 'lifting the veil'. We may note a family resemblance between this language and the *'invisible interconnectedness'* that Leo Bersoni, in his study of Thomas Pynchon's *Gravity's Rainbow*, identifies as the essence of the 'paranoid intuition'.[11] In the world of the 'paranoiac', disparate phenomena are interpreted as the (visible) symptoms of a single underlying, and deliberately hidden, system or plot. Similarly, Rita Felski uses the less pejorative term 'suspicion' to describe those interpretive practices that rely on metaphorical oppositions of surface and depth, apparent and hidden. Felski's investigation concerns not paranoid fiction, but what she characterises as a pervasive 'critical mood' in scholarly writing in the humanities and social sciences.[12] Work dominated by this mood is deemed suspicious because of its tendency to assume that texts, people, or social phenomena are hiding something; they can only be 'explained' in terms of hidden motives, deep structures, or sinister intentions. Felski acknowledges that suspicion can perform important critical work: exposing often ignored injustices, unearthing surprising links between ostensibly separate concepts, bringing sense and order to a chaotic universe, bestowing authority on its practitioners. And yet, she warns, when suspicious readers assume their critical mood to be the only one – when reading, in other words, becomes synonymous with suspicion – they become indifferent to the element of chance, the contradictory and often incompletely articulated interests of various actors, the complexity of historical causality, and the innocence of groups and individuals. The desire to pronounce a verdict – 'explanation-as-accusation', as Felski calls it – overrides the ability to see and read justly.[13]

Let us return now to the twin theories of Coca-Cola and the Great Pyramid. If we assess them according to the standard of 'research engagement' or committed political critique, one appears interesting while the other appears aberrant, fantastical, absurd. If we view them both as an exercise in suspicion, however, the relation between them becomes much less mysterious. In both cases, an uncanny object solicits the protagonist's attention. The object is uncanny either because of its ubiquity and proximity to major events, as with the Coca-Cola bottle, or because of its intricate design and unknown origin, as in the case of the Great Pyramid. Suspicion kicks in, and each object is assumed to be hiding something. Interpretation is required, and strange links and connections come to light. Each new item of information becomes evidence of a larger design, clues to solving a crime. In both cases, the mystery is solved with the discovery of a masterful scheme behind the scenes: the special science of a crypto-Jew, or the pervasive influence and indomitable will of an American corporation.

We should be careful not to assume, however, that suspicion is a mood the protagonist has chosen consciously of his own free will, and for which he alone is 'guilty'. (Who chooses to be in a mood?) Although he claims that his investigative techniques constitute an 'innovative method' (72) – in other words, the fruit of his concerted efforts and autonomous reasoning – the novel also implicates a number of other factors that contribute to the reign of this particular and contingent critical practice. One important dimension of suspicion is sexual desire. This will be explored in more detail in Chapter 4, but it bears mentioning here. At one point in the novel, the protagonist finds himself witnessing an act of sexual harassment on an overcrowded public bus. He does not entirely disapprove of what he sees:

> I'm the first to admit I have a thing for that protruding part of the female body and am an aficionado of stolen moments in a crowd. From my point of view, this behavior, which some may condemn and which arises from our reality and independent character, is nothing other than an Arab substitute for Western dancing in which people pursue such business face-to-face. But our national substitute fulfills a more complex role than the mere release of repressed desires. It is a successful way of fighting the boredom arising from overcrowding and frequent long delays in streets jammed with private cars. Likewise, for me, it is an important means of releasing tension and one *method of acquiring knowledge.*
>
> A woman is a mysterious creature, the object of a thousand speculations, especially if she appears haughty and hostile, until, at the light brush of a leg, she suddenly reveals herself [– *like a book* –] by indicating her consent or objection. (144–5; emphasis added)

It is remarkable that the translation has left out the phrase 'like a book' (*ka-kitāb*) (112), which is the most significant part of this scene. Suspicious reading – the practice of penetrating surfaces to reveal hidden meaning – is linked explicitly with the pleasure of 'knowing' a woman. The point here is not that the protagonist's critical mood is at root, and only, a reflection of an unconscious urge to sexually harass women on public buses, but that his overwhelming tendency to 'lift the veil' off secret truths is, at least in part, indebted to the same structure of desire. Thus, interpretation is not a pure and disinterested intellectual pursuit, but one that relies on passions and pleasures to which the protagonist himself admits.

A second factor that contributes to the protagonist's suspicious reading practices is the undeniably oppressive and mysterious reality in which he finds himself. Before he even faces the members of the Committee, he finds 'a shroud of secrecy veiling their names and jobs' (7). Then there are the questions themselves, which are so vague as to leave open the door to any manner of speculation. The protagonist is required to produce knowledge, but at the same time, he is implicitly forbidden from requesting clarification (33). Furthermore, even after deciding on a topic around which he may formulate a response, his efforts are thwarted at every turn by censorship, unwelcoming archive staff, and the constant gaze of the Committee and its agents. Eventually, he is confronted directly by Committee members, and told to either drop his investigation of the Doctor, or find an approach that does not implicate them or their powerful allies in a wider criminal plot. As a result, the protagonist's 'passion for knowledge' (123) is not only his own, but is repeatedly and cruelly provoked, seduced, and demanded by the Committee.

A third and crucial factor is intertextuality. In a scene quite reminiscent of Don Quixote's stockpiling of books of chivalric romance, a Committee member scrutinises the protagonist's personal library and finds it full of 'detective stories' (97; *al-riwayāt al-būlīsiyya*, 77). The protagonist explains that he is a 'devotee' of the novelist Georges Simenon and his hero, Inspector Maigret (100). Indeed, if we look back at the protagonist's bouts of archive diving and hunting down of clues, we will recognise the basic elements of the murder-mystery genre. Felski elaborates on the similarities between the police detective and the practitioner of suspicious critique: 'a penchant for interrogating and indicting, a conviction that deceit and deception are ubiquitous and that everyone has something to hide, a commitment to hunting down criminal agents and a reliance on the language of guilt and complicity'; *'like the detective, the critical reader is intent on tracking down a guilty party'*.[14] Our protagonist does not deny these similarities; he takes great pride in them. His research would not have any merit, he says, if he did not hold true to Balzac's famous maxim, 'Behind every great fortune is a great crime' (94).

Turning back to the protagonist's quest, we can see how his commitment to the role of detective plays out. In his final appearance before the Committee, he announces that he has found the hidden link that connects everything: 'diversification' (124; *al-tanwī^c*, 96). This term has been chosen not only because the 'phenomena and mysteries' that elicit his attention happen to be characterised by 'multiplicity' (*al-tanawwu^c*) – that is, 'they are not related to just one facet of life, but extend through diverse facets' – but because, he asserts, they are the product of a deliberate strategy of 'diversification' in global governance.[15] Asked to explain what he means, he offers a detailed response that is worth quoting at some length:

> [']As my example, I will take a subject known to us all, Coca-Cola. Many obscure phenomena are linked to the evolution of this well-known beverage.
>
> 'For example, I read of a far-reaching crusade launched in 1970 in the United States over the mistreatment of a quarter million migrant workers on farms controlled by Coca-Cola. I mean farms, not factories. This crusade spread to television and from there to Congress. Senator Walter Mondale, at that time a member of the Committee for Migrant Workers, summoned the president of Coca-Cola to answer officially, before the United States Senate, the accusations levied against Coca-Cola.
>
> 'Not three years later, the president of Coca-Cola participated in selecting that same Mondale for membership in the Trilateral Commission I told you about in our first meeting. Then he selected him as vice president to President Carter.
>
> 'At the same time as Coca-Cola was accused of the theft of a handful of dollars from its workers, we read that it dedicated vast sums for charitable and cultural works ranging from an entire university budget to an important prize for artistic and literary creativity. It also presented a huge grant to the Brooklyn Museum in 1977 to rescue Egyptian pharaonic antiquities from collapse.
>
> 'Coca-Cola, according to statistics for 1978, distributes two hundred million bottles of soft drinks daily throughout the world, leaving tap water as its only rival. So, now we see it sponsoring projects for the de-salinization of sea water, relying on the Aqua Chem Company that it bought a few years ago, in 1970 to be precise.

'These contradictions confused me, so I did several studies on Coca-Cola. Its policy was to remain committed to the two basic principles set down by its great founders. The first principle was to make every participant in the Coca-Cola enterprise rich and happy. The second was to restrict its energies to creating a single commodity: the well-known bottle.

'But the winds of change that blew in the early '60s forced a choice between the principles. In order not to sacrifice the first, Coca-Cola preferred to diversify its products. It began by producing other types of carbonated beverages, then extended its interests to farming peanuts, coffee, and tea. It had extensive holdings in that same state of Georgia where it was founded. Its farms neighbored those of the American president Carter, which perhaps was behind its involvement in public affairs, both domestic and international, and thus its policy of diversification grew all out of proportion.

'Obviously, this policy couldn't help but be successful. In this regard, it is sufficient to mention the return of the familiar bottle to both China and Egypt through the initiative in both countries of brave patriots, who acted on their principles.

'However, this success produced a strange phenomenon. With modern methods and lower production costs gained by relying on poorly paid migrant workers, Coca-Cola became the largest producer of fresh fruit in the Western world. But, sadly, it found itself forced to dump a large portion of the yield into the sea to keep the world market from collapsing.

'There was no solution to this problem except to continue diversifying. Coca-Cola exploited its great assets and expertise in the field of agriculture by sponsoring many nutritional programs in underdeveloped countries, among them a project to farm legumes in Abu Dhabi, undertaken by its subsidiary, Aqua Chem. Likewise, it extensively researched the production of drinks rich in proteins and other nutrients, thereby compensating consumers for the surpluses it had been forced to dump in the ocean.' (124–7)

The protagonist stops to take a breath, before going on to use 'diversification' as a 'key [to] open many other locks': the 'slogans' and 'goals' of Arab regimes, the influx of foreign weapons and automobiles, the spread of housing projects for rich and poor alike, the changes in Egyptian cigarettes, the increase in cases of depression, cancer, 'sexual impotence, religious fanaticism, apathy, slovenliness', and 'insanity' (127–30). He concludes: 'Thus you see, gentlemen, how the process of diversification leads in and of itself to explaining the many phenomena in our contemporary life and how it joins them as links in a strong chain' (130). But what kind of explanation is this, exactly?

'Thus you see, gentlemen': so speaks the detective of so many stories, after he has assembled a room full of suspects, witnesses, and police officers, and made his explanation-as-accusation. In his commitment to uncovering a hidden design and attributing blame, the detective has reduced an incredible range of diverse phenomena to a deliberate strategy of control. This slight of hand is captured nicely in the move from *tanawwu^c* to *tanwī^c*: general and random diversity becomes, through the lens of suspicion, a sign of causality. There are certainly differences between Inspector Maigret and Sonallah Ibrahim's hero. While the former would typically uncover a murderer, the latter has not pointed blame at an individual criminal, but has rather implicated the nature of the crime, and insinuated the guilt of a number of individuals such as the Doctor, Coca-Cola executives, and the members of the Committee. Nevertheless, both characters begin their quest with a presumption that a crime has been committed, and end up locating a guilty party.

To dwell on the metaphorical, emotive, and intertextual dimensions of suspicion is not cause enough for questioning the viability and significance of its results: as Felski herself admits, thought and discourse cannot proceed in any meaningful way *without* relying on familiar scripts, figurative language, and emotions or 'moods'.[16] Moreover, one cannot deny that the detective does important work. He solves a mystery that others cannot, and, in apprehending a criminal, he allows for justice to take its proper course. But we may question whether this is always and necessarily the best and only model to follow for economic, social, and political analysis. For one, detectives do get things wrong, and not every officer of the law has the intellectual and moral perspicacity of Maigret, Poirot, or Miss Marple. More importantly, the critic's assumption of guilt and criminality – an understandable suspicion when the issue is tracing the bullets in the back of a corpse to a murderer with a gun – becomes problematic when attending to more complex phenomena. What if there is no actual crime, no individual criminal agent or group of agents? What if Coca-Cola is not (only) a criminal act of empire, but (also) a method devised by Arab Spring revolutionaries to mitigate the effects of tear-gas and overthrow dictators? What if a Samsonite briefcase is not (only) a sign of Egypt's economic submission to foreign corporations, but (also) an object of sentimental value for its carrier, a gift from husband to wife, a blunt instrument wielded against a capitalist parasite, and, indeed, the very receptacle that holds the fruit of the protagonist's painstaking investigative labour? When suspicion reigns, 'only' prevails at the expense of the possible, the hopeful, and the also-real.

Yet it is not only that the protagonist's critical mood risks being unfair to particular people and phenomena, or that his obsession with rooting out malice leaves him no time to consider the bright side of life. These are risks that, under certain circumstances, many an ideologue would be willing to take. A potentially graver risk concerns not the single-mindedness or suspicion of the protagonist's critique as such, but his deference to particular figurations of agency that coincide with those of the Committee. In the following section, we will consider the extent to which suspicion, particularly in its conspiracist variety, not only fails to deliver its subject from tragedy, but reinforces the same structures of domination that have condemned him.

The Detective Eats Himself

In her seminal article on 'paranoid reading', Eve Sedgwick outlines the principle characteristics of an interpretive practice that, she argues, has come to dominate many areas of the humanities and social sciences. Among these characteristics is what she calls paranoia's 'faith in exposure': the assumption that the hegemonic forces that rule the universe will become undone merely through the public presentation of their crimes or contradictions.[17] Thus, to use one of her examples, a radical queer theorist may believe that the performance of drag, almost by itself, deconstructs and dismantles the ruling and oppressive binaries of gender. That the performance may fail – that, at the end of the day, patriarchy and heteronormativity have not yielded an inch – is, to the paranoid reader, almost unthinkable. In a similar manner, we may say that the protagonist of *al-Lajna,* to borrow Sedgwick's words, places 'an extraordinary stress on the efficacy of knowledge per se – knowledge in the form of exposure'.[18] By simply 'lifting the veil', he is not only acting in defiance of the Committee, but setting the scene for the eventual, if not immediate, collapse of the globalised economic empire that it supports.[19]

We may note here how crucial this 'faith in exposure' is to the detective of many popular novels. Hercule Poirot, for example, always assumes that the police are waiting in the wings, ready to arrest the culprit he has just exposed to an audience of suspects. But what if the police are not there? A more sinister prospect: What if the police have the criminal's back, and are only waiting for the detective to finish his entertaining performance before they riddle his body with bullets and throw him to the crocodiles?

Indeed, by the end of the protagonist's journey, the order he challenges remains firmly in place. If anything, it appears even stronger than before, as its lone challenger is eliminated, having accepted the sentence of autophagy so furtively suggested to him. Sedgwick suggests a plausible reason for this cosmic irony: the 'hermeneutics of suspicion and exposure', in the end, serves only to grant greater range to 'violence that was *from the beginning* exemplary and spectacular' (140; emphasis in the original). That is, hegemonic forces reproduce themselves precisely in their repetition, performance, and ostentatious visibility; terror cannot rule without an audience.

To fill in the details on how this process works with the discourse of conspiracy, we may turn to an important article on the topic by anthropologist Paul Silverstein.[20] Writing about transnational communication practices in the context of the Algerian civil war, Silverstein describes how conspiracy theories emerge amidst a scarcity of reliable narratives on major events like assassinations, massacres, bombings, and changes in government. In contrast to much recent research on conspiracy theory that suggests it is either a discourse of the margins, or inherently opposed to the hegemonic structures of the state, he notes that all parties in the conflict, whether secular or Islamist, 'street' or establishment, engage in the practice with equal intensity. While acknowledging that radical suspicion and scepticism may constitute a form of critique and sense-making for many Algerians, Silverstein argues that conspiracy theory 'cannot be contained within a category of "resistance," for all reinterpretations that uncover state, military, or Islamist conspiracies simultaneously grant to these forces stability, agency, and control that they do not otherwise or necessarily enjoy'.[21] This is especially so during civil conflict, when the ability of any one actor or agency to monopolise violence is called into question. So conspiracy theory constitutes a 'discursive prop' to a fragile political authority.[22]

Even in the absence of open civil war, power is no less threatened by contingency, accident, disobedience, detours, distractions, trespassings, and trapdoors. Practices of popular suspicion – in particular those that fetishise the influence of large and identifiable actors, and place great emphasis on intentionality and design – not only give corporations and capitalists more credit than they deserve, but constitute one quite effective mechanism through which these entities exercise and exude what authority they have. This may go some way in helping us to understand why, in fact, the protagonist is summoned before the Committee in the first place: his conspiracy theories are not for his edification alone. From the beginning, his suspicious 'critiques' are prodded and incited by the Committee members, both through their targeted questions about 'momentous' events and 'luminary' individuals, and the veil of secrecy they impose upon everything. He is thus led to focus specifically on powerful forces, and left to develop his wildest speculations about their influence and reach.

In this vein, we may also note how seldom the Committee objects to his theories. After his first exposé on the Coca-Cola company, his interrogators appear more bored than antagonised; upon completing his theory on the Great Pyramid, they seem rather amused:

> I felt the tension clouding the room lift and the hostile atmosphere ease. The Committee members had listened to me with intense interest; even the fat man sitting at one side lowered his eyes from the ceiling for the first time and fixed them on me. When I finished, one of the officers looked at me with approval, which cheered me up. (28)

When the Committee members *do* object to the direction of his research, it is after letting him elaborate at some length on the hidden machinations of power. Even then, they do not command him to halt his research into the Doctor, only to find a different approach. When he persists nonetheless, they keep listening, allowing him to present his fuller thesis on the grand conspiracy of 'diversification' and its agents.

To be sure, the Committee does not agree with everything the protagonist says. But it would appear that their disagreement is not with conspiracy theory as such, but with the implication that they or their allies have committed some wrongdoing. This becomes evident during the final encounter, when the Committee offers its only sustained rebuttal to particular accusations. In mourning the loss of a colleague, who has just been murdered by the protagonist, the member known only as 'the old man' speaks:

> From the beginning the Committee has put itself at the service of revolutionary objectives, ethical principles, and religious values. Its members have supported everything that would strengthen basic freedoms and expand the democratic process.
>
> Naturally, we thus aroused the animosity of evil and destructive elements, which did their utmost to resist us. In this connection, let me draw your attention to the carefully manufactured uproar over the methods we use in our work and to the charges, sometimes of sadism and sometimes of demagoguery, that are liberally levied against us.
>
> These forces have always tried to link us to political coups d'etat, sectarian massacres, and limited conflicts happening now in the Arab world, and even to some unexplained suicides, a few sporadic incidents of persons missing without a trace, and other persons who fell from rooftops or were killed in chance traffic accidents. (114–15)

It would appear that the member is rejecting conspiracy theories. And yet, we should note that he has not explicitly denied any of these accusations – he has only mentioned that they were levied by 'evil and destructive elements'. More important is the curious fact that he has mentioned these accusations at all, and in some detail. At the very least, it would seem a poor rhetorical strategy for the Committee to bring up these accusations in the first place, if it would rather have them suppressed. At the most, it is possible that the old man and his fellow members delight in these accusations, as in a most sadistic fashion, they provide evidence of how powerful and insidious they can really be. The only thing more gratifying than broadcasting these accusations themselves is to listen, watch, and record in sumptuous silence as the protagonist, at once impassioned and humiliated, goes on to eloquently spin out the narratives of their domination all by himself.

Throughout his quest, the protagonist is intent on exposing the scandal of his fellow citizens' enslavement to the hegemons of globalisation. He delights in telling us that 'the Doctor' 'holds the political threads of the future in his hands' (71), and that a handful of corporate behemoths have effectively transformed 'the workers into machines, the consumers into numbers, and countries into markets' (18). Yet if statements such as these are intended as invective, they are received rather as panegyric, as tacit recognitions of corporations' otherwise contested and temporary grip on consumers. It is quite telling, then, that the protagonist prefaces this latter accusation by saying, 'I suspect you agree with me, your honors, that ...' (18). In fact, they are all too happy to agree with him that corporations and committees are the uncontested rulers of the world. This is to them not a shameful exposé, but a generous compliment offered by a potential critic.

None of this is to suggest that the Committee is consciously and deliberately promoting conspiracy theory, or has plotted from the beginning to set up the protagonist as an exemplary practicioner of suspicion – such a suggestion would only reinforce the notion of hegemony we have been intent on complicating. Perhaps some members of the Committee are more aware of their rhetorical and interpretive strategies than others; perhaps some assume such strategies, but fail to see them through to their desired effect. In addition, we should not assume that, conscious or not, the 'discursive prop' of conspiracy theory necessarily or automatically re-establishes the hegemony of the corporate overlords. As a discursive object in the world, conspiracy theory, whatever the intentions behind it or the effects it claims, requires technologies of circulation, enthusiastic spokes-persons, faithful consumers, and a receptive audience beyond those subjects assembled in the Committee's interrogation room. That is to say, propping up the powerful is a *risk* that the conspiracy theorist takes; it is not an inevitable outcome.

These qualifications aside, we must not forget the protagonist's grue-some end. Although it would be simple to view him as the victim of an unjust verdict pronounced by a cruel and all-powerful Other, we should also consider the role played by his own discursive practices. After all, he has not been explicitly ordered, much less physically forced, to commit suicide by self-consumption. By agreeing to appear before the Committee, by never questioning the premises of its questions, by dutifully conducting research, and by reproducing and thus gratifying its dream of global hegemony, he has, to a significant extent, contributed to the narrowing of his own horizon and the inevitability of a retreat into the hidden depths of his body.

Conclusion: Yes and No

It is inevitable that a critical reassessment of a celebrated protagonist will arouse some suspicion. In an attempt to assuage any doubts about this chapter's ulterior motives or ultimate goals, let us list some of the arguments that we have *not* made:

(1) The protagonist is only a conspiracy theorist; his claims about corporate power are untrue and possibly pathological.
(2) The protagonist's theories are borrowed from detective novels, and are therefore fanciful.
(3) The protagonist is not a true radical. His theories are naively complicit in hegemonic structures; he is not suspicious enough!
(4) Suspicion only leads to auto-cannibalism; resistance is futile; Quietists of the world, unite!

The first claim belongs more properly to the conservative or reactionary critic who feels threatened by the novel's anti-imperialist tones; it is the claim made by the Committee itself. Yes, this chapter has argued, Ibrahim's protagonist *does* partake in a critical mood that shares much with conspiracism; no, his accusations are not totally misplaced or delusional. Raising the spectre of conspiracy theory is not intended to challenge the veracity of particular accusations levelled by the novel's protagonist – multinational corporations like Coca-Cola certainly do exert influence on politicians, consumers, and global culture. To be sure, one may wish to question the assertion that Cheops, builder of the Great Pyramid, was 'the secret king of the Israelites' (27; cf. 99); that the Trilateral Commission, together with the Coca-Cola company, plotted to install Jimmy Carter as president of the United States, and hand-picked his Vice President, Walter Mondale (22, 124); or that there really exists a figure in every country who, like 'the Doctor', has had a hand in every major commercial deal and political event of the last thirty years (71). But to deny that sugary beverages are a threat to public health, or that capitalism wreaks havoc on workers and consumers, or that money buys influence, is as much to suggest that all that is true must be good.

The second claim constitutes a non-sequitur. Yes, this chapter has shown that the protagonist's interpretations rely much on tropes and narratives of detection. This is not an argument; the protagonist proudly admits as much. However, this is not to cast aspersions on the sincerity of the protagonist's quest, or to imply that his theories are totally fictitious. Rather, it is, first, to challenge the claim that suspicion is an 'innovative approach' that differs fundamentally from other approaches. All quests for knowledge must rely to some extent on narrative, and detection is no exception. More importantly, calling attention to the protagonist's guiding models and metaphors allows us to assess their shortcomings as tools of interpretation and knowledge production. If sniffing out a crime is a suitable disposition for the officer of the law, it becomes much more problematic when applied to the broader realm of human and non-human action, where guilt and innocence, if not totally irrelevant categories, may easily coexist, in varying degrees and for differing periods of time, in individual persons, pyramids, bottles, and boxes.

The third claim is an extension of the protagonist's own logic of suspicion, folded back in on itself. Suspicion is now eyed with suspicion, as a once innocent-looking tool of resistance turns out, in a moment of Orwellian terror, to be yet another tentacle of the octopus of hegemony. This chapter has argued, indeed, that conspiracy theory risks shoring up the very forces it opposes. This risk is inherent in its attribution of supreme agency either to individuals like the Doctor, or to entities like the state, multinational corporations, or the Committee. But this is only a risk – conspiracist discourse does not create institutional authority from nil, nor does it constitute the only pillar of this authority. Moreover, its effects should not be exaggerated. 'If misreading, overreading, or bad reading is at fault,' Rita Felski submits, 'it is one that we are all prone to commit on a regular basis: more like a traffic violation than a capital crime' (122–3).

The fourth claim is admittedly tongue-in-cheek, but one cannot deny its appeal to those who may accept some of the previous claims. Indeed, the thrust of this chapter has been to cast the protagonist's critical project in a less positive light than it has previously enjoyed. Yet this is not the same as rejecting it *en tout*, and running over to apply for membership on the Committee. First, a thorough, non-hypocritical reckoning with suspicion and conspiracism must acknowledge the positive aspects of these practices.

To borrow a phrase from Eve Sedgwick, 'Paranoia knows some things well and others poorly' (130). That is to say, there are many good truths to be derived from the protagonist's assertions, however exaggerated or misplaced they may sometimes be. Hidden injustices must be brought to light, and connections between disparate phenomena must be unearthed. Beyond the knowledge it produces, the suspicious quest also bestows emotional, moral, and aesthetic benefits on the Quixotes and Maigrets of the world. al-Musawi is absolutely correct in noting that the protagonist's research 'works to create identity, to elevate an empty life to a new one of purpose and discovery'. Similarly, Chris Stone rightly points out that, prior to the novel's fateful twist, the protagonist's 'life has been changed for the better', a fact that shows 'the benefits of activism' (145–6). Indeed, the protagonist repeatedly invokes these benefits, saying that his quest 'had given some meaning to [his] life after a long spell of hopelessness' (105); at one point, he even characterises his research as amounting to a drowning man's 'life preserver' (83). We may express concern over the protagonist's over-commitment to suspicion, and still recognise that it does him some good.

Finally, we should not conclude that critique is synonymous with solipsistic, self-defeating suspicion, and therefore abandon all efforts to resist and deconstruct dominant forces. There are many alternatives to conspiracist discourse. These may be articulated either as a change in mood – a turn from suspicion to guarded optimism, patient concern, and even love – or as a change in tactic that abandons reductionism in favour of recognising the complex trajectories of intentions and designs, the distributed nature of agency, the possibility of surprise, the fragility of monsters, and the political and ethical ambivalence of both everyday objects and extraordinary committees.

As was insinuated at the beginning of this chapter, these issues of interpretation and critique concern more than just the protagonist of a single novel. Having elaborated on the risks and limits of suspicion, let us now turn back to our opening scene: the mysterious case of the leftist turned authoritarian. This case is mysterious only if we assume, as readers have often assumed of the protagonist of *al-Lajna*, that Sonallah Ibrahim's public persona is that of a committed 'leftist', 'liberal', 'Marxist', or 'progressive'. Indeed, his persona is this, but only if we understand that such terms indicate not an ideological stance or set of rigid intellectual positions, but rather a critical disposition or mood (let us call it a 'style') that forever assumes a crime has been committed, distrusts surfaces and appearances, delights in the pleasures of unveiling and sideways glances, emphasises and exaggerates author intentionality and influence, and discounts chance, accident, innocence, or incoherence. In other words, we may better understand how a critic has become an apologist if we trade the concept of critical theory for conspiracy theory. It is only natural that the exposer of globalist parasites and their local agents, the critic of effeminate and feminising cultural forces, and the detective of sundry shadowy plots should find common ground with an ostentatiously masculinist regime whose raison d'être is a conspiracy of traitors and namby-pamby global elites against the nation. Thus, the 'authoritarian turn' is not a turn at all, but a consistent and logical denouement for the narrative of conspiracy and suspicion.

As previous readers have suggested, there is much in *The Committee* that relates to Sonallah Ibrahim's own experience as a critic, author, and public intellectual.[23] In addition, we suggest, there are important parallels to be drawn between the protagonist's articulation of conspiracist suspicions and Ibrahim's own public performance of such theories. We may observe this connection with a final example. In his interview with *al-Yawm al-Sābiᶜ* cited above, Ibrahim offered the following claim as part of his diagnosis of Egypt's current crisis:

> First of all, we must understand that there are plans/plots (*khitat*) arranged in research centers in Germany and America to analyze our political and social conditions. Their goal is to maintain their control over us. The plans/plots are carried out through the planting (*zarᶜ*) of a number of personalities in our midst that can be used for their benefit. Among these personalities is Dr. Mohamed ElBaradei.

From a certain perspective, this accusation may appear strange. Yet in many ways it is anticipated in the sinister figure of 'the Doctor' in *al-Lajna*. Both ElBaradei, a Nobel Peace Laureate and former head of the International Atomic Energy Agency, and the fictive Doctor are leading figures in international organisations; both have moved between the roles of policy maker, diplomat, and activist; both are perceived by critics as failing to project the desired masculine charisma; both are seldom mentioned without their preceding title. *Al-Lajna* was written, of course, long before ElBaradei achieved his present 'luminosity'. It is as if, in attempting to fit the present political chaos into a coherent narrative explanation, Ibrahim has lifted more than a few pages from his old book.

Ibrahim was not alone in his perception of ElBaradei. A few weeks before the novelist gave his interview, and before ElBaradei had resigned the post of vice president in protest at the Rābiᶜa Massacre, another famed Egyptian author wrote the following:

> I began observing [ElBaradei] as though I were watching a character in a novel or a play. In terms of his appearance, with his spectacles and tall, insecure build, he appeared to have just stepped out of a film with Laylā Murād. (Resembling, most of all, the musician ᶜAzīz ᶜUthmān.) In terms of his words and ideas, I observed that he didn't propose anything of any value. He appeared unfamiliar with the culture of the age. Graver still was that fact that the man appeared strange, foreign, an Arabist (*mustaᶜrib*), indeed exactly like an Arabist. Perhaps that has to do with the long time he spent outside of Egypt. Why did he return at this precise time in 2009 [that is, shortly before the 2011 Revolution]? Could it be he had connections to the Muslim Brotherhood and the Islamists?[24]

The author of these words was Gamal al-Ghitani, whose engagement with conspiracy we take up in the following chapter.

4

Gamal al-Ghitani's *Ḥikāyāt al-Khabīʾa*: The *Fitna* of Sexual Deviance

He went on to say, 'There are secret reports telling of the spread of sexual deviance (*al-shudhūdh al-jinsī*) among our country's leadership class, at all levels, such that they now constitute ten percent. This is connected to a foreign plot to gain complete control of the country's decision-making and destiny.'[1]

Muḥammad ʿAbbās, an extremist Islamist author and television pundit, provided this frightful portrait of an Egypt overrun by homosexuals in an article published in May 2002. (His source – an anonymous 'prominent member of Parliament' – had considered this a 'very grave matter' that warranted immediate exposure.) Simply titled 'Liwāṭ' ('Sodomy'), the article appeared in the wake of the infamous Queen Boat case of the previous year, when police arrested fifty-five men on charges of 'practicing debauchery'.[2] Incensed that the men had not been punished severely enough – apparently, he either did not know, or did not care, that the detained had been brutally tortured – the author accused the Egyptian regime of 'championing sodomites' and playing into the hands of a gay international plot.[3]

There is reason to believe that ʿAbbās's source was real, even if his story was not. Upon their arrest, the defendants in the Queen Boat case found themselves accused by security officers, as well as by the media, not merely of committing private moral offences, but of conspiring to form 'a cult eroding moral values, a subversive network threatening state security'.[4] In particular, the interrogators alleged, the men belonged to a group called the Agency of God on Earth, which, apart from Satan worship, embraced the prophethood of Lot (Lūṭ) and the Abbasid-era poet Abū Nuwās (756–814).[5] Subsequent investigations revealed, however, that these accusations of conspiracy – and perhaps even the alleged 'sexual deviance' – were likely the product of the security services' own interpretive excesses and narrative elaborations. The case had begun with the interrogation of one man who, under torture, happened to recant a 'dream' involving the Prophet Muhammad and a prophecy concerning a 'Kurdish boy'.[6] Their oneiromantic fantasies aroused, security officers – according to one hypothesis – deemed their prisoner a homosexual, based on nothing other than the casual mention of a boy in a dream. They imagined, furthermore, that their prisoner was the leader of a secret society. The subsequent arrest of more than fifty individuals, many of whom were randomly abducted from the street and had no relation to the primary prisoner, was conducted in order to corroborate the theory of the alleged network, and give the narrative the actors it needed to be performed.

In Muḥammad ʿAbd al-Nabī's *Fī Ghurfat al-ʿAnkabūt* (In the Spider's House) (2016), a novelistic dramatisation of the Queen Boat case, a character recounts the formation of the security services' conspiracy theory thus:

> They alleged that [the prisoner] narrated (*rawā*) to them, suddenly and without any clear context, a dream – or, in the official report's language, a 'vision' (*ruʾyā*) – he had fifteen years ago. He had dreamt that the Prophet Muhammad was visited by a blonde lad, and that the Prophet said that this Kurdish lad will appear and take revenge on the whole world – Jews, Christians, and Muslims – because they did not try to stop the Turks from attacking the Kurds. What have the Turks and the Kurds got to do with us? It was probably just Samir [the prisoner] suffering delusions after a case of indigestion. Or, perhaps it was the creation (*ibdāʿ*) of an anonymous author in the security services, who finally was able to release his suppressed literary talents to compose an elaborate tale about the [so-called] Agency of God on Earth organization.[7]

The character goes on to imagine this anonymous author penning away at his story, 'like an ingenious novelist'.[8] In this way, ʿAbd al-Nabī's novel calls attention to the imaginative – indeed, literary – practice that generated the charges of conspiracy, undermining their pretence of legal and logical authority. Accusations of a vast homosexual plot against the nation are revealed to be founded on an act of suspicious misreading – in part deliberate, in part whimsical – shot through with the suppressed and sublimated pleasures of literary creation.

The '(sexual) deviant' (*al-shādhdh*) – in particular, the homosexual or effeminate man – has long featured as a trope of considerable potency in conspiracy theories and paranoid plots, and not just those that emerge from the fringes of Islamism or state security. A striking example we have already encountered is that of the opportunistic *khawal* in Nagib Surur's *Kuss-ummiyyāt*. Although considerably more subdued, the protagonist of Sonallah Ibrahim's *al-Lajna* conjures up this image, too, both in his allegation that 'The Doctor' has 'latent homosexual tendencies',[9] and in the recurring metaphor that links capitalist crimes to the penetration of the anus or, more specifically, homosexual rape.[10] Examples are by no means limited to Arabic literature. In North America, one may think of the recurrent right-wing allegations about a 'gay agenda' or 'homosexual lobby'; even ostensibly leftist cultural forms, such as Oliver Stone's film *JFK* (1991), may have been implicated in the transmission of a conspiracist 'homosexual panic'.[11] In imagining the homosexual as supremely manipulative, singularly influential, and everywhere at once, such narratives represent something more than homophobia. Indeed, 'phobia', as we will see, may be only one part of a tempestuous, often unpredictable cauldron of affects that includes shifting proportions of disgust, delight, panic, and pleasure.

The nexus of sexual deviance, conspiracy, and contagious affects finds a unique literary expression in Gamal al-Ghitani's novel *Ḥikāyāt al-Khabī'a* (Tales of the Treasure Trove) (2002), which appeared in the same year as the article quoted above. The novel dramatises the rise to prominence of Fayrūz Baḥrī, a so-called *lūṭī* ('sodomite') whose proximity to the executives of an unnamed 'foundation' provokes overwhelmingly negative reactions among fellow employees. The first section of this chapter engages with several well-known 'suspicious' readings of the relationship between paranoia and homosexuality, and assesses the extent to which we may understand the reactions of characters to Fayrūz in terms of subliminal 'anxieties' and 'panics'. Yet while Fayrūz repels, he also attracts. In the second section, we will see how his male rivals derive pleasure from their carefully cultivated practices of detecting, unveiling, penetrating, and recording the secrets of his private and professional selves. Both wittingly and unwittingly, Fayrūz himself stimulates the interpretive practices of his rivals, seducing them with the prospect of rarefied knowledge and special powers through a playful oscillation between absence and presence, ostentation and obscurity. These men are also attracted to Fayrūz because he appears to embody the model of unobstructed, conspiratorial agency that they desire for themselves. The gossip and rumours they produce about him thus contain exaggerations that are more a reflection of their own fantasy of control than of Fayrūz's actual influence and reach.

After considering the affective bonds that tie characters within the text to Fayrūz Baḥrī, we turn in the third section to show how the author extends this very game of seduction to the reader. By alternating between transparency and obscurity in his description of uncannily familiar personalities – including the use of character names that rhyme or echo with those of members of Egypt's cultural and political elite – al-Ghitani constructs a *roman à clef* that seduces readers into digging up secrets behind the text and 'cracking its code'. In other words, the novel makes its reader suspicious. Specifically, *Ḥikāyāt al-khabīʾa* leads us to read beneath the surface of its text the public feud between the author, Gamal al-Ghitani, and Egypt's longstanding minister of culture, Farouk Hosni (Fārūq Ḥusnī, whose name is echoed by 'Fayrūz Baḥrī').

In the conclusion, we follow up on these suspicious insights by speculating on the affective dimensions of Egyptian cultural politics at the turn of the millennium. In particular, we will consider the extent to which the panics and passions in the novel may help us understand the mysterious rivalry, and subsequent reconciliation, between al-Ghitani and Hosni.

Panic and Pathology

Ḥikāyāt al-Khabīʾa is in fact the sequel to, or second part of, Gamal al-Ghitani's *Ḥikāyāt al-Muʾassasa* (Tales of the Foundation), which was published in 1997, five years earlier.[12] The two novels share not a common plot or cast of characters, but a *topos*, namely, 'the Foundation' or *al-muʾassasa*, a veritable behemoth with its hands in just about everything but nothing entirely specific: unnamed technological innovations, the latest in corporate managerial schemes, national and international politics and espionage, and the queer acronyms of globalisation like COMESA, FIFA, FAW, and Benelux. The long-deceased 'Founder' (*al-muʾassis*) whose presence haunts the two books is the object of nostalgic reverence for some, and of negligence and apathy for those who have managed, or yet desire, to occupy his office through intrigue and corruption: a group of mostly technocrats, bureaucrats, prostitutes, and freaks. By the beginning of the second novel, *Ḥikāyāt al-Khabīʾa*, the simple, paternalistic vision that had guided the Foundation through its early days has been all but erased by a wave of young professionals whose business sense is decidedly neoliberal, and whose actions fall behind an increasingly thick veil of obscurity. In this context there is whisper of one 'Fayrūz Baḥrī'.

Who is Fayrūz Baḥrī? His name first appears amidst much noise, as the latest in a series of secretive figures promoted to sensitive positions during the term of the fourth and current chief executive. In the middle of *Ḥikāyāt al-Khabīʾa*, he is appointed 'Head of the *Fuyūḍāt* Sector': it is a nonsensical phrase, one among the many new position titles that parody the illegible and disorienting signscape of the technocratic sublime. While *fuyūḍāt* lacks any meaning in Modern Standard Arabic, it is a derivation of the root *f-y-ḍ*, which denotes 'excess', 'abundance', 'fluidity', or 'flood'. Quite appropriately, then, Fayrūz is a figure that is always over the top, but also fluid in his seductive elusiveness: he can never quite be pinned down. Moreover, his position makes him responsible for the 'Treasure Trove' (*al-khabīʾa*) of the novel's title: a labyrinthine vault of artefacts and artworks that are as priceless as they are nameless, located beneath the ground floor of the Foundation's central building.

Fayrūz's entrance is through rumour: 'A single sentence, nearly uniform in content, was whispered and pronounced in secret and in the open: "There's a sodomite [*lūṭī*] in the new administration"' (150–1). It is rumour, too, that translates this character to readers for the length of the novel. We, along with the Foundation's employees, are treated to precise details about the types of boys he likes (168, 209), the ribald sex parties he calls 'freeing the reigns' (250; *iṭlāq al-ʿinān*), and – if there were any doubt remaining about the nature of his 'deviance' – rumours of accounts of leaks of direct audio and visual recordings made of Fayrūz in bed with his partner (244, 248, 260). There are, of course, allegations of corruption and mismanagement, too, but it is gossip of a sexual nature that dominates.

Scattered signs of a Foundation-wide panic about sexual deviance erupt even before the appearance of Fayrūz Baḥrī. This suggests that the murmurings that later surround him have perhaps more to do with the prejudices and anxieties of Foundation employees, than any verifiable acts committed by Fayrūz. The Foundation's chief executive is an early conduit for these anxieties. It is said that 'His Excellency' – this is the chief executive's recurring epithet – had the habit of curling up like a ball in the back seat of his car and, invisible to the rearview mirror, would pose strange questions to his driver. Once, out of the blue, he is said to have asked, 'Can a man become a sexual deviant late in life?' A second version of this question is reported: 'Can a man, who has not known sexual deviancy in his entire life, suddenly find his desire strengthen in the opposite direction, and strive for a man to penetrate him?' Yet a third version of the question is circulated: 'Can a man turn into a sexual deviant after fifty?' (76). We do not know the driver's response, and the question is as bewildering to the reader as it is to the employees of the Foundation. The chief executive is known to have a wife and children, as well as numerous mistresses. There is no context to cause us to expect this question, apart from the appearance of a 'well-groomed' chauffeur who suffers from one of the chief executive's notoriously capricious and unexplained grudges.

This same anxiety finds other outlets for expression, such as an equally random and unexpected warning that several parents issue to their children. In one instance, a stepmother cautions her adopted son 'not to take off his clothes in front of anyone, not to play English leapfrog, and not to let anyone touch his rear' (164). This echoes an earlier incident in the novel's prequel, in which a secretary, caught in traffic, lets her mind wander to concerns about her two sons. Of the youngest, she expresses 'her constant fear that someone will play a trick on him, as she had also feared for his older brother. She has tried … to warn them against playing games in which a boy must bend over, or in which boys jump over each other.'[13]

The appearance of Fayrūz Baḥrī, midway through the novel, effects a sudden increase in the volume of these phobic reverberations. While many employees in the Foundation are content to pass on the rumours of his 'sexual deviance' without comment, others are driven totally mad by the alleged impropriety and exert no effort to conceal their opinions. These include a newspaper editorial warning of the dangers of 'this type' taking office (154), a website that digs up salacious reports on Fayrūz's 'deviant' activism (218–19), and an older employee who bursts out into the hallway shouting, 'Anything but this sodomite!' (200). As the supervisor of the Treasure Trove becomes more intimate with the chief executive, and especially one of his mistresses, a number of the Foundation's erstwhile powerbrokers grow increasingly incensed. At least one of these rivals, however, pauses for a brief moment of self-reflection. 'ᶜAzab al-Mīdūmī' asks himself the following:

> So, why does he attack Fayrūz? Why does he take such a fierce position against him?
>
> Is it because he is known for his sexual deviance [*shudhūdhihi*]? Or because he has risen to a sensitive position?
>
> Every person is free with his own body, but when it comes to filling such sensitive positions, it is necessary to perform the proper examinations.
>
> Examination of what? Is he kidding himself?
>
> Examination of what?
>
> Doesn't he know that this is the time for all invalids [*maᶜṭūbīn*]? (228)

These equivocations allow the narrative voice to maintain a pretence of critical distance from the base fears and hatreds expressed by the mass of employees, while ultimately reaffirming the irredeemable otherness of non-normative sexualities (if that is what they are).

Thus, the question remains. Why, indeed, do he and others attack Fayrūz? Stepping back a bit, we may situate these reactions in literary terms as common tropes within the tradition of pre-modern Islamic apocalyptic writings (for example, *al-fitan wa al-malāḥim*, *ᶜalāmāt al-sāᶜa*), with which al-Ghitani, famous for his rich intertextual engagement with the canon of Arabic literature, was surely familiar. Walid Saleh has shown how medieval Sunni renditions of this genre regarded women with a particular anxiety. Immoral women, seductive women, and the increase in women both in the general population and in leadership positions were perceived not only as threats to the social order, but as integral to the horror of the end times. These anxieties, Saleh notes, extended to homosexuals as well.[14] Similarly, in *Ḥikāyāt al-Khabīʾa*, the rise of Fayrūz occurs within the context of a more general eschatological panic. As in 'ᶜAzab al-Mīdūmī's self-reflection above, characters often express that they are living in a particular 'time' of deviance and decline. It is the 'Age of Occultation' (*ᶜaṣr al-khafāʾ*, 150) – a reference to the pervasive secrecy in the Foundation; it is the 'Era of al-Glādiyūs' (*ḥiqbat al-glādiyūs*, 104) – a reference to the special status afforded to the chief executive's mistress; it is, most especially, the 'Time of Rears' (*zaman al-muʾakhkharāt*, 169) – at once a reference to the spread of (both hetero- and homosexual) anal intercourse, and a possible pun on the 'end times' or the 'Last Day' (*al-yawm al-ʾākhir*). These apocalyptic themes have a particular resonance in the lead up to the new millennium, in anticipation of which many of the novel's events take place.

But what makes the homosexual, in particular, the centre of attention? This question applies as much to premodern apocalyptic texts as it does to the present novel. One way of attending to the specificity of the homosexual anxiety is through Eve Sedgwick's re-conception of 'homosexual panic'. While 'homosexual panic' had been deployed, in the United States beginning in the early twentieth century, as a legal defence for accused murderers of homosexual men, Sedgwick's 'theft' of the term is intended to explore the emotive, psychological, and political dimensions between men in English literature and society (2008: 20–1). It is conceived not as individual psychopathology, but as a structural principle that renders nearly all men fearful of the implication of homosexual relationships, whether as paranoia about one's one latent homosexuality, or the fear of being taken advantage of by other homosexuals. Sedgwick historicises this panic, situating its emergence in the middle of the nineteenth century, when it became 'an endemic and ineradicable state' for men, specifically those in high-powered professional settings (185).

While the panic studied by Sedgwick, no less than the word 'homosexual' itself, may be the object of such analysis that rightly aims for a degree of historical and cultural specificity, one cannot fail to recognise the aptness of her concept in describing the anxieties that surround Fayrūz.[15] It is (ostensibly heterosexual) men who show him the most extreme animosity, which cannot be reduced simply to a matter of professional jealousy. The questions allegedly posed by the chief executive about the stability of sexual orientation become rumour, most likely because they index an anxiety shared by many other men: perhaps you, perhaps me, perhaps your best friend, could turn into 'one of them'.

Another way of understanding the fears that motivates the attacks on Fayrūz is in terms of what Timothy Melley has called 'agency panic'.[16] One hears, in the narrative murk of *Ḥikāyāt al-Khabīʾa*, repeated speculation about the powers-that-be, and a confusion about the precise sources of action and discourse. Who, really, is in charge? These questions multiply soon after Fayrūz's appointment, as anonymous voices ask: 'Who is planning? Who is making the decisions? [*man yukhaṭṭiṭ? man yuqarrir?*] It is difficult to determine, what's happening now is strange, deviant [*shādhdh*] from everything familiar' (184). Fayrūz's sudden appearance provokes such questions in an environment where authority (the ability to plan, make decisions, and exert influence) is defined in terms of normative masculinity. As a 'deviation' from this ideal, the homosexual, effeminate man, or woman who gains visibility represents not just a loss of authority, but the penetration of external forces into the community. Thus, one of Fayrūz's detractors argues that 'the danger of deviants and abnormals assuming sensitive positions' is due to the fact that 'they can be easily influenced, and penetrated through their weak spots' (154). The phrase is repeated almost verbatim by other voices (153, 154). The object of these fears is at once the mysterious puppet-master behind the deviant, and the deviant himself, to the extent that he threatens to penetrate (that is, dominate) other men.

One significant conclusion we may draw from these different theories of panic is that the anxieties surrounding homosexuality in the novel are far from specific to this Foundation, in an Arabic-speaking country, at the dawn of the third millennium. One may productively compare them to similar anxieties in medieval Islam, nineteenth-century English literature, or twentieth-century American culture. More importantly, (eschatological, homosexual, or agency) panic calls our attention to the unconscious drives behind the behaviour of many characters, which may otherwise be rationalised as conflicts of policy, ethics, or ideology. That is to say, there is more behind the opposition to Fayrūz than the characters themselves would care to admit.

There are, however, limits to reading suspiciously. For while panic provides a useful framework for understanding those who spurn, reject, and express disgust at Fayrūz, one cannot fail to recognise that he inspires as much passion as he does polemic. Sometimes, this passion exhibits itself in dramatic shifts in opinion or mood: the chief executive, despite his earlier bout of homosexual panic, is the one who appoints, and gives his unqualified backing to, the supervisor of the Treasure Trove; another character, despite initially opposing Fayrūz on account of the latter's sexual deviance

(154), suddenly changes his mind and announces his full endorsement of the newcomer (158). More often, the desires and delights that Fayrūz inspires in others are more subtly expressed, shimmering along the trims and trusses of putative diatribes, or betraying themselves in the frequency and volume of popular gossip. To account for these other emotions, we need a change of terms.

Fitna

The Foundation's employees detest Fayrūz, but they also cannot get enough of him. Perhaps a more appropriate word for the hold he has over them is not panic but *fitna*. Let us consider what this could mean. Previous research on the term, reviewed by Walid Saleh, has wielded some of the following definitions: 'temptation, trial, torture, straying from the right path, intra-communal political strife', 'apocalyptic battles and horrors', and 'the destructive influence of females on the social order and their role in the apocalypse' as well as 'the highest word of praise one can use to describe [female] beauty' (128–9). *Fitna* folds nicely around the affect-scape of *Ḥikāyāt al-Khabīʾa*, as it is capacious enough to capture both the negative and positive emotions that Fayrūz provokes. There is on the one hand apocalyptic horror and strife – in other words, eschatological/homosexual panic – and on the other beauty, temptation, and seduction. It is the latter grouping of concepts that we probe here.

A surprisingly productive concept of 'seduction', for our purposes, is provided by Jean Baudrillard. For the French postmodernist,

> [seduction] does not consist of a simple appearance, nor a pure absence, but the eclipse of a presence. Its sole strategy is to be-there/not-there, and thereby produce a sort of flickering, a hypnotic mechanism that crystallizes attention outside all concern with meaning. Absence here seduces presence.[17]

Whether or not it is a conscious strategy, and whether or not its effect is to 'crystallize attention outside all concern with meaning' – meaning of a specific kind is what is desired – the ostentatious disappearance (or discrete appearance) of Fayrūz Baḥrī seduces spectators with the prospect of hidden knowledge and value. It is the dominant preoccupation of the Foundation's employees to access this hidden knowledge, these secrets, and this they manage through the sundry tactics available to them: speculation, rumour, and constant, technologically mediated voyeurism.

Fayrūz's name mimics this process of seduction: the oscillation between absence and presence, between seen and unseen. In Arabic, *fayrūz* is 'turquoise', a gemstone to be unearthed; *Baḥrī* or *baḥarī* may occur in the colloquial phrase *ʿa-l-baḥarī*, meaning 'on display' or 'open for all to see', here with meretricious connotations. Thus, Fayrūz Baḥrī is at once a rare, secret stone and a show that bares all; he is once seen, then unseen. He is, moreover, supervisor of the 'Treasure Trove': the word in Arabic is *al-khabīʾa*, which in Egypt has connotations of archaeological digs and Pharaonic artefacts, but more generally implies something that is hidden, concealed, or kept secret. In this role, he stays true to this name. Many of his actions at the Foundation are *ʿa-l-baḥarī*, including his flashy television appearances, his projects for the renovation and display of the Treasure Trove, his proposal to make a film fictionalising the life of the elusive chief executive (180–81), and his organisation of what critics claim is celebration for the sake of celebration (254–5). It is even said that Fayrūz 'takes pride in displaying his condition' (214) – that is, his sexuality. At the same time, however, he remains just as obscure as the Foundation's other major power brokers. It is decided, after the whispering has become too loud, that Fayrūz Baḥrī and his suspected partner shall be officially included among the officials 'whom it is forbidden to observe, whose movements are not to be watched, and whose calls are not to be recorded' (261).

The word 'seduction' inevitably conjures up the twin images of a powerful, deliberate agent (the seducer) and a vulnerable, passive victim (the seduced). But this commonsense binary does not hold, whether in theory or in practice. In *Lisān al-ʿArab*, the verbs *fatana* and *iftatana* (whence our term *fitna*) may be either transitive or intransitive, referring either to the seducer or the one seduced.[18] Additionally, the passive participle *maftūn* ('[one] seduced') may also be used as a verbal noun synonymous with *fitna* ('seduction').[19] Baudrillard goes even further to explode our assumptions about agency:

> The cycle of seduction cannot be stopped. One can seduce someone in order
> to seduce someone else, but also seduce someone else to please oneself. The

illusion that leads from one to the other is subtle. Is it to seduce, or to be seduced, that is seductive? But to be seduced is the best way to seduce. It is an endless refrain. There is no active or passive mode in seduction, no subject or object, no interior or exterior: seduction plays on both sides, and there is no frontier separating them. One cannot seduce others, if one has not oneself been seduced.[20]

This is to say that seduction takes two (at least), neither of whom is the origin or prime mover of the action. Fayrūz seduces, but this is not necessarily a conscious and deliberate strategy. Nor is seduction a mechanism of total and complete control, rendering its object(s) brainwashed, unconscious, and defeated. In many cases, supposedly 'seduced' individuals are actively cultivating an attachment to the 'seducer', deriving pleasure from a disposition to detect and control.

In the Foundation, there is no shortage of those with the prurient desire to expose Fayruz's secrets; one employee, however, is more seduced/seductive than the rest: his name is ʿAbdū al-Namarsī, 'the pimp'. He is a grotesque figure who boasts of his ability to seduce any woman and transfer her desires to one of his wealthy clients. Throughout both *Ḥikāyāt al-Muʾassasa* and *Ḥikāyāt al-Khabīʾa*, the reader hears him recount the sordid details of the audio and video recordings he has made of his clients in the bedroom, which he desires one day to publish – not necessarily with the aim of destroying reputations, but rather to satisfy his interest in a recondite form of *scientia sexualis*. The essence of his practice, or 'gift' (*mawhiba*) as it is called, is the discernment of hidden knowledge and the seduction of women.[21] He is driven by 'a curiosity stimulated by the attempt to discern what the senses cannot detect'.[22] Indeed, al-Namarsī is the practicioner of suspicious interpretation who, much like the protagonist of Sonallah Ibrahim's *al-Lajna*, perceives women in the same way he perceives texts: each presents him with the challenge of 'opening messages' (*faḍḍ barīdihā*), of 'reading secret codes' (*qirāʾat shīfaratihā al-sirriyya*).[23] Much like the detective, he is always on the look out for traces of evidence, opportunities to sneak around, exclusive audiences to impress, and individuals to diagnose, accuse, and 'apprehend'.

When Fayrūz Baḥrī appears, he pushes al-Namarsī's voyeuristic abilities into overdrive, seducing him with the flickering prospect of a new kind of sexual knowledge. The pimp quickly declares his task:

> Fayrūz's condition and behavior astonish al-Namarsī, and he is absorbed in anticipation of what he will show next. Despite his aversion to such types, his curiosity is yet stronger … From now on, he will attempt to discern the details of the likes of Fayrūz. (168)

Everywhere that Fayrūz Baḥrī leaves a trace, ʿAbdū al-Namarsī eagerly gropes about for the hidden meaning. He begins, as always, with a reading of surfaces: Fayrūz's rear is thin, he observes, as opposed to his partner's 'full' rear (169; *muktanaza* – it is full of *kunūz* or 'treasures'). Over the course of several chapters, al-Namarsī builds a more and more complete narrative of Fayrūz's sex life, emotional attachment to his partner 'Farīḥ', and intimate relation with 'al-Glādiyūs', a 'whore' who has the ear of the chief executive. The more he discovers, it seems, the more he is seduced forward. This process is captured neatly in a single phrase: 'Fayrūz is taken to, but does not give' (167; *fayrūz yuʾtā wa lā yaʾtī*). The phrase is to be read, first, as a euphemism for the passive position in sexual intercourse (Fayrūz receives anal penetration, he does not penetrate). This is in itself a salacious detail in which al-Namarsī finds pleasure. But it also describes the seduction of secret knowledge: the phrase '*Knowledge* must be taken, it does not come by itself' (*al-ʿilm yuʾtā wa lā yaʾtī*) is attributed to Malik ibn Anas, the founder of one of the four main schools of Sunni Jurisprudence.[24] Thus, knowledge of Fayrūz must be sought after, for it does not yield itself. It is a seductive challenge that al-Namarsī takes up in total obsession.

The figure of the sodomite or sexual deviant aligns here with the *khawal* of Naguib Surur: he is the dazzling *sāqī*, the cup-bearer and mediator of occult knowledge who is jealously pursued by control-obsessed men of letters in a zero-sum game of sex and power. Indeed, it would appear that al-Namarsī's desire for this figure eclipses his seduction by others, even before the encounter with Fayrūz. Repeatedly, the reader is told of his desire for a particular kind of sexual object: a female who possesses many of the physical characteristics of the male.[25] It is not long before the pimp must begrudgingly admit to himself that Fayrūz Baḥrī is not merely an enemy or a rival, but a challenger who attracts him in a positive sense. 'Al-Namarsī always likes a nice game, even if he is against it' (181), and, indeed, when faced with Fayrūz, 'he cannot ignore that hidden sense of admiration that flows through him' (217). This sense, this seductive pull, strengthens every time he hears about Fayrūz's new schemes and projects for the Foundation. It is hardened into jealousy when he hears that Fayrūz is beating him at his own game: the custodian of the Treasure Trove is able to woo others with his uncanny ability to reveal hidden knowledge. 'The breadth of his knowledge is amazing, from color dyeing to the interpretation of dreams, in addition to urban planning, the design of gardens, and all so many civilized matters and sublime affairs' (243). This leads his friend and sponsor al-Glādiyūs to exclaim repeatedly: 'You know everything!' (245).

The *fitna* of Fayrūz has to do with power as well as knowledge. Al-Namarsī, along with other scattered voices, perceive Fayrūz in terms that are strikingly conspiracist: sudden changes around the Foundation are described as *mudabbar* (managed, pre-arranged) and *mukhaṭṭaṭ* (planned, plotted) by him (205), and he is implicated in a nefarious network made up of other 'deviants', the Russian mafia, and international paedophiles (211). The conspiracist rush reaches its climax in a scene when al-Namarsī thinks he has finally caught Fayrūz. He sends him an envelope containing sexually explicit photographs captured of him with his partner. But he is already outmanoeuvred: 'In what newspaper or magazine would you like them published?' Fayrūz asks his would-be blackmailer (261). Al-Namarsī is shocked and thrown off balance by the realisation that 'sexual deviants' control the press. The curtain is thrown back in dramatic fashion, offering the pimp a glimpse of what he believes are – what he desires to be – the hidden hands that manipulate the order of things in this strange post-industrial era.

We may be tempted to tie these conspiracist images up into a neat and satisfying theory of sexualised agency panic. Yet it is not altogether clear that al-Namarsī is terrified or panicky in the scene above, or indeed at any moment of his encounter with Fayrūz. If anything, he experiences a kind of agency passion. The image of this all-powerful, invincible sodomite is in many senses an exaggerated reflection of his own ambitions and desires. After all, it is only al-Namarsī's thoughts that we hear, and never those of Fayrūz: the latter is an object closed to narrative empathy and comprehensibility, and may only be accessed by wild speculation, rumour, and the inscrutable refractions and contortions of the urge to narrate and disclose. Here is an uncanny nemesis that emerges from obscurity and appears to accomplish what he himself aspires to. Just as al-Namarsī holds magical sway over a shadowy network of pimps and prostitutes, so does this phantom Fayrūz command a shadowy conspiracy of sodomites: the two fantasies mirror each other and exert a seductive pull on their subjects despite their partly illusory nature. And though we have little if any insight into the mind of Fayrūz Baḥrī that is not already polluted by the speculation of others, it is easy to imagine that such a conspiracy theory would be just as seductive to him: the fantasy of his magical control gratifies his own ambitions and projects an image of authority to which others, wittingly or unwittingly, submit. For the pimp, in any case, these conspiracy fantasies carry as much pleasure as they do paranoia. After his final encounter with Fayrūz, al-Namarsī is frustrated, but no less seduced: he fades into the background, and the last we hear of him, he cannot stop himself from expressing fascination and surprise (308).

Homophobia and homosexual panic provide seductively simple explanations for the pull that the *lūṭī* exerts on others in the modern *mu'assasa*. But this particular 'sexual deviant', at least, is the focal point of subtly expressed desires and fantasies that draw in even – or especially – some of his fiercest opponents. Where agency in this game of seduction resides is, however, a question that may be deferred endlessly: often, it would seem that Fayrūz intentionally plays hide-and-seek with his opponents in order to draw them in; just as often, it seems that al-Namarsī is predisposed to play this hide-and-seek, whether because of some inborn curiosity or, more likely, because of the hermeneutical habits and hobbies he has accumulated through his own occult occupation of pimping and scandalmongering. Thus, the revelations that al-Namarsī claims to have made about Fayrūz are as much revelations about his own interior proclivities, and reflect less the truth about his rival than the artful, if tastelessly graphic, work of his imagination. In this respect, one cannot fail to mention, al-Namarsī is not alone: the reader, too, is caught up in the seductive hide-and-seek, and motivated to fill in the gaps regarding all these characters who do not fully reveal themselves to one's comprehension. This is especially so when we take into account the historical context in which the novel was written.

The Seduction of the Reader

When it was published in 2002, *Ḥikāyāt al-Khabīʾa* inspired literary critic Fārūq ʿAbd al-Qādir to coin the term *adab al-talsīn* ('slander literature' or 'the literature of [malicious] gossip').[26] Having 'made quite a bit of noise' upon its publication, the book deserved this label for daring to enter 'a territory that had been previously restricted to gossip sessions and the chattering in the coffeehouse'; its author, one of the most revered in Egypt's republic of letters, stood accused of 'settling personal scores' under the transparently absurd pretext of disinterested literary work.[27] These 'tales' (*ḥikāyāt*) of Gamal al-Ghitani, as ʿAbd al-Qādir went on to say in his scathing review, were in fact more akin to 'the prattles of old pensioners in their cafés' than to any respectable form of literature.[28]

These remarks may very well shock readers of Arabic literature outside of Egypt, mostly because, compared to other works by al-Ghitani, *Ḥikāyāt al-Khabīʾa* has attracted little if any critical interest internationally. The novel is, certainly, much less known than other Egyptian novels of the same period that might be deemed 'scandal literature', such as Alaa Al Aswany's *ʿImārat Yaʿqūbiyān* (2002; The Yacoubian Building, trans. 2002), which Fārūq ʿAbd al-Qādir included in his account, or Ibrahim Eissa's *Maqtal al-Rajul al-Kabīr* (The Murder of the Big Man, 1998). Yet, however shocking or polemical ʿAbd al-Qādir's assessment may be, his reading is not wholly invalid: *Ḥikāyāt al-Khabīʾa* strikes even the most naïve reader as an obviously – even inelegantly – crafted *roman à clef*, with pointed words cast at particular members of Egypt's cultural and political elite.[29] For those familiar with these personalities, we suggest, the novel effects a seductive pull that mimics the affective bond between Fayrūz Baḥrī and ʿAbdū al-Namarsī. Readers are drawn by al-Ghitani's narrative strategy of hiding/revealing into a desire for more secrets and gossip behind the text.

ʿAbd al-Qādir unwittingly testifies to the effectiveness of this strategy in his scathing review of the novel and its prequel. 'The main problem with this work,' he complains, 'is its vacillation between showing and hiding, between expressing and insinuating, between what the narrator wants to say and what he is able to say.'[30] He goes on to describe this process as 'winking at the reader, seducing him to complicity [*ighrāʾ bi-l-tawāṭuʾ*]'.[31] This is a quite apt description of the type of seduction, or *fitna*, we encountered above: the oscillation between presence and absence, 'to be-there/not-there'.[32] The symptoms irrupt immediately on the critic's own tongue: in the following sentences, he is seduced by the aura of secret knowledge, and proceeds to indulge himself with an enumeration of the many points of comparison between the novel and modern Egypt. The novel's prequel, *Ḥikāyāt al-Muʾassasa*, he tells us, caricatures the Akhbār al-Yawm Foundation – the media conglomerate where al-Ghitani had begun his journalistic career, and whose literary weekly magazine, *Akhbār al-Adab*, he headed for nearly two decades. The absent Founder (*al-muʾassis*), mentioned in this prequel, is none other than the media tycoon Muṣṭafā Amīn, whose death roughly coincided with the novel's publication. Thus, ʿAbd al-Qādir is drawn into reproducing the very gossipy discourse he has denounced; he cannot resist, such is the hypnotic enigma of Gamal al-Ghitani's prose. Yet, with respect to *Ḥikāyāt al-Khabīʾa*, he refrains from mentioning specific names, with the exception of the author's, who seems to repel/attract the critic as much as the novel's other celebrities.

What ʿAbd al-Qādir describes as the novel's 'vacillation between showing and hiding' is not an idiosyncratic observation. It is plainly manifest, first, in the various species of speculation and hearsay that constitute the narrative stuff of the novel. Such formal techniques, common to many of al-Ghitani's literary works, may be characterised as resolutely 'dialogic', 'metafictional', or polyvocal, in keeping with the author's general ontological concerns, or perhaps his specifically Sufic obsession with pondering the hidden meanings of a fundamentally enigmatic universe. In the most general sense, the novel and its prequel may be read as behind-the-scenes accounts of the painful structural transformations endured by many 'foundations' or institutions in the post-colonial world over the last sixty years, as the charisma and paternalism of nationalist leaders like 'the Founder' gave way to the confused frenzy of military rule, which was in turn undercut by the displacements and disparities brought by neoliberal globalisation. Such structural changes have occurred at the level of the state – it may be said that *maṣr muʾassasa* ('Egypt is a foundation', that is, too big to fail) – as well as at the level of the various organisations that in Egypt are called *muʾassasāt* (foundations), from publishing houses and charities to public and private corporations.[33] More specifically, in *Ḥikāyāt al-Khabīʾa*, these gestures towards narrative open-endedness are interspersed with just enough hints of familiarity to compel a reading of the novel as, indeed, 'slander literature', or a *ḥikāya* of something outside the text. The key to all of this is, of course, Fayrūz Baḥrī.

Who is Fayrūz Baḥrī? The unusual name has the same syllable structure as Farouk Hosni (Fārūq Ḥusnī), Egypt's culture czar for more than two decades. His tenure as the flamboyant minister of culture, from his appointment by President Mubarak in 1987 until the revolution of 25 January 2011, was marked by periodic scandals – some of which, it was rumoured, had been ingeniously orchestrated by the minister himself. These included the display of his own rather mediocre paintings in Egyptian museums, the alleged leasing or sale of Pharaonic artefacts to foreign museums and collectors in exchange for personal benefits, a deadly fire at one of the ministry's theatres in Beni Souief in 2005, derogatory remarks he made about the hijab in 2007, his expensive and unsuccessful bid to become director-general of United Nations Educational, Scientific and Cultural Organization (UNESCO) in 2009, and the theft of a Van Gogh painting from a Ministry of Culture museum in broad daylight in 2010. In addition, his private life was – and to a certain extent remains – the subject of gossip and crude innuendo in the corridors of power, the national press, and the cafés of Cairo – much of which centred on his alleged homosexuality or 'sexual deviance'. The rumours would usually be embellished with details that the minister kept a palace full of handsome male servants, exploited his office to engage in loud orgies, maintained a flirtatious relationship with the president's wife and son, and enjoyed close ties to the security services and European organised crime.[34] Even since Hosni has left office, he has continued to provoke speculation about his sordid affairs with disreputable players – as when, seemingly out of the blue, he was awarded the Cultural Personality of the Year Award in Sharjah, UAE in 2013.[35]

The rumours about 'sexual deviance' can be traced back to October 1987, when Hosni was appointed Minister of Culture – a highly coveted position among Egypt's intelligentsia. Before Hosni had been sworn in to office, controvery flared up over the president's odd choice – odd, because Hosni was quite young compared to former ministers, whose age was meant to bestow upon them both experience and gravitas, and because his reputation was far from established in the cultural field. On 18 October 1987, the novelist and journalist Tharwat Abāẓa (1927–2002) published an article in *al-Ahrām* entitled 'Wujūm' ('Speechless'), in which he expressed his opposition to the new minister in coded language:

> My suffering is due to the news that struck me last week, rendering me speechless … It is this inability to speak (*sukūt*) that is the tragedy, for I have never been accustomed to be silent about what I believe to be true. I've lived my life saying what I believe is worth saying; nothing has prevented me from speaking since I first picked up my pen. When Egypt was beset by tyranny, we chose to write through symbolism (*bi-al-ramz*) rather than direct and honest speech, which the dictator had forbidden. We spoke, and people understood what we were saying; symbolism attained greater power of expression than candor … [But] today, [even] symbolism cannot assist our pens. Today, the honest word has no way of surviving.[36]

Abāẓa did not specific what 'news' had upset him, let alone mention the minister's name. But his message, even while eschewing 'symbolism', was clear enough: Egypt was now suffering from that very sin that dare not speak its name.

More explicit was an article written in the same issue by Rajab al-Banna, entitled 'Bidāyat Maʿraka Jadīda' (The Start of a New Battle), in which the author passed innuendo about the 'negative' (*salbiyya*) personality types – perhaps also a reference to the 'passiveness' (*salbiyya*) associated with homo-sexuality – and 'parasitic' (*ṭufayliyya*) characters that had recently 'spread and jumped to prominence'.[37] The newspaper featured another article in the same column several days later, in which a different critic denounced 'passive types' and 'parasites'. Again, the critic did not name names, but his language – he spoke also of 'grey' individuals (*ramādiyyīn*) who had 'burst forth and sprouted in a devilish manner', and 'deviants' (*munḥarifīn*) who had penetrated every area of public life – had an obvious referent.[38] Yet these critical voices were quickly drowned out by a backlash enjoined by the new minister's supporters. On 26 October, the magazine *Rūz al-Yūsuf* asked provocatively on its front cover, 'Why the Commotion around the Minister of Culture?' ('Limādhā al-Ḍajja ḥawla Wazīr al-Thaqāfa?'). The arti-cles within were overwhelmingly flattering – even if the minister's supporters, too, seemed unable to resist the crudest innuendo. One piece, drawing its title from the magazine's front cover, described the situation in the following dramatic terms:

> Egyptians awoke in the morning to find that war had suddenly been declared against the new minister of culture, Farouk Hosni! Attack came on all fronts, and made use of weapons both licit and illicit, and even the kind that explodes inside the body! … Intellectuals and quasi-intellectuals alike set about investigating the accusations made against the minister, attempting to determine whether they were true or false![39]

The author went on to specify that 'one of the reasons for the attack on the minister of culture was that he is young (*shābb*)!' Uttered in this context, the word 'young' or 'youth' – *shābb* – easily evokes the word *shādhdh* – '(sexual) deviant', that is to say, 'homosexual'. Similarly, a defence of the minister elsewhere in the magazine describes how his appointment had been tantamount to an 'electric shock' (*ṣadma kahrabāʾiyya*) to many; the article's author rebukes these critics, before concluding that the minister shall be judged according to whether his works turn out to be 'positive' (*ijābiyya*) or 'negative' (*salbiyya*).[40]

Husni himself seems to have largely ignored these insinuations. That is, until the former minister gave what was presented as a tell-all interview to *al-Ahrām* in the summer of 2011, in which he pointedly denied the rumour of his homosexuality, along with other accusations, and blamed Ṣafwat al-Sharīf – former henchman of the spy chief Ṣalāḥ Naṣr, and later one of the most reviled figures in the regime of Husni Mubarak – for inventing it.[41]

The more one discovers, the more one is driven on. As soon as Farouk Hosni reveals himself behind Fayrūz Baḥrī, the reader is drawn to the novel's other characters, who flash seemingly significant details like clothing, distinguishing features, and improbable names, and the text unfolds as a web of interconnected puzzles. ʿAbdū al-Namarsī, the pimp and major rival of Fayrūz Baḥrī, 'clicks' seductively with the father–son pair Mamdūḥ al-Laythī (1937–2014) and ʿAmr al-Laythī (b. 1970), both rumoured to be 'procurers' and rivals of Farouk Hosni within the cultural establishment.[42] The father, Mamdūḥ al-Laythī, one of Egypt's most famous scenarists and movie producers, had often attempted to dispel rumours about his alleged habit of blackmailing actresses with sexual secrets and turning them into spies. In the novel the two are hounded by charges of nepotism, and their names often confused (149, 156), just like their historical counterparts. The name al-Laythī, furthermore, resembles *al-layth*, 'the lion', just as al-Namarsī shares the same root as *al-nimr*, 'the tiger'. The prequel's unflattering physical description of the father, finally, bears a remarkable resemblance to that of his real-life counterpart.[43]

The *Ḥikāyāt* have more to tell us. Who, the reader may ask, is Zahrān al-Ḥusnī, the character who serves as a stepping stone for Fayrūz Baḥrī and is later moved to work in the Cairo suburb of Giza (185)? Isn't he Zahi Hawwas (Zāhī Ḥawwās) (b. 1947), former chief inspector of the Giza pyramids plateau and a caricature of himself in fact as well as in fiction? More than anything, we want to know who is al-Nabrāwī, a capricious figure who vocally protests the ascension of Fayrūz Baḥrī on account of his sexual deviance (154–5), but then suddenly reverses his position at a packed meeting of a major cultural club (158–9)? Al-Nabrāwī rhymes with ʿAbd al-Raḥmān al-Sharqāwī (1920–87), author of the novel *al-Arḍ* (1954) (*Egyptian Earth*, trans. 1992) and one of the most revered littérateurs of twentieth-century Egypt. Indeed, al-Sharqāwī did vocally oppose Fārūq Ḥusnī's appointment as Minister of Culture in 1987, before scandalously reversing his position for unknown reasons and passing away a few months later.[44] The novel reveals about al-Nabrāwī/al-Sharqāwī 'what no one else has discovered' (171): an elaborate story of a lost will, which is thought to prove al-Nabrāwī's ownership of the entire Alexandrian shoreline, unfolds over the next several pages. Somehow, Fayrūz Baḥrī promises to help with the legal difficulties so that al-Nabrāwī gets his land back (171–6). But before anything else is revealed, al-Nabrāwī dies of 'an overdose of Viagra' (321), and our sense of curiosity is overwhelmed. We are still seduced: who is the chief executive? And who is Frédéric, the Frenchman fluent in Arabic who is encountered sifting through old gramophone records near al-ʿAtaba Square as he is preparing a doctoral dissertation on antique Egyptian music (278–9)?

Suspicion has its limits, however: while the reader is led to ascertain these apparent truths, many of the putative correspondences between the text and the world are more likely to be distorted products of the reader's own interpretive enthusiasms. One may draw, for example, any number of improbable connections between the novel's 'al-Glādiyūs' and Egypt's former First Lady,

Suzanne Mubarak: *glādiyūs* may be a corruption of *glādiyūlus* (gladiolus), which is a flower of the iris (*sawsan*) family (*sawsan* resembles 'Suzanne'). Just as al-Glādiyūs delights in the company of Fayrūz Baḥrī, who charms her with his knowledge of all things beautiful and sublime, so was Suzanne Mubarak rumoured to be responsible for the rise of Farouk Hosni, who allegedly assisted in the selection of her wardrobe. Such hidden links, however, are tenuous at best. This uncertainty plagued the seduction of ʿAbdū al-Namarsī, too, as his lustful quest for knowledge of Fayrūz turned up as much 'truth' as it did personal fantasy.

On the one hand, for readers unfamiliar with the novel's historical intertexts, all these sordid details may have the feeling of just so much trivia. On the other hand, for those called out by the seduction of the author's gossip and innuendo, *Ḥikāyāt al-Khabīʾa* attains another level of significance. In this way, al-Ghitani's text offers to enrich our understanding not only of the dynamics of personal and literary seduction, but of the affective background of cultural politics in Egypt during the time of the text's composition. In particular, the text brings into view the ambivalent emotive dimensions of the author's public feud with Farouk Hosni, to which we now turn.

The Seduction of Farouk Hosni: From *Engagement* to *Engouement*

'Farouk Hosni's management of the Ministry of Culture has been no less disastrous for Egypt than the Naksa of 1967.'[45] Gamal al-Ghitani is alleged to have uttered these words, comparing the reign of President Mubarak's longest serving minister to the most traumatic political, military, and cultural defeat suffered by Egypt in the twentieth century. The statement was the most dramatic made by al-Ghitani in his decade-long campaign against the minister, which unfolded in the form of virulent polemics and investigative reports published in *Akhbār al-Adab*, the weekly cultural journal he had run since 1993. This campaign, which had begun sometime in the late 1990s and continued into the new millennium, was fuelled in part by the scandals that repeatedly flared up around Farouk Hosni, as enumerated above.

It is worth mentioning that feuds between littérateurs and cultural administrators are not a new phenomenon in modern Egypt. Samia Mehrez offers valuable insight into the quarrels between Hosni and Egyptian writers in her book *Egypt's Culture Wars: Politics and Practice* (2008). The minister's heavy-handed dealings with artists and intellectuals, she argues, exacerbated a much older tension between the cultural and political 'fields' in modern Egypt. While focusing on cultural politics in the late Mubarak years, Mehrez's study thus includes an important historical dimension. Mehrez notes that littérateurs, and intellectuals more generally, have maintained fraught alliances with the 'political field' since Muhammad ʿAli's sponsorship of secular civil servants in the early to mid-eighteenth century. A defining feature of this 'cultural field', as Mehrez calls it (following Bourdieu), is its dependence upon, and manipulation by, the state. If artists and intellectuals have depended on state funding, the state, for its part, has sought to sponsor or control this secular cultural field in order to counter the parallel power structure of religious groups and institutions. As Mehrez puts it, 'cultural producers maintain the most ambiguous relationship with the state that is at once their patron and their persecutor'.[46] The terms of this relationship have shifted, but not radically changed, over the course of the twentieth century: Abdel Nasser's establishment of the Ministry of Culture reaffirmed this relationship; Sadat's sidelining of the cultural field led to a resurgent Islamism; Mubarak's renewed engagement with the cultural field found its boldest expression in his constant support for Farouk Hosni. As Minister of Culture, Hosni sought to radically reaffirm the state's role in culture through ambitious and costly projects and campaigns and by seducing many artists and intellectuals into the government's 'pen' (*ḥazīra*, a common characterisation).[47]

Al-Ghitani's attacks on Hosni owe much to this broader history, as well as the specific improprieties committed by the minister. At the same time, this particular feud remained something of a puzzle to some observers, given the manner, frequency, and tone of the novelist's polemics, as well as the startling aloofness with which the minister responded. In 2007, asked by reporters what al-Ghitani's problem was, Hosni responded coolly, 'Don't ask me, ask him.'[48] The plot took a further twist when, in the same year, al-Ghitani accepted a literary award from the Ministry of Culture with remarkable enthusiasm – an event that marked a sudden reversal in the author's position towards the minister.[49] Seemingly overnight, feud had become friendship, and not long afterwards television reporters caught al-Ghitani smiling approvingly at one of Hosni's personal art exhibits in Cairo.[50]

Gamal al-Ghitani's quarrelsome, then cordial, relationship with Farouk

Hosni would pass as little more than a curiosity if it were not for the way in which the discourse traded between the two men effectively fashioned 'cultural politics' – its terms and tropes, ironies and intensities – as it was waged in Egypt at the dawn of the third millennium. At least for consumers of Cairo's cultural press and rumour mills, the author-critic and the 'artist-minister' appeared to hold a monopoly on defining the major issues, drawing the lines of debate, and posing problems and solutions, albeit from opposing sides.[51] It would appear all the more significant, then, that behind the highly formalised veneer of principles and partisanship that ostensibly bound together these two men there persisted some personal – and even emotional, erotic – motive of equal potency. This much is suggested by the equal intensity of al-Ghitani's attack and retreat, a nearly inexplicable change of position on the face of it.

For followers of cultural politics in Egypt, it can be tempting to adopt the drama between al-Namarsī and Fayrūz Baḥrī as a template for reading the relationship between al-Ghitani and Farouk Hosni, and to appeal to the emotive undertones of the former to explain the ineffable vicissitudes of the latter. In her brief review of the novel's prequel, Mona Zaki makes the important observation that al-Ghitani 'portrays al-Namarsi in the way he would like to present himself: a pimp with a personal philosophy on his "art", a connoisseur of the female species, an assessor of beauty, an opportunist'.[52] Al-Namarsī is not al-Ghitani – more likely, as we have speculated above, he caricatures Mamdūḥ and ʿAmr al-Laythī – but the psychological identification is close: he is the only character who plays a prominent role in both *Ḥikāyāt al-Khabīʾa* and its prequel, and one of the few who are given any subjective complexity beyond their caricatural shells. And their seduction of/by Fayrūz Baḥrī/Farouk Hosni is comparable. There had always been scattered hints in the press and gossip cafés that there was more to the novelist's attack on the minister than matters of cultural policy. As early as 2005, as al-Ghitani was still penning away at his challenger with allegations of corruption, a former media adviser to Hosni released an 'exposé' of the Ministry of Culture in which he deemed the conflict between the two men to be nothing but a big 'joke'.[53] Interviewed in 2007, the minister himself declared that he did not harbour any bad feelings towards the author, and that his critiques were all just part of 'the cultural game'.[54] In other words, we may say, the two were engaged in an exchange of challenges, a game of seduction, each attempting to claim the role of seducer and not that of the seduced.

At the very least, *Ḥikāyāt al-Khabī'a* appears crafted to cast light on the emotive mechanisms that structured the responses of famous personalities to the ascension of Farouk Hosni to the Ministry of Culture, and thus fits in with its author's broader corpus of '*narratives on history*' that 'question and subvert the official, exclusionary versions of history'.[55] In this sense al-Ghitani is eager in this novel to expose aspects of modern Egyptian history that the personalities implicated would have preferred to sweep under the rug, to wit, their phobias, panics, passions, and pleasures.

Having admitted as much, however, it would hardly be a stretch for the reader to implicate al-Ghitani, too, in the emotionally charged power games so described, and to draw some important conclusions. First, and most broadly, the feud between the author and the minister reveals itself to be suffused with an irreducibly emotional charge, which is precisely why it lends itself so well to narrative embellishment through fiction. Panic, paranoia, and, indeed, *fitna*, play as much a role in the formation of literary subjectivities, political ideologies, and interpretive strategies as do conscious decision making and calculated postures and positions. In other words, culture and cultural politics are as much *engouement* (infatuation) as they are *engagement* (commitment or *iltizām*). More specifically, the attraction aroused by Fayrūz Baluī in the fictional text – in his relationship with al-Namarsī and others – prefigures the 'admiration' that al-Ghitani would later express for his rival. To register the affective pull of *fitna*, in other words, goes some way towards explaining the abrupt shift that occurred in the relationship in 2007, as hostility turned to hospitality and the two men appeared to regard each other as friends.

It must be said, in closing, that in drawing attention to such inscrutable forces as love and hate, we do not seek to 'expose' the 'hidden' inclinations of 'pathological' authors and actors, and thus to devalue their projects of criticism or initiatives of *detente*. Rather, pursuing such an investigation allows us to enrich our understanding of complex events by adding previously neglected motives and mechanisms to an ever-evolving narrative of (literary) history. Placing emphasis on emotions – as opposed to, say, immutable ideologies or overdetermining histories – allows us to leave room for different futures: feelings, after all, are liable to change. Apocalyptic terror prevails for a time, nourished by subterranean currents of homosexual panic and paranoia, but may suddenly recede under unpredictable shifts of tone and taste.

5

Paranoia in the Second Degree: Three Recent Novels

'Is there a difference between paranoia with and without quotation marks?'[1] The question is posed by Svetlana Boym in an insightful article on the sundry mutations of *The Protocols of the Elders of Zion* in European literature, across the presumed boundaries of fact and faction. Boym traces the textual evolution of this central conspiracist tract from the gothic novels and detective thrillers of the nineteenth century, to 'a fictional political pamphlet' originally directed against Napoleon III, to the anti-Semitic polemic proper, and on to the 'self-conscious' conspiracist novels of Umberto Eco and Danilo Kiš. In doing so, Boym not only casts a critical eye on the notorious acts of plagiarism and 'deadly intertextuality' that birthed the *The Protocols* – that is to say, the reliance of an ostensibly non-fictional work on fictional predecessors – but examines how later works of fiction, through ironical appropriation ('paranoia with quotation marks'), serve to undermine that text's enduring influence. Specifically, a novel like Umberto Eco's *Foucault's Pendulum*, in dramatising the paranoid exploits of three book editors in Milan, offers 'ethical insights into, and unique heuristic tools for understanding' (and critiquing) conspiracy theory.[2]

This chapter directs Boym's question to three recent novels that put conspiracy theory within quotation marks: *Kitāb al-Ṭughrā: Gharāʾib al-Tārīkh fī Madīnat al-Mirrīkh* (2011) (*The Book of the Sultan's Seal: Strange Incidents from History in the City of Mars*, trans. 2015) by Youssef Rakha; *ʿĀm al-Tinnīn* (The Year of the Dragon) (2012) by Mohammad Rabie; and *Istikhdām al-Ḥayā* (2014) (*Using Life*, trans. 2017), written by Ahmed Naji and illustrated by Ayman Al Zorkany (Ayman al-Zurqānī). Each of these novels deploys conspiracist tropes and themes, not as expressions of strongly held convictions or acts of political posturing, but as experiments in irony, or parodical imitations of predecessors and contemporaries in literature and society. This is not to say that each unequivocally condemns or departs from conspiracy theory as a critical practice. At its simplest, 'irony' may be understood as 'the intentional transmission of both information and evaluative attitude other than what is explicitly presented'.[3] The 'evaluative attitude', Hutcheon explains, is where irony gets most tricky. It is not always apparent when confronting a work of irony whether it is intended to tentatively appraise, quietly applaud, elbow in the side, or hack to pieces the position it pretends to adopt, the author it subtly references, or the work it imitates. Conspiracy theory may be placed between ironical quotation marks, but this does not mean that it has been marked for deletion.

Boym answers the question posed above with a tentative 'yes' – paranoia may be decentred, deconstructed, or undone when placed between the quotations marks of a carefully crafted literary work. Eco's novel, in satirising the circular pursuits and passions of leisure-class occultists, treats the reader to the interpretive delights of conspiracy theory while implicitly admonishing anyone from following their example. Our own answer to the question, with respect to the three novels under consideration, will be, respectively, an unfortunate 'no', an ambiguous 'yes', and an optimistic 'perhaps'. Before elaborating further, it is worth spending some time introducing each of the three authors, who, in contrast to those hitherto examined, have not yet received significant critical attention.

Authors and Avatars

Recent scholarship in Arabic literature has begun to theorise the emergence of a 'new generation' of Arabic authors in relation to the political and aesthetic practices dominant in previous decades – particularly in Egypt, where generation has long served as a basis for literary classification.[4] Sabry Hafez, for example, has argued that novels by the '1990s generation' of authors, in their turn towards quotidian and ontological concerns, represent a 'radical departure' from the work of their elders (the '60s generation'), who tended towards realism, recognisable (and for the critic, non-suspect) forms of political committedness, and a more carefully maintained Standard Arabic.[5] Literary genres of the new millennium – hypertext, blogs, graphic novels, and comics – have also been brought into the debate about paradigm shifts and epistemic ruptures, as have the novelistic experiments of Egyptian authors like Ghāda ʿAbd al-ʿĀl (b. 1978), Basma ʿAbd al-ʿAzīz (b. 1976), Ḥamdī Abū Julayyil (b. 1967), Muḥammad ʿAlāʾ al-Dīn (b. 1979), Aḥmad al-ʿĀyidī (b. 1974), Manṣūra ʿIzz al-Dīn (b. 1976), and countless others.[6] It is not just genre that is redefined in these new texts. As Tarek El-Ariss has argued, the Arabic author has mutated from engaged litterateur into a 'scandalous, sensational, and vulgar' trickster-type, as the literary 'scene' has shifted from the Habermassian public sphere to the cacophonous and contested crossroads of technology and culture, and the act of writing itself has been re-configured as hacking, exhibitionism, and *faḍḥ* ('scandal, exposure').[7] By most accounts, Arabic literature is not what it used to be.

Enter Youssef Rakha (b. 1976), Mohammad Rabie (b. 1978), and Ahmed Naji (b. 1985), three emerging authors whose fiction, while eschewing any simple categorisation, may easily be located within this context of innovation, rupture, and return. Aesthetically, they have much in common: each playfully mixes words with images, text with hypertext, and multiple styles and registers of Arabic in order to creatively redefine the 'novel'; each has only recently arrived at the novelistic craft after initial 'practice' with other genres, namely cultural criticism and poetry (Rakha) and blogging (Rabie and Naji). Socially, they are quite close: each enjoys both personal and professional ties with the other, to the extent that we can be sure that their work has emerged out of an intimate and ongoing dialogue that shall remain, in part, inscrutable to the majority of readers. Yet their work also demonstrates notable differences in style, intention, and maturity, and thus it is worth considering each author separately.

Before *Kitāb al-Ṭughrā* – his debut novel – Youssef Rakha was known primarily for several collections of poetry, as well as his work for the cultural pages of *Al-Ahram Weekly Online*, the English edition of Egypt's flagship state-run newspaper. His poetry may very well situate him within the '1990s generation' described by Hafez above – indeed Rakha's second novel, *al-Tamāsīḥ* (2013) (*The Crocodiles*, trans. 2014), is to be read as a partly fictionalised history of certain poets of that generation. Yet his alienation from this group can be detected in the same novel, as well as in *Kitāb al-Ṭughrā*, whose impetus seems to have been, at least in part, a quite personal settling of scores with those 1990s-generation poets he felt had never given his poetry its due. (This private dimension of the novel will remain beyond the scope of the present chapter.) While this local context matters, it is clear that Rakha – a graduate of the University of Hull who also writes beautiful and complex works of fiction in English – is keen to be read as contributing to 'the larger conversation that is the contemporary novel'.[8] This is particularly evident in *Kitāb al-Ṭughrā*, which, in addition to its rich engagement with pre-modern Arabic literary and historiographical works, abounds with intertextual gestures to the novels of Umberto Eco, Thomas Pynchon, Paul Auster, and William S. Burroughs.[9] Rakha continues to maintain a blog, *The Sultan's Seal* (yrakha.com; previously *The AntiArab*, previously *The Arabophile*), which provides links to his work in a variety of publications, as well as the work of other emerging authors of poetry and prose in Arabic and English.

Mohammad Rabie and Ahmed Naji can be more closely linked with each other than either to Rakha. Both began crafting their writerly subjectivities in the early 2000s through what would become two of the most creative, sustained, and eccentric literary-cultural blogs in Egyptian cyberspace.[10] Rabie, despite a successful career in engineering, now works as an editor at the publishing house Dār al-Tanwīr, having established himself as a uniquely skilled storyteller and a novelist of considerable promise. His debut novel, *Kawkab ʿAnbar* (Amber Planet) (2010) – an experiment in magical realism that relates, among many other things, the impossible translation of Luigi Serafini's *Codex Seraphinianus* into Arabic – won first prize in the emerging writers' category of the Sawiris Cultural Award. *ʿĀm al-Tinnīn* (The Year of the Dragon), which we will consider here, was published in 2012, and was nominated for the same award. Recently, his third novel, the hard-boiled, post-apocalyptic *ʿUṭārid* (2014) (*Otared*, trans. 2016), was shortlisted for the International Prize for Arabic Fiction (IPAF), unofficially known as the 'Arabic Booker'. In addition to his background in blogging, Rabie's novels are informed by an eclectic array of literary and non-literary texts and traditions. In *ʿĀm al-Tinnīn*, for example, one may detect echoes not only of recognised authors like Jorge Luis Borges and José Saramago, but of Rājī ʿInāyit (b. 1929), the author of a popular series of putatively non-fiction books on paranormal phenomena. (Books in this series bear titles such as *al-Haram wa Sirr Quwāhu al-Khāriqa* (The Great Pyramid and the Secret of its Super Powers) (1981) and *Sirr al-Aṭbāq al-Ṭāʾira* (The Secret of Flying Saucers)

(1980)). Rabie was an avid reader of ʿInāyit's books in his childhood, and finds them a continued source of inspiration – not as repositories of historical truths, but as low-brow 'literary' texts whose powers of imagination may be said to exceed those of certain consecrated members of the Egyptian literary canon.[11]

From approximately 2005 to the end of 2009, Ahmed Naji was known to many only as 'Bīsū', the digital avatar behind the blog *Wassaʿ Khayālak* (Widen Your Imagination).[12] In this capacity, he developed a reputation as a sort of trickster whose double-voiced polemics against state-sponsored intellectuals, meddlesome family members, and other bloggers could display as much aesthetic ingenuity, intellectual rigour, and linguistic play as the short pieces of fiction that he would occasionally post as well. In the meantime, Naji was establishing himself as a regular contributor to the prestigious literary review, *Akhbār al-Adab*, and had published several creative and critical works: his first novel, *Rūjirz* (Rogers) (2007), a Pink Floyd-inspired tale of adolescent rebellion and schoolyard conspiracies; *Sabʿa Durūs Mustaqā min Aḥmad Makkī* (Seven Lessons Learned from Ahmad Makki) (2009), a short collection of essays parodying contemporary postmodern theory-speak; and a 'history' of the Egyptian blogosphere, released by the Arabic Network for Human Rights Information (ANHRI) in 2010.[13] *Istikhdām al-Ḥayā*, the work we shall consider in more detail below, is Naji's second novel. Upon its publication in Lebanon and distribution in Egypt, the novel was an immediate sensation. A special book signing and exhibit was held at the Medrar artists' collective in downtown Cairo (24 November–1 December 2014), which featured Ayman Al Zorkany's drawings in a variety of printed formats, including T-shirts and coffee mugs, and was attended by major figures from the local literary scene. Portions of the novel have subsequently been adapted to a variety of formats, such as Al Zorkany's recent short film entitled *al-Raqṣa al-Akhīra li-Dhubābat al-Ist al-Zarqāʾ* (The Last Dance of the Blue Anus-Fly) (2016), and an interpretive dance performance held at the cultural centre Darb 1718 in Cairo in late 2015. Yet the novel had at least one detractor. After an allegedly 'obscene' excerpt from *Istikhdām al-Ḥayā* was published in *Akhbār al-Adab*, an obscure lawyer brought a case against the author for 'harming public morals'. In spite of an initial full acquittal, upon retrial the author was sentenced to two years in prison – an unprecedented verdict for a literary work in Egypt. At the time of writing, Ahmed Naji has been released after spending ten months in prison, although his case awaits retrial.

The bi(bli)ographies of these three young authors are far from extraneous to their fiction. This is not only because a literary work needs to be read in relation to the textual and intertextual networks from which it emerged. In the three novels under consideration, the authors themselves appear in different dramatic guises. Muṣṭafā, the protagonist of *Kitāb al-Ṭughrā*, shares both personal and professional details with his author. Naʿīm, the protagonist of *ʿĀm al-Tinnīn*, shares little with Mohammad Rabie, with two notable exceptions: the profession of engineer, and a personal photograph, which the author has inserted in his novel to portray his hero. Bassām in *Istikhdām al-Ḥayā* is an act of misdirection. He shares with his author the moniker 'Bīsū', yet his likeness is inspired by another individual, whose anonymity we prefer to preserve. The presence of Rakha, Rabie, and Naji within their fictional works attests both to the self-reflexivity of these novels and their sharp ironical edge.

Kitāb al-Ṭughrā: Naive and Sentimental Paranoia

'This world fills my heart with a sickness, whose only cure is departure to a world beyond,' declares Mustafa Nayif al-Shurbagi (Muṣṭafā Nāyif al-Shūrbagī), as he casts off the shackles of a sorely regretted marriage, giving himself over to a springtime caroming across the bridges and boroughs of a post-millennial, but pre-revolutionary Cairo (36). The textual imprint of this *raḥīl* ('departure, journey'), as he calls it, is the book before us. Almost encyclopaedic in scope – each 'section' or 'journey' doubles as 'a scientific study or article on a particular topic' (12); every page adds, through techniques of pastiche and parody and direct quotation, to a postmodern palimpsest of classical, medieval, and modern Arabic *adab*; multiple appendices include a thoroughly pedagogical dictionary of Egyptian Arabic; casual doodles render the protagonist's bodily and geographic shocks, displacements, and translations – *Kitāb al-Ṭughrā* holds little if anything back from its putative addressee, Mustafa's London psychiatrist.[14]

During his three-week *raḥīl*, Mustafa drives, shops, kvetches about neoliberalism, attends a wedding, and reads history. Before long, he is consumed by the feeling that he is the victim of 'a secret organisation'. While its essence is mysterious, its signs are everywhere: coworkers and city crowds perceived as brain-snatched automatons; the kitsch rampant at malls and on highway billboards; the hypocrisies of former friends. The organisation's aims include not only the mental enslavement of Mustafa (his transformation into a 'zombie'), but the complete and comprehensive hollowing out of any and all genuinely local experiments in modernity. Not all is hopeless, however. For at the same time that he uncovers this malicious conspiracy, another, more appealing one stands presented to him in the form of the ghost of Muḥammad Waḥīd al-Dīn (Mehmed VI), the last of the Ottoman Sultans. The ghost, who possesses an elderly coworker, lays at Mustafa's charge the recovery of a Qurʾanic manuscript fragment that is key to the vanquishing of the secret organisation. Our grumbling divorcée's new heroic trajectory is given a stamp of strange inevitability, as he discovers that his apparently random sojourns around the city follow rather precisely the loops and lineaments of the Sultan's calligraphic seal – the *ṭughrā* of the title – as plotted on the map of Cairo.

Before considering what is odd about Mustafa's journey, let us recognise how utterly typical it is. There is, first, the central motif of the Conspiracy. This is revealed to Mustafa gradually. Initially, it occurs to him as little more than a 'delightful danger' (29) – the peculiar affective aftertaste of a conversation he barely remembers with a friend, having something to do with his wife. In the moment, he pauses, searching for the image that best matches the feeling: 'something in a story about a far-reaching gang, or a secret organization. Yes, that's it: a secret organisation, of such might and muster that it controls the whole wide world' (28). The sensation is enriched and entextualised when Mustafa starts hanging out with Amgad Ṣalāḥ, a *sunnī* or Islamic fundamentalist who, while enabling of his companion's delusions and oddly endearing, is held in too much contempt to be a true Sancho Panza. It is Amgad who, having travelled abroad and been in and out of insane asylums, has acquired enough contemplative space to 'canonise' his anxieties about hidden powers into a full-blooded conspiracy theory (147–8). In particular, it is 'the zombie' that he fears – a senile fellow cubicle-troglodyte who always seems to appear out of nowhere – as the prime agent of 'the Organisation' (*al-tanẓīm*). With the exception of a passing reference to 'Israelis' he has encountered in Canada, however, Amgad discloses little about this organisation's identity.

Mustafa, initially sceptical, takes it from here. 'There must indeed be such an organization,' he reasons, which has been causing him bizarre dreams and strange encounters not altogether different from those of Amgad (149). He, too, suspects that there is something preternatural about their 'zombie' coworker, Waḥīd al-Dīn, and the suspicion is confirmed as the latter transforms one night into the undead Sultan Muḥammad Waḥīd al-Dīn. Illuminating for Mustafa the nature of his quest, the Sultan expounds on the enemy at large:

> Amgad Effendi did not intend to lie to you, but he was truthful in only one detail of what he narrated to you. There is indeed a well-wrought conspiracy, what he called 'the Organization': a conspiracy wider and deeper than you, the people of the lower stations, can fathom. But those of the higher dimensions, such as I, are indeed able, by the Divine Will, to understand its true essence. Suffice it to say, my son, that it is like a vicious circle that has no beginning or end. (190)

Despite his obscurantism, the Sultan is able to provide Mustafa with two additional details. The first is that the Islamist Amgad, as well as a Coptic friend, are together agents of the conspiracy, whether they know it or not. The second is that Mustafa's own personal crises 'accurately symbolize' the conspiracy's various elements (190–1). This would seem to confirm Mustafa's abiding suspicion that his unhappy marriage had somehow been part of a grander scheme against him – in fact, he is to find out later that his wife had a previous relationship with his Coptic friend. Such personal treacheries Mustafa later identifies as constituting the 'lesser conspiracy' (*al-muʾāmarah al-ṣaghīra*) to the 'greater conspiracy' (*al-muʾāmarah al-kubrā*) wrought against Muslim civilisation (295–6).

There is little in this image of conspiracy that one will not recognise from, say, the verses of Naguib Surur. The secret organisation is omnipotent, ubiquitous, and eternal; its orders are carried out by religious or ethnic Others. The figure of the zombie, furthermore, recalls Surur's *mitnāk* ('fucked one'), the enslaved consumer of Sonallah Ibrahim's *al-Lajna*, or the people-cum-herd of so many conspiracy narratives: it is the embodied metaphor of the hero's fretting over agency. The corollary to this figure is the hero's assumption of the role of saviour: 'Mustafa' (*muṣṭafā*), he comes to realise, means

'The Chosen One', an epithet of the Prophet Muhammad.[15] His quest, in turn, takes on apocalyptic tones, which reverberate in his repeated complaint about the 'collapse' or 'destruction' of 'the world' (54, 77, 92, 104, 125, 152, 161 ...), and his fear of a zombie plague, for which he concocts the phrase *ṭulūᶜ al-mayyitīn* (also *ṭalaᶜān al-mayyitīn*) ('the rising of the dead') (74, 77, 97, 131 ...).[16]

Nor is there anything original about the sheer vitriol and venom that Mustafa pours on his ex-wife – this, too, was Surur's point of departure. It is in line with paranoiac's fear of, contempt for, and desire to control all manner of feminising forces. With Mustafa, these themes emerge subtly at first; later in the novel, he appears all but reconciled to his 'counter-revolutionary stance against women's rights' (420), and a nearly unequivocal admission that feminism is 'oppressive, stupid, and criminal – acceptable only to a man who is a coward' (376). It is no surprise, under this rubric, that his ex-wife is held responsible for perpetrating the 'smaller conspiracy' to the Organisation's 'greater conspiracy', and that homosexuals and effeminate men earn a significant share of the protagonist's mockery, derision, and disgust. There are, for example, the 'foreign old geezers' who sleep with local youth, enumerated among the signs of Cairo's decay (76); there is Aldū Matanzīkī, a corpulent Mozambican coworker likened to 'an effeminate water buffalo' (307), whose 'goosing of letters' (*baᶜbaṣitu li l-ḥurūf*) (59) and 'sodomite smile' (320, 322) annoy Mustafa as much as his insistence that the latter 'can't draw' (*mush biᶜiᶜruf ilrslm*) (59, 321–2) – so tightly does aesthetic failure align with personal failure under the projected phantom of emasculation.

One more trope that Mustafa al-Shurbagi shares with the conspiracy hunters of previous generations is personal (and collective) redemption through research. At the outset of his journey, Mustafa escapes from the drama of his pending divorce and takes refuge in the musty clutter of his father's library, which he imagines as another planet. Later, inspired by his encounter with the living-dead Ottoman Sultan, he succumbs to a second bout of hermeneutical fever, and spends a full three days rummaging through Ottoman and Egyptian history. He browses the Internet, fills his notebook with scraps and sketches, neglects his appearance, and smuggles himself into various archives. As Mustafa reflects on his readings, he envisions them as contiguous with his physical journey around Cairo: 'The pleasure of wanderlust [*mutᶜat al-tisfār*] comes from the search, from the activity of reading, which is the best way to get out of this sense of confusion and fragmentation I've been in' (211). His experience thus mirrors quite closely that of Ibrahim's protagonist in *al-Lajna*, who also spoke of archival research as a form of 'pleasure' (*mutʿa*) and a means of reinvigorating an empty life. This pleasure is not simple and ordinary, it is self- and world-redeeming: Rakha's protagonist, like Ibrahim's, perceives his discoveries and unveilings as the only possible means of defeating the Conspiracy.

In spite of these rather striking affinities, there is one thing that distinguishes Mustafa's paranoid flight from that of his predecessors, namely the use of the figurative quotations marks. Mustafa is not one who would allow his departure into the ebullitions and enthusiasms of delusion formation, and its probable causes and crochets, to escape his own shamelessly flaunted powers of observation, diagnosis, analysis, and justification. From the beginning, he admits to being 'self-obsessed', and to the possibility of being inflicted with 'a neurotic form of self-love' (34). The word *al-pārānōyā* itself recurs throughout the novel (112, 117, 128, 131, 268), whether as self-diagnosis, or as a broad but poignant index of Cairo's harrowing epistemic murk and mayhem. The *kitāb* is, after all, an extended letter to Mustafa's psychiatrist, and thus the spectre of analysis looms as a possibility even when the protagonist would allow the narrative gaze to shift away from his own internal torment, which is not often. Moreover, the almost picaresque, and undeniably comic, mode of the novel suggests that, at least for the reader, there is little to be taken seriously in Mustafa's conspiracist fantasies. We are compelled to laugh at, rather than emulate, this zombie-fearing anti-hero. At one late point in the novel, Mustafa, too, seems to adopt an attitude of ironic detachment towards his paranoia, as his musings about the Organisation are likened to 'the tone of a big intellectual at a cultural conference' (297). His plot, we may say, is just so much performance.

One may be tempted, in light of these gestures towards self-reflexivity, to read the protagonist of *Kitāb al-Ṭughrā* as a vehicle for the author's critique of an old and familiar 'type': the bourgeois Cairene cultural-worker-cum-conspiracy-theorist. The reader may be impressed by the protagonist's ability to make light of his own fantasies – a welcome departure from the dark seriousness of, for example, Bakathirian drama – and by the author's subtle winks and nods at famous paranoiacs in Arabic, European, and North American literature. Yet it is important not to confuse irony with criticism. Unlike his paranoid predecessors in history and literature, Mustafa comes to recognise that there probably is no Cosmic Conspiracy as such, and that his revelations and researches have been compromised by excesses of delusion and delinquency. *Only he does not care.* Instead, Mustafa finds in conspiracy theory a useful fiction for piecing back together a subjectivity shattered by traumas both personal and political. Rationalising his irrationality, he asks rhetorically, 'What could get me up and going again, and fill me with the energy of a boxer just entering the ring, better than a conflict of super cosmic proportions that defies the laws of nature?' (228). In other words, his con-spiracist *Weltanschauung* is the perfect remedy for his *Weltschmerz* (divorce, alienation, artistic and professional infelicities, and so forth). Indeed, his embrace of paranoia as a reparative practice, rather than a debilitating one, would seem to be confirmed by the novel's ending. When we leave Mustafa, he has been comfortably installed in a hotel in beautiful Beirut, invigorated with the prospect of more romance and adventure. That beats eating oneself *à la al-Lajna*, to be sure.

In *Kitāb al-Ṭughrā*, irony operates not in order to deconstruct, desta-bilise, or decentre conspiracy theory, but to elevate its protagonist above others who share his assumptions about agency, masculinity, and the clash of civilisations. In this sense, Mustafa's journey has much in common with what John Farrell (1998) has called the 'paranoid slant' of Sigmund Freud (1996 [1911]: 1). In a caustic reassessment of Freud's critical oeuvre, Farrell deems the father of psychoanalysis 'paranoid' in reference to the latter's excesses of suspicion, self-regard, and solipsism. This style or slant, Farrell argues, was something Freud had quite self-consciously borrowed in part from some of his own patients. But the psychoanalyst was keen to separate himself from his other:

> Freud's paranoid has the character of an overly credulous intellectual, a reli-gious zealot who can neither distinguish wish from reality nor preserve the proper level of skepticism toward his own thought. Freud knows himself to be smitten with the same curse as the paranoid, to be an irrational being of the same kind, only he, as a scientist, has kept his credulous tendencies

moderately in check. What distinguishes the scientist from his paranoid patient is not so much a superior understanding of the world, or even of other people's motives, as much as it is a superior awareness of his own irrationally self-aggrandizing nature. It is the difference between naive and sentimental paranoia. (3)

Farrell's remarks prove useful for understanding Mustafa's relationship with his only 'friend', the Islamist brute Amgad. It is, indeed, the latter who introduces the first full articulation of conspiracy theory in the novel, after travelling abroad and spending considerable time upon his return in insane asylums. Mustafa recognises that Amgad's rantings about a conspiracy of zombies and Israelis are ludicrous, but finds that they can provide, with some minor editing, a good plot for his otherwise meaningless existence. Does this mean, then, that the Western-educated intellectual with secular literary ambitions should express some degree of solidarity, commonality, or friendship with a person he looks upon as a simple-minded tool in the hands of international Islamic fundamentalism? Far be it! Rather than acknowledge any debt to Amgad, Mustafa allows himself to enjoy the interpretive delights and intoxicating reductionisms of conspiracy theory, while distancing himself from the practice's association with unworthy 'others' through an ironic stance that is as sharp as it is exclusionary. That is to say, to borrow Farrell's Schillerian gesture, he becomes the sentimental, rather than the naive, conspiracy theorist. But conspiracy theorist he remains.

Mustafa's final statement on the Conspiracy reinforces the true meaning of his ironic stance. In a note to his psychiatrist, he appears to rethink the nature of the enemy:

Organization. Conspiracy. The bite of the zombie. The reason behind the catastrophe … Maybe the story's not like we thought – a group of people consciously hatching cosmic plots. Even though, without the CIA, there'd be no Taliban. Maybe the Conspiracy isn't a matter of a particular dirty deed committed or caused by the advanced nations. It's not the humiliation and torture of blacks in South Africa, for example, or the forcing of dervishes to stop their whirling. It's not the rape and slaughter of refugees at Sabra and Shatila in 1982, or the inmates dressed up in orange overalls and squatting in chains in Guantanamo since 2001. The Conspiracy, perhaps, is just a way of looking at the world, or a style of thinking, which first sprang up among the residents of northwest Europe and became stamped with the color of their skin. The Enlightenment, the Industrial Revolution, colonialism: all these creatures of modernity that abolished Islamic history in the most complex and convoluted ways, and filled my heart with a sickness of this world … All are products of this way of thinking, this perspective. Perhaps this perspective is little more than a virus that first infected those sullen faces, who then passed it on to other peoples. That the whole world is against me, or that Muslims are all just a bunch of beggars and lowlifes mired in a culture of terrorism and superstition: maybe it's all down to a deadly virus, a virus of such might and muster that it controls the whole world … It occurred to me that the Conspiracy is a virus like this, and that it must be treated, whether we hate white people or not. (454–5)

These remarks may first appear to constitute a radical turn against conspiracy theory, and, by extension, a critical departure from the ideology of many intellectuals and littérateurs, psychiatrists and Islamists, who occur here as a disingenuously inclusive 'we'. Mustafa suggests that the 'story' (*ḥikāya*) of Conspiracy has been mistaken: there is no vast, secret organisation controlling everything on the planet, only a 'way of thinking' or 'perspective' that has infected everyone like a virus. And yet, this conceptual turn is equivocal. For although Mustafa has jettisoned the notion of a plot 'consciously' wrought by human beings, his fundamental perception of the universe has not changed: 'the whole world is against' him, 'Muslims' are still 'beggars and lowlifes', and *something* – a virus, a perspective – has 'such might and muster that it controls the whole world'. Moreover, he clings to the old reductive logic of self and other, articulated here in markedly racial or ethnic terms ('northwest Europe', 'Islamic history', 'sullen faces', 'Muslims', 'white people'). 'Maybe', 'perhaps', the Conspiracy-as-Organisation has left the picture, but the story is still very much the same.

Although it would be unfair to deny a literary work, especially one as ingeniously constructed as *Kitāb al-Ṭughrā*, its potential for ambiguity and ambivalence, it should be apparent that in its ironical spin on conspiracism, celebration is more operative than critique. Initially, the sharpness and absurdity of Mustafa's delusions, as well as his moments of deep self-reflexivity, would seem to position him as a mockery of the conspiracism of well-known writers, past and present. And yet, the pride and pleasure he takes in paranoia as a research project, an instrument of post-marital revenge, and a salve for his world-weariness, as well as his abiding commitment to the fundamental precepts of conspiracism, at novel's end, would suggest rather that Mustafa is here to satirise the credulity and 'naivete' of less successful authors, while re-telling their story in a more contemporary, high-brow form.

Ambiguity in Death: The Year of the Dragon

Published less than a week after the ouster of President Husni Mubarak on 11 February 2011, *Kitāb al-Ṭughrā* did not predict this event, but gives peculiar expression to the world-weariness that made it inevitable. Mohammad Rabie's *ʿĀm al-Tinnīn* (The Year of the Dragon), published a year later, pretends that the event never happened. The title is a reference to the year 2012 – the 'year of the dragon' in Chinese zodiac – and to Mubarak who, at novel's end, declares an absolute monarchy to become himself the Hobbesian Leviathan or *tinnīn*. The president, however, is largely absent from the novel. The reader is treated instead to the story of one Naʿīm ʿAbd al-Naʿīm Aḥmad Abū Sabʿa (henceforth: Naʿīm), a bookbinder-cum-engineer who fakes his death in hopes of collecting on the insurance. The chapters that constitute Naʿīm's story alternate at irregular intervals with letters of advice, sent by one unknown government official to another, on the tools and techniques of ideological domination. Through their juxtaposition, the two narrative strands that comprise *ʿĀm al-Tinnīn* invite the reader to become paranoid about the penetration of state power into the lives of ordinary citizens, while also revealing gaps, inconsistencies, and points of comparison that complicate any simplistic model of conspiracy or hegemony.

We first meet Naʿīm in his living room, where he weeps uncontrollably in the presence of his wife, his children, and a doctor who has agreed to forge for him a burial permit in exchange for a hefty bribe. It is the doctor alone who attempts to console him; his family pretends, as they have always, that he is already dead. Naʿīm is then silent. He heads out to the street where, joined by neighbours and curious passersby, he begins his funeral march. He walks too slowly for his mourners, who hoist him on to their shoulders, assault him with 'goosings' (*baʿābīṣ*), and carry him to the mosque and then to the graveyard where, humiliated, he is forced to lay down in a recently dug hole so that the gravedigger, if asked, can genuinely say that the man was interred. But this is just the beginning. Dying, Naʿim discovers, is considerably more complicated.

The chapters that follow shift back and forth between various events in the life of our anti-hero. We learn that, as a child, he was apprenticed at the bookbinding shop of one Wahīb Wahīb; that, some nine years later, he left the shop to become a fairly successful engineer; and that, after another nine years, his life took a turn for the worse as the result of a rather curious incident. Although he had fathered an unspecified number of nameless daughters, Naʿim is pressured to father a son. To this end, he is 'ordered' by his wife, ʿAṭiyāt, to venture into the 'graves' – a reference, most likely, to Cairo's City of the Dead – and place a cloth containing magic spells in the mouth of a corpse (16). Naʿim obeys and, whether as the result of a curse, a bug, or chance bout of ill health, he is stricken a few days later with what a doctor identifies as Wernicke's aphasia. The condition becomes so debilitating that the arrival of his first son nine months later is little consolation. In the short term, his aphasia causes him to lose his job and return to work at the bookbinding shop; in the long term, it exacerbates a brewing marital crisis that, thirty years later, drives him to attempt insurance fraud.

Naʿim's subsequent journey into the chthonian world of Egyptian bureaucracy is equal parts Borges, Kafka, and Gilgamesh. A pretend funeral and burial certificate are necessary but not sufficient steps towards his goal, and his son, after managing to procure rare forms and documents that allow him to procure yet rarer forms and documents, informs him that his fate ultimately depends on obtaining an obscure 'rose-colored death certificate'. With the help of a certain 'Muḥammad ʿUmar' – an Utnapishtim/Khiḍr-like super-centenarian credited with designing bureaucratic regimes across North Africa – Naʿim accesses a parallel universe underneath Cairo's Garden City, and emerges with his magical leaf of death. Although we do not get to see him collect the million-pound life-insurance policy, we understand that he has indeed prevailed.

Ostensibly separate from Naʿim's narrative are the mysterious letters that punctuate it at numerous points. With the exception of the first letter – an obsequious pledge of allegiance addressed to Husni Mubarak just as he has assumed the presidency – each is addressed to a certain 'Ṣalāḥ', who we understand is a member of President Mubarak's inner circle. Of their author, we know only that he works for, or associates with, some branch of Egypt's sprawling security services. Each letter expounds on a different rhetorical or disciplinary mechanism intended to help Mubarak extend his authority over an increasingly recalcitrant public. These include, among other things: more careful editing of the president's speeches; more subdued boot-licking in the press; a comprehensive 'plan of distraction'; rumourmongering; revved up Malthusian biopolitics and gradually implemented sterilisation campaigns; planned confusion; the fantasy of a perfect and aesthetically appealing database of information on every Egyptian citizen; the creation of both real and illusory enemies; fear, fear, and more fear.

As much as they exude confidence in the techniques they propound, the letters also belie an anxiety about the fragility and impermanence of the state's power to conspire. We begin to hear echoes and murmurings of change: the president's image has been defaced and trampled upon; the bloggers are making trouble (170–1). Things come to a head when the author of the letters reports on the curious case of a man who has successfully mulcted a life-insurance company out of one million Egyptian pounds (LE). This is not merely a grand heist, but an existential threat to the state, as the man has managed to forge – or, more incredibly still, genuinely obtain – the multitude of documents and forms necessary to prove his death. This man, the letter writer demands, must be crushed. In a subsequent letter, however, an extraordinary coincidence is revealed: the letter writer and the fraudster share the exact same name, Naʿīm ʿAbd al-Naʿīm Aḥmad Abū Sabʿa, and live in the same neighbourhood. Whether as the result of a genuine confusion or a deliberate misunderstanding, the letter writer finds that he, and not the fraudster, is wanted by the authorities. He is confident that he can evade them, however, and the last we hear of him is a letter outlining numerous justifications for the coronation of King Husni Mubarak, 'the Dragon'.

A first-degree reading would suggest that the narratives of the two Naʿims comprise yet another gloomy chapter in a long tradition of dystopian fiction. The letters of advice evoke most immediately the pessimism of Orwell's *1984*, the cynicism of Machiavelli's *The Prince*, and the general thrust, as suggested by the novel's title, of Hobbes's *Leviathan*. In reducing politics to a matter of hidden agents deliberately and directly moving a herd-like public, they amount to a conspiracy theory of power that differs only from Bakathirian drama as regards the identify of the perpetrators. The conspiracy takes on a more familiar form late in the novel, when we are given a short history of the so-called 'Peacocks' (*ṭawāwīs*): a secret society of *éminences grises* who have been advising the rulers of Egypt since the time of al-Ḥākim bi-Amr Allāh. (We may understand that Naᶜim the letter writer is a member, although this is not stated explicitly.) With the triumph of the Dragon in the end – if not a warning about Mubarak himself, then perhaps this is an uncanny prediction of the rise of ᶜAbd al-Fattāḥ al-Sīsī, 'the Lion'[17] – the novel's dystopian trajectory seems complete.

Yet *ᶜĀm al-Tinnīn* differs in important ways from the typical conspiracy narrative that ultimately undermine the novel's apparent dystopian closure. First and quite remarkably, Naᶜim the bookbinder is *not* paranoid. By all rights he should be. His lifespan reads like a history of modern Egypt: aged ten in 1963, we may calculate that he was born shortly after the inauguration of the 'July regime', or the succession of military dictatorships that ruled Egypt since 1952; his work as an engineer coincides roughly with the period of the Sadat presidency;[18] his affliction with aphasia is dated roughly to late October, 1981 – in other words, right as Mubarak was assuming the presidency; his attempted death happens 'thirty years later', or at about the time in 2011 that history would sweep the president into its dustbin. At another level, Naᶜim's attempt to cheat death mimics, or perhaps mocks, Mubarak's famed longevity. There are, in addition, more subtle connections that the reader may draw between Naᶜim's personal crises and the schemes cooked up by politicians-on-high. One might suspect that his fertility crisis, or lack of male offspring, has something to do with the secret plan, suggested by his letter-writing doppelganger, to contaminate the water supply with anti-contraceptive agents (53). One may also link the letter writer's desire to see the Egyptian people collectively assume the sexually suggestive position of 'bending over' (*falʾasa*) (143), with the 'goosings' (*baᶜābīṣ*) that Naᶜim receives from the small children of the neighbourhood, who ultimately succeed in sodomising him with a hot red pepper (166–9).

But Naᶜim does not make any of these connections. He does not read history, he reads *al-Ahrām* – especially the obituaries. His ignorance of the tap-water conspiracy – if that is what it is – contrasts markedly with one of the central obsessions of Sonallah Ibrahim's *al-Lajna*. Unlike Naguib Surur, he is totally unaware of his uncanny 'double'. (Like Surur, he gets into trouble for shouting the profanity, '*maᶜarraṣ*' – only he does so unintentionally, as the result of his peculiar aphasia.) Naᶜim is not a conspiracy theorist, not a detective, not a police officer – if anything, he is the quintessential fool, a boring and bumbling anti-paranoiac who fails to see the big picture.

Naᶜim's 'naïve' anti-hermeneutic – if we may call it that – is best symbolised in his relationship with the first book he is asked to bind: *Naṣiḥat al-Muluk* (Advice to Kings), a treatise on statecraft by the tenth /eleventh-century jurist Abū al-Ḥasan al-Māwardī (67). This, more than the texts of Orwell, Kafka, or Hobbes, is the true intertextual template for the letters written by Naᶜim the adviser. In fact, we find out later in the novel that the mysterious customer who finally purchased the tome was none other than this latter Naᶜim, long before he had risen to his current position in government (85, 223). We can assume that his letters of advice – in essence, a serialised conspiracy story – owe much to his careful reading of this pre-modern work. Book-binding Naᶜim, too, spends a good deal of time with *Naṣiḥat al-Mulūk*. But he never actually reads it. Instead, he spends months binding and re-binding the book, experimenting with different applications of glue, qualities of leather, and serendipities of balance and form until he reaches perfection. His relationship with the text is entirely superficial. And, yet, it is precisely because of this epi-textual aloofness – his preference for the aesthetic over the hermeneutic – that he prevails in the end. Unconcerned with hidden plots, undisturbed by the diabolical intentions of his double, Naᶜim is crazy enough to challenge Egypt's bureaucratic behemoth and think he can win.

Naᶜim the adviser admits as much in one of his final letters. Addressing a member of Mubarak's inner circle, he writes:

You are able to rule people through fear, through terror … It is fear that has kept Mubarak in power all these years.

This pseudocide (*muddaᶜi al-mawt*) no longer fears the law. By playing dead, he's broken every barrier of fear that's been set up before him. Is there anything more frightening than death? He's broken and smashed to pieces a good number of laws: forged a death certificate, gone walking through the streets without an identity card … All these actions clearly indicate that the pseudocide fears not the law, fears not any punishment. Perhaps he does not even fear the Great Terrors (*al-fazzāʿāt al-kubrā*): not the specter of economic collapse, not chaos, not even Israel. (220–1)

The state's fear-mongering, and its deployment of conspiracy theory in particular ('the Great Terrors', 'not even Israel'), has had no effect on Naʿim. Whereas previous world-weary heroes sought salvation *through* paranoia, Naʿim is saved precisely through his avoidance of it. His victory, moreover, gives lie to the idea of a carefully wrought, effectively executed Conspiracy that thwarts every act of resistance and incorporates all deviations from its rule. Whatever dark scenarios the government may direct, and however 'draconian' the head of state appears to become, at least one member of the audience is bored to death and decides to hatch a plot more to his liking.

There is, no doubt, more than a little ambiguity about Naʿim's victory. At his best, he may be celebrated as a cunning trickster, the Certeauian *bricoleur* or hacker who exploits a weakness in the system to carve out a small space of resistance. His literary precursor is not the advice-to-kings genre embodied by *Naṣīḥat al-Mulūk*, but the various premodern tracts on the *ḥiyal* ('tricks, ruses') of underground types like beggars, thieves, parasites, and buffoons.[19] Naʿim's trick is all the more effective because of its subtlety: he has merely exploited a small 'gap' (*thaghra*) (23, 27, 57), not committed himself to a utopian, world-changing 'revolution' (*thawra*). But to what end? Naʿim is an aphasic about to turn sixty, and his new fortune cannot reverse the cruelties and afflictions he has suffered throughout his life. He has lived to die, and then died in order to live, but death is still just around the corner.

The ambiguity of Naʿim's end returns the reader to potentially endless lines of interpretation, and is enough to remind him that meanings are not fixed by pre-ordained plots, but by the ordinary wit and will of determined fools and world-mumbling aphasics. Through its very lack of closure, *ʿĀm al-Tinnīn* untethers the story of conspiracy from its traditional moorings and sets the scene for alternative scripts and stagings.

Using Life

'I agree, of course, that Cairo's a miserable, hideous, filthy, rotten, dark, oppressive, besieged, lifeless, enervating, polluted, overcrowded, impoverished, angry, smoke-filled, simmering, humid, trashy, shitty, choleric, anemic mess of a city. But isn't it the architect's job to find ways to combat all this?'

'Sure, my friend. But at a certain point, one will find it simply impossible to work with the way things are. The only way out then is just to demolish everything and build again from scratch.' (130)

The question is posed by Bassam Bahgat (Bassām Bahjat), a twenty-something intern at a film-production company, and protagonist of the novel *Istikhdām al-Ḥayā* (2014). The response is that of Ihab Hassan (Īhāb Ḥasan), professor of comparative literature, world-renowned theorist of postmodernism and, in the context of the novel, the recently deposed head of secret global cabal called the Society of Urbanists (*jamʿiyyat miʿmārī al-madīna*). Over the centuries, the Society has shaped political regimes, geographical boundaries, reigning ideologies and religions, not through brute force but rather, as its name suggests, through changes to urban architecture, design, and the environment. Its latest plot, adopted after an internal coup, represents a dramatic shift in strategy: the cities of the world are to be wiped out, redesigned, and built anew, and placed under the direct control of the group's board of directors. Ihab was opposed to the plan, and now finds himself huddled together with his friend Bassam in a secret bunker somewhere underneath the Garden City neighbourhood of Cairo. Above ground, the city they both love to hate succumbs to an apocalypse of sandstorms, earthquakes, and sinkholes.

Istikhdām al-Ḥayā presents itself as 'no more than a collection of papers and memories gathered in secret, over a number of years, by a lonely old man' – that is, the future Bassam Bahgat, now in his late forties, who also describes this as 'a lengthy epistle addressed to the past, a mendacious trick made to resemble an advice column or a travel guide' (10). The 'novel'[20] may also be described, with respect to Ahmed Naji's background in blogging, as a 'wiki' of all things frivolous and fantastical: the sexual fetishes and fantasies of Cairo's forlorn twenty-somethings, the mating rituals of cockroaches, tropes from international comics and manga, intimations of a secret history of the Saint-Simonians, scenes remixed from Egyptian cinema, music and folklore, and spaces left open for reader contributions. Illustrations by Ayman Al Zorkany, and irregularly placed footnotes full of historical anecdotes and arcana, at once complement, and digress from, the main text. The narrative matrix that shelters these disparate elements concerns events in Bassam's life before, during, and after the Catastrophe that destroys Cairo.

In many respects, this is a classic conspiracy story: a sexually frustrated male, alienated from the decay and corruption of the capital city, finds himself caught up in the machinations of a secret society (the Society of Urbanists) determined to shape the world in its image. The dystopian *denouement* of Bassam's story – a future where every aspect of life is engineered to pristine perfection by the Society's chief architect of evil, Paprika (*Bābrīkā = Bābā/ Māmā Amrīkā?*) – evinces a politics and aesthetics of hopelessness, cynicism, and hegemonic doom that, at first glance, would appear all too familiar. But a closer look reveals that the plot is not so simple. Rather than piecing together the totality of the narrative, we will here consider an assortment of scenes and images that demonstrate the novel's departure from the conspiracist mould, in particular as this concerns the distribution of agency and the prospects for survival in a city on the brink of collapse.

Bassam's attitude towards Cairo – it is indeed an 'attitude', for the still maturing twenty-something lacks any recognisable ideology – is expressed concisely in his question quoted above. It is an attitude of extreme ambivalence: Yes, the City is a wasteland; No, this does not mean that it needs an apocalypse. The attitude is also expressed in the novel's most graphic scenes, where grotesque language or images function as mixed repositories of danger, delight, *bricolage*, and banality. This is in contrast to the traditional conspiracy story, where such elements function as symptoms or symbols of the hero's defeat by some ruthless hegemon. In commenting on the city's social life, for example, the narrator finds more than meets the untrained eye:

> On the surface, Cairo's residents appear as a wretched assortment of women wrapped in layers of cloth, and pitiful men whose ravenous sexual appetites go forever unfulfilled. A more penetrating view, however, reveals this city of twenty-odd million to be buzzing with shadowy gatherings of all sorts, each with its own secret rituals and languages. The casual visitor will be unable to crack their code, unless, by happy coincidence, he stumbles upon someone who holds the keys. Cracking the code by yourself, or acquiring your own personal key, requires a long and toilsome journey in which you abandon

yourself to the city in all its filthiness, until it becomes part of you and you become part of it.

The secret societies of the Cairenes include: religious fanatics who move about in cohorts of brothers and sisters; homosexuals who organize cocktail parties and meet-and-greets in homes out in Duqqī and Muhandisīn; young artists drowning in rivers of beer stretching from Zamālik to downtown; wife-swapping groups in Imbaba; street children overdosing on soda in the shadows of slums and abandoned railroad yards; hashish dealers making the rounds in the brothels of Dār al-Salām; a Church that's maintained its control and influence over its flock for centuries; bodybuilding fanatics; boxers obsessed with their fists; mendicant musicians and worn-out belly dancers in the backstreets of Fayṣal and the Pyramids District; gluttonous businessmen organizing hunting trips to begin after midnight; junkyard dogs; foreigners who ride motorcycles in Maᶜādī; youth committed to charity and public service in ᶜAjūza; folk singers in Shubra; S& M fans in apartments that overlook the Nile in Maᶜādī; families begot of incest with a biological map stretching from the corniche at Rawḍ al-Faraj over to Aḥmad Ḥilmī Street; fornicators with donkeys in ᶜIzbat ᶜAntar; the men in black, defenders of security and stability; dog catchers and dog dealers roaming about in bands in the desert; private security firms in the Fifth Settlement; killers-for-hire hiding out in al-ᶜAtaba … All these secret societies grow up and mature in close geographic proximity to each other. They greet by sniffing each other with the tips of their noses, or by licking each others' necks, or by looking each other in the eye: each one's secret is safe with the other. (59–60)

These local, grassroots 'secret societies' stand in an unresolved ontological tension with *the* secret society, the Society of Urbanists, which plots to rule the world. Perhaps, the narrator means to suggest, the existence of one implies the existence of the other. Or perhaps it is that the local societies represent a form of opposition, however unwitting, to the global Society. What is certain, in any case, is that Bassam's list is not merely a register of sins. It is worth contrasting this passage with a remarkably similar one in *Kitāb al-Ṭughrā,* in which the novel's narrator enumerates the sordid manifestations of civilisational collapse that he has witnessed in downtown Cairo:

I've seen drugs of all different kinds, the corresponding differences in class and mood among their users, what effect they have on them and their lives. I've seen the kind of men that prefer sleeping with men or children, and the kind of women who do likewise. [I've seen] a whole little world centered downtown, made up of foreign old geezers and the street-savvy youth who sleep with them in exchange for any number of things – money being the most obvious, and rarest, among them … I've seen people murdered, cases of torture in police stations, and nervous breakdowns that don't always end in an asylum. [I've seen] demonstrations and fights break out in the street, movie stars shooting themselves up in the bathrooms of bars, professional prostitutes who wear the hijab, and kids swiping cans of gasoline from each other. (76–7)

In this instance, Rakha's novel partakes of a conservative, almost reactionary ethics, in which the corruption of the inner city portends a broader civilisational collapse. Utterly irredeemable, Mustafa's Cairo needs an apocalypse and a conspiracy to save it. Bassam's journey into the city's underbelly, by comparison, is as much a rescue and recovery operation, as it is an inspection of vice. Or rather, it is neither: Bassam is concerned merely to document, rather than to celebrate or condemn, the many groupings of Cairenes he encounters. He mentions 'cracking the code' (*fakk al-shifra*) of the secret groups – but rather than suggesting the violent apprehension implicit in the interpretive quests of the detective, the pimp, or the paranoiac, the production of knowledge is here achieved through total immersion. 'Cracking the code,' Bassam tells us, 'is a long and toilsome journey in which you abandon yourself to the city in all its filthiness, until it becomes part of you and you become part of it.' The hermeneutics of suspicion is eclipsed by a hermeneutics of entanglement, which allows our protagonist to access Cairo's secrets without becoming paralysed by fear.

The diversity of lifestyles and lifeforms in the city is also on display in a section entitled 'The Animals of Cairo'. Each of the eleven creatures in this human bestiary is represented by a grotesque illustration and brief caption. While a few of these – 'The Black Rat' and 'The Tiger Shark', for example – function as transparent denunciations of assorted authoritarianisms (the police state, and Islamism, respectively), most others – 'The Slimeball',

'The Veiled Girl', 'Junkyard Dogs', 'The Egyptian Woman of Today', 'The Biological Taxi', and so on – are difficult to fit into any strict axiological taxonomies. They are debased, but not damned. In marked contrast to the image of the people-cum-herd, whose loss of agency points to the existence of a totalising Conspiracy, these 'animals' are above all survivors who have adapted – through complicity rather than rejection – to the filth and corruption of the city. Consider 'The Wild Rhinoceros':

> Certain creatures are able to adapt to the pollution and filth of Cairo through mutations in their genes. Their voice acquires a particular coarseness. The voice box is replaced with a live frog that subsists on carbon monoxide and dioxide, sucking up cigarette smoke and the exhaust of automobiles.
>
> During childhood, the skin of the wild rhinoceros undergoes a process of shedding and regeneration. The flesh becomes covered in a thick, inorganic mix of dust particles and noise pollution. This unnatural coating serves to protect the animal's internal organs, but at the same time seals him off from any communication with the outside world. A stone has been placed upon their hearts, or their hearts are like stone. (95)

The smudgy image accompanying this caption depicts a pair of bloated, pustule-ridden feet settled into a pair of worn leather sandals with double buckle-straps. The feet are human, but their skin suggests that of a pachyderm. This creature is 'unnatural', 'inorganic', and sealed off from 'any communication with the outside world' – yet the moralistic connotation of these terms is undermined by the final line that, vaguely Qurʾanic, smacks of the same irreverant tone in which other religious phrases and discourses are voiced within the novel. The boundaries between animal and human, organic and mechanical are blurred, but this does not signify the loss of some putatively autonomous model of subjectivity. Instead, it serves as a graphic recognition of the entangled existence of all lifeforms, which is neither good nor bad. The Wild Rhinoceros, then, shares much less with the *dābbat al-arḍ*, or apocalyptic beast, than it does with Donna Haraway's 'cyborg' – a figure designed for us to reflect on the interdependence of the biotic and the abiotic, the semantic and the material, the human and the non-human. At its best, the cyborg provokes us to consider possibilities for adapting to, rather than retreating from, the strange new worlds in which we find ourselves.[21]

Sexuality is another domain in which the protagonist of *Istikhdām* shrugs off the familiar bugbears of the conspiracist. This is particularly evident in the chapter entitled 'A Cocksucker's Reprimand to His Fellow Cocksuckers' ('Hādhā ʿItāb al-Khawal li al-Khawalāt'). (The title parodies 'Love's Reprimand to the Lovers' ('Hādhā ʿItāb al-Ḥubb li-al-Aḥbāb'), a poem by Fārūq Juwayda.) The *khawal*, as we will recall from previous chapters, often appears in conspiracist discourse as the locus of fears about the dissipation of agency and the defeat of traditional masculinity. It is to these fears that Bassam Bahgat speaks when he says, in conclusion to this chapter,

> Give yourself a break. You aren't in control of yourself, you aren't in control of anything in this city. It's she that controls you. You're nothing but a cocksucker among cocksuckers. Quit the drama, little one, and enough blaming yourself. In the end, it's not so bad to be a cocksucker in Cairo. Just relax and take it all in. You might even find that cocksuckery (*khawlana*) guarantees a certain amount of protection, a certain amount of security, a good deal of prowess and an incredible lightness of being. (66)

The tone of this passage will strike the reader as tongue-in-cheek: Bassam doesn't really want to be a *khawal*. Bassam is not outing himself, nor is he raising the banner of gay liberation. Yet this is not a homophobic text. It is a double-voiced taunt directed, on the one hand, to the 'drama' of self-flagellating masculinity, and, on the other, to the bourgeois erotics expressed in Juwayda's poem.

Although suffused with the tropes of conspiracy theory – secret societies, dehumanised citizens, sexual deviance – *Istikhdām al-Ḥayā* strips these of their moralistic connotations, and places them instead within a gritty cityscape where possibilities for survival emerge precariously alongside harbingers of the end. This is not to say that the novel negates all the pessimism and gloom of its narrative precursors. Rather, *Istikhdām al-Ḥayā* elaborates a tension that is implicit in its title: between the negative 'exploitation' of life, on the one hand, and its positive 'appropriation' on the other. This tension emerges from an ambivalent conception of power as totalising, dehumanising, and inescapable, yet also sustaining, transformative, and available for use. Perhaps there is a Conspiracy, but perhaps, Bassam would suggest, it is possible to live with it.

Conclusions

'Conspiracy theory': what difference do the quotation marks make? In the above, we have suggested that the answer ultimately depends on the individual work, and the evaluative stance implied by the quotation. While parodying conspiracist fantasies, Rakha's novel ultimately decides on a stance of aristocratic irony that distances itself from pedestrian credulity while embracing the central scripts and reductionisms of the conspiracist worldview. This stance may be contrasted with the more ambivalent novels of Rabie and Naji, which stretch conspiracism to imaginative extremes and confound, qualify, or cast away its narrative of pessimism and dystopian closure.

These conclusions require a few final qualifications. First, it is worth stating the obvious: there is more to each of these novels than an evaluative stance on conspiracy theory. Especially when engaging a capricious mode like irony – where what is said contradicts, complicates, or conflicts with what is intended – the ultimate meaning assigned to a text depends as much, if not more, on the reader than on the author. More fundamentally, these texts are not political manifestos, but literary experiments that entangle the reader in labyrinthine plot-lines and multiple modes of existence, feeling, and thought. This is not only because, in Deleuzian terms, literature is at once concept, precept, and affect – distinct but complementary modes of knowing. More locally, the works in question cultivate a relationship to the political that may be said to separate them from preceding literary paradigms in Egypt. Youssef Rakha contends as much in his reading of Muhammad Rabie and other 'post-nineties' novelists, whose work he characterises as 'post-political as opposed to apolitical, in the sense that (unlike the nineties novel) it does not shy away from politics per se, but never endorses a political argument'.[22] One may add that, not only are the novels of Rakha, Rabie, and Naji political or post-political in some new sense, but that each represents only the beginning of its author's literary journey, and thus can only tentatively be tied to a coherent conceptual, preceptual, or affective paradigm.

Which brings us to our final qualification. To what extent do these ironical adaptations of conspiracy theory represent a new paradigmatic shift in Arabic literature? It has become fashionable in some circles of literary and intellectual history to posit a linear evolution of narrative forms that begins with assorted romances and realisms of the first degree and ends with the triumph of second-degree parodies and pastiches. This sort of teleological (and one may add, ideological) telling of the story rests on a specious *argumentum ad novitatem* and lacks historical depth. In the case at hand, irony, parody, and self-reflexivity have, to varying degrees, certainly always pervaded, countered, and confused the styles and discourse of Conspiracy. One need only the return to the first chapter of the present monograph, where we discussed the conflicting dramaturgical strategies of Bakathir and Idris, to perceive that anti- or post-conspiracism is nothing new in Egyptian literature. Rather than herald a 'new generation' of enlightened ironists over an 'old generation' of naive conspiracists, perhaps we as readers would do better to allow each author a range of intentions and designs, paradigms and plots, beyond what their history or ideology may suggest. Reading with charity may prove more rewarding than reading with suspicion.

Epilogue

To review the uses and acceptations of the idea of plot in revolutionary ideology would be an unending task, for it was truly a central and polymorphous notion that served as a reference point for organizing and interpreting action. It was the notion that mobilised men's convictions and beliefs, and made it possible at every point to elaborate an interpretation and justification of what had happened … Above all, it was marvelously suited to the workings of revolutionary consciousness … Like the Revolution, [the plot] was abstract, omnipresent and pregnant with new developments; but it was secret whereas the Revolution was public, perverse whereas the Revolution was beneficial, nefarious whereas the Revolution brought happiness to society. It was its negative, its reverse, its anti-principle.[1]

Historian François Furet speaks here of the French Revolution, although his words may also serve as an apt description of national political discourse in Egypt since 25 January 2011. Like France in the late eighteenth-century, Egypt in recent years has, by many accounts, witnessed a veritable explosion of conspiracy theorising by both revolutionary and counter-revolutionary voices, as well as those who belong to neither of these two currents.[2] Although this is not the place for an extended comparison, we may note, as an aside, some of the eerie textual correspondences between the two revolutions: rumours of *brigands* and *balṭagiyya*, of kidnapped children and abducted Muslim girls, of the death of the king and the death of the president, of foreign invasion and neocolonial plots.[3] As in the French case, too, 'conspiracy' in Egypt has meant many different things to different people, and provoked a range of emotional, indeed artistic reactions and counter-reactions that has been neither monolithic, nor entirely predictable.

A beautiful synthesis of some of these conflicting perspectives on conspiracy theory is offered in the two-part autobiography of novelist Radwa Ashour (Raḍwā ʿĀshūr) (1946–2014). *Athqal min Raḍwā* (Heavier than Radwa) (2013) and *al-Ṣarkha* (The Scream) (2015), Ashour's final published books, interweave vivid reflections on the advances and setbacks of the Revolution with sober descriptions of her battle with cancer.[4] Conspiracy theory is not the primary focus of these two books, but operates as one especially charged node of emotive, literary, and political meanings. Her first remarks on the topic are defensive. 'It's quite often,' she writes, 'to see a guest on a television talk-show deny conspiracy theory (*naẓariyyat al-muʾāmara*), to disparage or make light of it.'[5] This strikes her as odd, 'because a large part of our modern history has been defined and determined by conspiracy'. In this vein, Ashour's narrative voice proceeds to cite the example of the Sykes–Picot Agreement, the 1916 accord through which the major European powers codified their hegemony over the modern Middle East. Compelled by this historical reference, ʿĀshūr fears that the current revolution is threatened by a conspiracy no less grand.

This defence of conspiracy theory may at first appear curious, given that many of the loudest conspiracy theories of recent years have been voiced by figures *opposed* to the Revolution. Even before demonstrators stormed Tahrir Square on 25 January 2011, the broadcast voices of what pro-democracy forces would call the 'counter-revolution' (*al-thawra al-muḍādda*) began speaking in a language quite reminiscent of that used by the Free Officers in their early years on stage: the demonstrators, they claimed, were part of a 'plot' to carve up the Arab World; the youth in Tahrir were 'agents', or had been 'led astray' by 'hidden hands', 'destructive ideas', and free fast-food; this so-called 'revolution' was nothing but a 'conspiracy'. This conspiracist rhetoric did not end with the removal of President Mubarak on 11 February, but mutated into newly fantastical, grotesque forms as evidenced in the television seances of 'trickster' figures such as Tawfīq ʿUkāsha, Aḥmad al-Sayyid al-Mandūh (AKA Aḥmad Sibaydar or 'Ahmad Spider'), Muṣṭafā al-Bakrī, and Ḥusām Suwaylim.[6] The performances of these actors have been challenged through the creative work of comedians, cartoonists, and bloggers, whose fashioning of a potent anti-conspiracist discourse has truly been one of the most remarkable developments in Egyptian public culture in recent years.[7]

Ashour's engagement with conspiracy theory, however, differs from both sides of this debate in the manner in which she conceives of the practice. First, although she repeatedly identifies her moments of suspicion and pessimism as constituting *naẓariyyat al-muʾāmara*, the claims she puts forward under this label are quite sober when compared to the rather extravagant forms of conspiracism we have examined in this book. Mubarak, Ashour surmises, has been 'sacrificed' along with his entourage so that the regime may survive essentially intact. The Supreme Council of the Armed Forces (SCAF) will do its best to buy time and concede as little power as possible, as its generals order the forceful dispersal of demonstrators, and the mass arrest, torture, and murder of anyone who opposes them. Ashour calls this 'a hellish plot ... a conspiracy'.[8] But the manner and content of what she proposes, far from devolving into the reductionist logic of 'conspiracy theory', comes much closer to a rather plain description of historical events. In other words, what she has described is much less a secret, totalising plot, than the very public crimes of the counter-revolution.

Ashour's 'conspiracy theory', moreover, is enriched through a series of images and metaphors that draw attention to its aesthetic and emotive intensities. She describes her doubts about the revolution as deriving from *waswasa* (208) or *waswās* (280), a habitual or nagging 'suspicion'. The demonic associations of the term are made explicit later in the autobiography's second part, when the author, using Qurʾanic language, describes her suspicions as emanating from 'Slanderous Satan (*al-waswās al-khannās*), who whispers (*yuwaswisu*) into the hearts of those like me' (154). Like the Devil, conspiracy theory, for Ashour, is a force that comes and goes, attacks and retreats. Like demonic possession, conspiracist suspicion is neither a wholly natural experience, nor an entirely pleasant one. It is in fact distinctly painful: 'the idea of conspiracy', the author states, 'lays a nest in my head'; it is 'a rat playing around in my clothes' (370). Thus, conspiracy theory establishes a parasitic presence on its subject that, although detrimental to physical and psychological health, cannot so easily be gotten rid of.

These metaphorical strands merge in the eerie coincidence of the author's actual illness, which she identifies early in the book as 'a pestering tumor behind my right ear' (23). Through its metonymic link to the Devil, who whispers (*yuwaswisu*) into the ear, the author's cancer operates in a manner strikingly similar to the described paroxysms of conspiracism and suspicion. The coincidence of images is not lost on the author, who casually remarks on the similarities between the ongoing trauma of her illness and the drama of revolution. She observes, for example, how one particularly excruciating journey through the international medical bureaucracy happened to coincide with the coup that ousted President Muḥammad Mūrsī (28). Later, a friend comments on how 'strange' it was that her surgery happened to occur at the same time as the al-Rābiᶜa Massacre (58). As these coincidences mount, Ashour is compelled to ask, 'Is Egypt in a similar state [to mine]?' (159). Yet no sooner does she detect this connection than she dismisses it as 'a silly metaphor, quite nearly delusional (*al-halwasa*)' (160). The dismissal of metaphor here is more than just a reflection of the generic incongruity between literary fiction, where such figurative language can run wild, and autobiography, where connections of this sort would appear narcissistic. Rather, in depicting a quick, reductive figuration as 'delusional', the author performs one final act of resistance against the temptation of suspicious interpretation. Disease and revolution are separate stories that, in spite of their imbrications and correspondences, cannot be reduced to a single cosmic Plot.

As a text with both conspiracist and anti-conspiracist narrative gestures, Radwa Ashour's autobiography provides an appropriate ending point for our book. While defending conspiracy theory under specific circumstances and positing its inevitability, Ashour also presents it as an insidious and debilitating force that one should resist for the sake of one's own, as well as collective, well-being. Conspiracism, or *waswasa*, alerts us to lurking dangers, but it also constitutes a danger in and of itself. In this sense, Ashour would seem to suggest that suspicion and trust, fear and hope can coexist within a common repertoire of attitudes, styles, practices, and critical moods – each with its own strengths and weaknesses, narratives and digressions. Finally, it must be remembered that Ashour was not only a literary author, but also a scholar, a professor, and a critic of literature. Her final work thus serves as a recognition that all of us – authors and academics, readers and writers, revolutionaries and counter-revolutionaries – may be implicated in the theories of conspiracy in and around modern Egyptian literature.

Appendix

Selections from 'The Mother-Cunt-ets of Naguib Surur'
(*Kuss-ummiyyāt Najīb Surūr*)

The text below reproduces the complete *Kuss-ummiyyāt* proper, in addition to relevant sections of the 'Sequels' (*Mutatābiᶜāt*), following the version published online by Shuhdī Surūr (S1). Endnotes belong to the author, and have been reproduced with their original annotation (for example, *hāmish* 2, *malḥūẓa* 1). The original orthography, including inconsistencies, has also been preserved; however, a few edits have been made to correct what are obvious typographical errors in the original. For translation and discussion of select verses, see Chapter 2. Full citations for all versions (S1, S2, S3) are provided in Chapter 2, endnotes 32 and 33.

The following edits have been made. Line numbers have been added to facilitate reading. Stanza division has been revised in a few instances where the original has conjoined verses of separate quatrains. A footnote has been inserted to provide the variants to lines 6 and 7 that occur in the audio recordings (S2, S3). Finally, the author's prose introduction and concluding note have been removed.

كُـــسْ أُمّـيَّاتْ نجيب سرور

1	الأوله آه
2	والتانيه اُفْ
3	والثالثه أحّوه !
4	يا نيك يا نيك يا ليل ..

5   يا نيك يا نيك يا عين !

6   منين اجيب ناس لمعناة الكلام يتلوه

7   شبه المحرّق إذا شافوا خول وناكوه . *

8   عجبى عليك يا زمن فيك الخول مُخرج

9   وكمان مدير يا زمن يا ابو الميزان اعوج

10   لما المـعَّرص فى فرقة فنانين يحكم

11   وفوقه أعرص وفى المسرح بيتحكم

12   يبقى عليه العوض فى الفن يا جدعان

13   ويبقى حل الفساد والخبص والتعريص

14   (والكوسه والباميه والملوخيه .. ما تعدش!)

15   يا عم سيبك بقى قللى كلام ينفع

16   وكس ام الشرف نفعنى واستنفع

17   الفن يا عم بورصه يعنى خد وادفع

18   ووَطّى أنيكك وصلى ع اللى فيك يشفع .

19   وقلنا ننضف بقى قالوا بلا وكسـه

20   والله لتحصل بدال النكسه ميت نكسه

21   بلد المنايك بلدنا الكل ناك فيها

22   شوف الخريطه تلاقيها فاتحه رجليها

23   ربك خلقها كدا راح تعمل ايه فيها

24   يا نيك يا نيك يا ليل ..

25   يا نيك يا نيك يا عين !

26   الفن قسـمه ونصيب قول بخت يا ابو بخيت

27   ما هوش مواهب ولا شهادات ولابعثات

28   الفن يا معرصين له عندنا حواديت

29   تغطى مليون سنه موجات على قنوات

---

*. في S2: "شبه المحرّق إذا شافوا يهودي ناكوه" ، وفي S3: "شبه المحرّق إذا شافوا خول ناكوه \ تاني: منين أجيب ناس لمعناة الكلام يتلوه \ شبه اليهودي إذا شافوا يهودي ناكوه \ تالت: منين أجيب ناس لمعناة الكلام يتلوه \ شبه الماسوني إذا شافوا ماسوني ناكوه \ أحّة".

30	طب مين هايخرجها .. ؟!
31	بسـيطه ..
32	هاينقوا واحد عرص م العرصات
33	ومـش ضرورى يكون علاَّمه فى الاخراج
34	كفايه يبقى جنابه رد جرسونيرات
35	ولما يخرج لبن .. برضو بلاش احراج !
36	جايز يكون مرخى جايز حضرته متناك
37	ومالو .. بس المهم يبان بتاع نسوان
38	يسهر ويسكر ويعمل نفسه قال فتَّاك
39	وتيجى تكشف تلاقى العرص بس بيضان
40	السهره سخنت وفاكرين الجدع دبور
41	طب تعمل ايه اللى هايجه ونفسها فى الدور
42	ويعمل ايه اللى نفسه يحللى من غير نار
43	اللحس ليه انتشِر ؟! .. عشـان مافيش إزبار
44	اخر شياكه وفاتح حضرته قزازه
45	مش طافيه .. لأ وسـكى .. والشرموطه على حجره
46	سلام يامخرج لكن من اين لك هذا ؟! هامش2
47	لازم علاوة غلا ومخصصه لزبره !!
48	ماهيته يعنى مش خمسين ولا ميَّه
49	ولا يعنى وارث ولا من عيله سلطاني
50	اه يا بلد إنما الاخراج بالنيَّه
51	نْويتُ أخرج وانيك واخرج وأنيك تاني
52	الفن قسمه ونصيب يعنى النصيب قسمه
53	قاسمنى بالنكله وادى الإذن للصراف
54	اهبـش وشيَّل وشِيل واهجم على اليغمه
55	ما تخافـش هو اللى فوقك يعنى كان بيخاف ؟!
56	"النص" جاهز ومكتوب لك ومتفصَّل هامش3
57	والدور كدا تلبسـه وتنام عليه وتقوم
58	نافق وعرَّص ودلَّك وانحنى توصل
59	وتبقى بين يوم وليله يا علق نجم نجوم
60	وانتى يا شرموطه دورى كل يوم مرَّه

61	على المكاتب بميكروجيب من الغنَّاج
62	يعنى يادوبك كدا سنتى على الصُّرّه
63	ها تفهمى م الرياله يعنى إيه إخراج
64	يارب صاحب امانه نبعته مرسال
65	للمسئولين اللى فوقنا فى السما السابعه
66	يقول لهم ع اللى حاصل واللى ما ينقال
67	وان كانوا يستغربوا يحلف على "الرابْعه"
68	الست متجوزه .. يا عم خلصنا
69	بلاش تمثَّل كفايه عليها هم البيت
70	والتانيه مطلقه .. اعمل لها استثنا
71	وهاتها على ودنه فاضيه ولسه خربه البيت
72	والتالته يادوب على وش .. وش طلاق
73	ناقصها اسْفين ويصبح نيكها ع الطبطاب
74	فهّمها إن الزنى بقى سيِّد الأخلاق
75	حلقات على سهرات .. يامريَّحه العزابْ
76	وصاحبنا عامل شريف فى اليغمه ومفلس
77	خليه شريف يعنى جوَع كس دين امه
78	ولما يتعب هايجى بنفسه ويفنس
79	ويجيب مراته كمان .. يمكن يجيب امه
80	وارُءس الناس فى "الاستوديو" واقموا، عجبى ⟨هامش4⟩
81	مين اللى وَطَّى ومين لسه ما وطاشي
82	واحط ايدى من الحسره على زبي
83	واقوله أوطى .. يقوللى عيبه مترضاشي
84	الفن كس امه بس لامنى ع الفگَّه
85	خرمان يا عالم و انا ف ايدى السبع صنعات
86	واللبوه آخر مزاج بالغنجه والضحكه
87	يارتنى لبوه وادوق "الكنت" يا عرصات ⟨هامش5⟩
88	عجبى على اللبوه والعربيه شيفورليه
89	ولباسها باين وحتى كمان عليها الاكس
90	حظر وفظر وقوللى اللى جاب ده إيه
91	مش كس ؟! .. يبقى خد زبى وهات لى كس !

92   اللبوه قاعده وفاشخه كسها شبّاك

93   بكلوت نيلون ونايكون والسيجاره الكنت

94   اقول لروحى ودين امى انا المتناك

95   علشان بعيش بالشرف وبدخن البلمونت

96   اللبوه داخله على ابن اللبوه فى "المكتب" هامش6

97   تغمز وتغنج .. وأف .. وأحّه .. الى اخره ..

98   صاحبنا رَيَّل .. ونَزّل .. عنها قام يركب ..

99   وهوه مركوب .. ونشف بالورق زبره !!

100   شويه داخل وراها جوزها ذو القرنين

101   يحسب ويقبض ويعزم ع البضاعه العال

102   البُق له شفتين والكس برضو اتنين

103   اربع شفايف يغنوا للخول مَوّال .. !

104   مزاد ياغاويه افتحى رجليكى للطابور

105   ألا اُونا بالدور وبالدَوره ونيك واجرى

106   واعمل حسابك من دلوقت ع الدكتور

107   سيلان مصيبه خفيفه البلوى ف الزهرى !

108   معاك سيجاره ؟ .. بسلامته طلع العلبه ..

109   "لاكى استرايك" يا عالم لايقه ع الوسكي

110   اقطع دراعى لو امّك جت من التربه ..

111   ماتعرفك .. اصلها بيّاعه فى الموسكى !

112   "ياشَبعَه من بعد جوعه يا بنى يا معَرّص

113   دانا كلتها بدُقّه وجعت سنين عشان تِتْخنْ ..

114   طالع لمين يا بنى متخيّط ومتبعبص ؟!

115   لازم لأبوك اصل أبوك زيك كدا والعن "

116   يا نيك يا نيك يا ليل ..

117   يا نيك يا نيك يا عين !

118   انا حظى دايماً مدُوحَسْ حتى فى النسوان

119   وعرفت شرموطه م الشراميط وقلت تتوب هامش7

120   التوبه تابت وهى ف كسها سرطان ..

121   ميتوبش .. يعنى الزنى على كسها مكتوب !

122 فزّوره بنت الحرام .. تتناك ولو فى الصين

123 وف يومها برضو تلاقيها منيِّكه ف قليوب !

124 عجبى على لبوه " فانتوم " لبوه بجناحين ..

125 فى ايدى إيه اعمله غير رميها بالطوب !

126 القدره تكفيها تلقى امها هيَّه ..

127 وهيَّه برضو أمها واللبونه م الأم

128 الحيه باضت وجابت زيها حيّه

129 طب يعمل ايه الطبيب والمنيكه فى الدم !

130 انا معرَّص ؟! .. فشر .. طب وذنبى ايه ..

131 وانا لا خاين ولا عكاك ولا خوَّان ..

132 فيه حد فينا بيعرف امه عملت ايه ..

133 بلاش مراته زنت .. ماهى كلها نسوان !

134 طب أمنا حوّا مش نامت مع الشيطان ..

135 بنص تفاحه .. واحنا مش ولاد حوّا ..

136 اقول يا ناس النياكه طبع فى النسوان ..

137 وحتى ادم ضرورى أمه على جوّه ؟!.

138 لو تسـألوها أنا نييّك تقول ايوه ..

139 نييّك و فى النيك معلم يعنى برضو ياريت !

140 طب اسألوها وليه اتناكتى يا لبوه ..

141 تقول الفلوس بتهد أجدع بيت .. هامش8

142 جعان وعريان وعاطل بالسَّبع صنعات ..

143 والست تعبت .. يا عم لا يمها ع الفكَّه ...

144 هاتوا المحافِظ وايديكو يللا ع الشـيكات ..

145 ونظره يا اللى جايين الليله من مكه ...

146 فلوس ووسكى وصعبه العمله .. والصَّعبه

147 يسهل عشانها الشرف وإركب بنات الناس !

148 عرضى وعرضك بقى فى السوق ولا اللَّعبه ..

149 امير و متناك ومرخى هو ده اللحَّاس !.. هامش9

150 وانا أمير بس للشعرا بكس أمى ..

151 يافرحتى بزبى والاشعار وطُظ ف طُظ ..

152 عشان اعَرّص هاتولى دم غير دمى ..

153	دا حظى دمى .. ودمى برضو هوّه الحظ !
154	صبرت ياما ولا أيوب ولا غيره ..
155	يارب تفرجها بس اعفينى م التعريص
156	وتمر ليام أقول الجوع ده من خيره ..
157	وبكره تفرج وبس ما اكونش م البلاليص !
158	ألاقينى برضك معرص من ورا ضهري
159	والكل عارف وانا ف مولد مالوش صاحب
160	لو حد كان قاللى كنت حلفت له بربري
161	إنى ولا اعرف ومولد بس انا الغايب !
162	صدر قرار الوزير ميت مره بالتعيين .. هامش10
163	لكن قرار الوزير باطل ولا التأبيظ !
164	افهمها .. ليه الوزير تعيينه مش تعيين ..
165	طب يرفدونى مادام الوش أصبح طيظ
166	وزير سيادتك .. وماله بس دبّرني
167	تدابير تخش الدماغ مش طَظُّه تقلب طُظ
168	لما الوزاره وسيّه تساع ولا تسعنى ..
169	دا يبقى تعريص وزارى ولا يبقى حظ ؟!
170	ثروت عكاشه خول والعهده ع الراوي
171	وزير ويغلبنى طبعاً لما اكون عاطل
172	وينيك مراتى وامانه تسألوا الصاوي
173	طب يعمل ايه الضعيف لا حق ولا باطل
174	مخرج .. ممثل .. مدير .. حتى الوزير ناكها
175	حتى اللى انا ياما عنه كتبت واسمه "نجيب" هامش11
176	شوفوا حكاية الزنى دمغه على وراكها
177	وقولوا بعدى "نجيب" رد الجميل "لنجيب"
178	يا نيك يا نيك يا ليل ..
179	يا نيك يا نيك يا عين !
180	بلاش أقول أمها .. طب شوفوا عمّها مين !
181	تلاقوه يا عالِم رئيس المكتب المخصوص ..
182	يعنى داسسْها عليه ياليل يانيك ياعين

183	وانا واخدها نياكه ولابس البعبوص !
184	شرموط وطالق علينا كس بنت اخوه
185	ومسلّطه ع الغلابه نيك وجاسوسيّه
186	إوعوا من الكس ده الكس ده مشبوه !
187	واقطع دراعى ان بنت اللبوه يهوديه !!
188	طب اسألوا عن تاريخه هو قاتل كام ؟!
189	ياما يا جيلنا قتل يا شُهدى ياعطيّه .. هامش12
190	يادم ساح ف السجون والشهر شهر حرام
191	ولا حد قال ياضحايا للقتيل ديه
192	صبرت صبر الإبل ودّونى ع اللومان هامش13
193	وقالوا خانكه .. وخانكه يعنى فين يوجع
194	يعنى عدوّك بقى ع الضرب فى المليان
195	عامللى يابن الفطْس بين العلوق مجدع ؟!
196	انا قلت كس امكم مجدع واموت مشنوق
197	مكدّبوش الخبر شنقونى بالفوطه .. هامش14
198	ومرتين اتشنقت ويومها بصيت فوق
199	يارب خدنى دانا مش ابن شرموطه
200	دانا إبن مصر اللى فيها الشنق ولاكوليرا
201	من عهد خوفو وخفرع واللى قرع الباب
202	او يشنقونى اليهود فى السرّ إيه بحرى
203	هايقولوا مجنون شنق نفسه وانا الكداب
204	أشنق ودّيتها حقنه قبل وقف النبض
205	يصحى وتانى اشنقه وبحقنه تانى يفوق
206	وقلت يومها يارب الموت علينا فرض
207	والحقنه بتقوللى كس أمك خد الخازوق
208	نفسى اتشنق بس اقولها كلمه للرَّيس هامش15
209	ياعرابى ياعرابى من اندالنا خد بالك
210	اسمع كلامى انا بس اسمعه كويس
211	ولو قالولك انا صهيونى عقبالك
212	يقولوها ليه والصهاينه بره مش جوه

213	يبقى الصهاينه يا ريّس جوه مش برّه
214	لحد امتى حتفضل مصرنا لبوه
215	حمار وجوّه البلد مستنياه مُهره ؟!
216	ليه كل مصرى وراه قناصه زى صقور
217	وراه ليرقد .. وراه م الباب وم الشـباك
218	وقولوا ليه المواهب تنخطف بالدور
219	طبعا عشان نتنكس يعنى عشان نتناك
220	سيد يادرويش يا نابغه ليه تموت مسـموم
221	والشعب ملبوخ فى رجعة سعد من منفاه
222	ميت فى يوم القيامه مين على المرحوم
223	هيبكى ..والكل اصبح وشّه زى قفاه ؟!
224	ده كله شغل اليهود يا مصر فى الضلمه
225	ديابه سارحه ورا ولادك بقالها سنين هامش16
226	تعابين فى برج الحمام بس البلد نايمه
227	يعنى بقى مش غريبه نبقى منكوسين !!
228	انا عطّشونى تلات تيام فى عز الحر
229	لحد ما عميت وع الفناطيس ودلونى
230	وفضلت أقرب لقيتنى طرمبه يعنى بَهُر
231	أتاريه ما هوش ميه .. ده جاز .. ياصبايا دلونى
232	فين السبيل والسبيل مسموم وانا العطشان
233	مدد ياسيدنا الحسين نظره ياجيل الجاز
234	خربت محاشمى تقولش انْصَبْت بالسرطان
235	يافرحتى بالخنافس يرقصوا ع "الجاز"
236	اطفال وزى ابنى قدام عينى ناكوهم
237	يعنى اللى بتشوفه ده مستقبل إولادك
238	يعنى مفيش فايده واولادك هايرموهم
239	للنيك وللجاز وشرحه كانوا أجْدادك
240	طيب على الطلاق من كوع دراع امى
241	لتشربوا الجاز وتتناكولنا يا خولات
242	ولو نفدتوا النوبا دى يبقى كس أمى
243	وكس أم اللى يكتب كس أميات ! هامش17

244 طيب ما جايز ناكونى مره وانا نايم ‏^{هامش18}

245 مش قصدى نوم ربنا قصدى بحقنة بنج

246 ويجوز كمان صورونى وربنا العالم ملحوظة 1

247 يعنى كمان حرَّموا ع المتناكين الغنج ؟!

248 هاتناك ضرورى ولازم كلنا نتناك

249 عشان ما يفضلش فيكى يا مصر ولا راجل

250 لو كتفونى وناكونى أبقى مش متناك

251 عيّان وبينيّك فى ميت يبقى مات راجل !

252 يا هيك فى علم النيك ..

253 يا نيك فى علم الهيك ..

254 قالوالى ليه كل حاجه تقولها فيها نيك

255 بطلت ليه السياسه والكلام فيها ؟!

256 يامتناكين ما السياسه هيّه برضو النيك

257 والنيك سياسه وحاميها هوّه حراميها

258 الجارسونيرات مش عشان ليالى الانس

259 والشرب والكوسه والملوخيه والباميه

260 البلوى مش فى النياكه .. زب داخل كس

261 بسيطه بس النياكه وراها جاسوسيه !

262 تتناك يا شاطر وتبقى نجم فى السِّيمه

263 وتجيب لنا معلومات عن أى شئ ينفع

264 والطبل والزمر والأبواب ببريمه ..

265 ها تنفتح لك وسيّه يعنى كُلْ واشبع

266 تتناك يالبوه ؟.. أيوه !. وعقد شرطه نور

267 تنورينا كده مين .. فين .. بيعمل ايه ؟!

268 وتسافرى لبنان والمانيا على حنطور

269 وتيجى متريّشه ولا حد عارف ليه ؟!

270 تتناك سيادتك ؟.. ياريت !. بكره هاتبقى وزير

271 تصفّى جوه الوزاره اى شئ مصرى

272 ده يعيش وده يموت ودا يطلع يبيع جرجير

273 كرخانه يعنى ومفتوحه ع البحرى !!

274	وزير من الوِزر .. مش صدفه ولا تلفيق
275	هاتولى واحد نزيه وشريف ويبقى وزير
276	هاتوا الدفاتر يا عالِم واعملوا تحقيق
277	تلاقوا طيظ الوزير م النيك فى غوْطِ البير
278	ليه وكل حته بروحها باشم ريحه النيك
279	تقولش باتناك بقالى من السنين ألوفات
280	طيب أقول ايه وقدامى ووَرايا نيك ..
281	ما عادش فى ايديه الا الكُس أميات
282	مش عيب اقول كس أميات وانا مطرشق
283	ما عادش فيها خشـا ولا عيب ولا نيله
284	ومصر قدام عِنّه كسها مرشّـق
285	م النيك .. دمامل وما باليد ولا حيله
286	خول تجيبه مره .. منصب يجيب شرموط
287	فلوس تجيب ده وده .. جدول ومتفنط
288	وكل خانه بخيانه والحساب مظبوط
289	وانا وانت لامؤاخذه يعنى قول بنتخيط
290	تسرق شلن تبقى هيصه وبلوه وجَريمَه
291	تسرق أُلوف الألُوف تبقى م الابطال
292	وكل ما السرقه تكبر .. القانون سيمه
293	وكل ما السرقه تصغر .. فيه حرام وحلال
294	وتيجى تُجْرُد تلاقى الحسبه عال العال
295	مسددين الخانات والمِيَّه فى المِيَّه ..
296	فيه خانه ناقصه ؟.. حريقه فجأة مش ع البال
297	وكس أمى إن لاقيت حنفية الميه
298	عقود عمل ع القفا بس العمل بره
299	هاجر وسيب البلد مفروشه للغربان
300	يعنى يا إما السجون يا الشنق يا الهجره
301	يا اما تهمه جنون يا العيشه ع الصلبان
302	يا اما تسْكر وتسْكر زيى ليل ونهار
303	ونهار وليل وانت شايف نكسه ع العتبه ^{هامش19}
304	اسقينى واعمِينى لو حتى بمِيّه نار

<table>
<tr><td>305</td><td>علشان ما احسش بإن السيف على الرقبه</td></tr>
<tr><td>306</td><td>ويقولوا باسكر وماله ؟ مش بدل ما اتناك ؟</td></tr>
<tr><td>307</td><td>أنا حتى لاقى !.. دانا وَلَّعت م الطافيه</td></tr>
<tr><td>308</td><td>لو كنت أفوق التقيهم امموا الكونياك</td></tr>
<tr><td>309</td><td>وداوينى بالتى كانت بلا قافيه</td></tr>
<tr><td>310</td><td>ماشى ف شوارعك يا مصر معايا شهدى ابنى</td></tr>
<tr><td>311</td><td>ومراتى حامل بدّور بس على أُوده</td></tr>
<tr><td>312</td><td>صبح الصباح والديوك كورس بيندبنى</td></tr>
<tr><td>313</td><td>أتارى دبح الديوك عند اليهود موضه</td></tr>
<tr><td>314</td><td>ماعدشى غير دمى يالا سيحوا دمى</td></tr>
<tr><td>315</td><td>انا صليبى تعب يا مصر من كتفى</td></tr>
<tr><td>316</td><td>انا ابويا انقتل يا مصر بعد امي</td></tr>
<tr><td>317</td><td>وانا كمان هانقتل وَلَّا هاموت منفي</td></tr>
<tr><td>318</td><td>مش ها انتحر حتى لو قتلوكوا يا ولادي</td></tr>
<tr><td>319</td><td>حتى لو الانتحار كان الخلاص يا مصر</td></tr>
<tr><td>320</td><td>انا خلاصى خلاصك قولوا يا بلادي</td></tr>
<tr><td>321</td><td>يا بلادى ليه الانتحار والوعد هوه النصر</td></tr>
<tr><td>322</td><td>بلدنا موعوده يا محرق تعالى اركب</td></tr>
<tr><td>323</td><td>يركب عليها ولادها يطلعوا شبهه</td></tr>
<tr><td>324</td><td>ويركب غيره وورركبه بعد ما يغلب</td></tr>
<tr><td>325</td><td>ولادها برضو ياقادر يطلعوا شبهه</td></tr>
<tr><td>326</td><td>أنور نسى .. كلنا بننسى على الكرسي</td></tr>
<tr><td>327</td><td>نسى العذاب والصياعه والضياع والجوع</td></tr>
<tr><td>328</td><td>والسجن .. يا مصر قولى أحّه يا كسي</td></tr>
<tr><td>329</td><td>مسكينه كل اللى بتضحيه مالوش مرجوع</td></tr>
<tr><td>330</td><td>يا يقتلونى يا اما محاكمه علنيه</td></tr>
<tr><td>331</td><td>للى شنقنى ولو كان انور السادات</td></tr>
<tr><td>332</td><td>اشمعنى يعنى المشانق تبقى سريه</td></tr>
<tr><td>333</td><td>ما تأمموها ونصبح كلنا خولات</td></tr>
<tr><td>334</td><td>بيوضى ورمت ما بين روسيا وامريكا</td></tr>
</table>

335   يعنى ما فيش مصر فيه يا معرصين شطرنج

336   واقرا الجرايد اقول يا ويكا يا ويكا

337   نياكه يعنى .. وأى نياكه عايزه الغنج

338   هيكل ده متناك بيكتب لسّه بصراحه

339   بصراحه خالص ومين يقدر يرد عليه

340   ومادام دى هيه الصراحه يبقى بوقاحه

341   أشْخُر واقول م الجرايد كلها احيه

342   البيك ياعم جحا كان قبلها فى دارك

343   وقلت وانا مالى جالك م الشيشان النيك

344   وقلت وانا مالى ناكك جار لجار جارك

345   ما عدش فيها بقى شبيك ولا لبيك

346   النيك بقى سياحه خد تأشيره تيجى تنيك

347   وفى أحسـن العائلات والكس سَيّاله

348   ادفع تخيط وبس افرد يا عرص ايديك

349   بالعمله والعمله صعبه ومصر حَصّاله

350   يهودى ليبى سعودى .. كله نازل نيك

351   فى بناتنا وشبابنا طالع دينه ومحرّق

352   يا شبابنا سيب الصابون قبّظ بحمض فنيك

353   دا النيك مغرّب فى مصر الثوره ومشرّق

354   مبروك عليك البلد يا موشى يا ديّان

355   مفتوحه جاهزه تخش تاخدها من غير حرب

356   أَمَلَه ما يحلم بيها ولا حتى جينكيز خان

357   اللـه يجازى اللى خللوا لبغل زيك زب

358   الجبهه داخليه خارجيه ع السـنجه

359   وجاهزه من كله .. فركه كعب ع النكسه

360   والنصر طاب ع الشجر يا موشى ولا منجه

361   تنتصرى ليه يا بلد متناكه يانجسـه ؟!

362   وتعالوا يا ولادنا شوفو المعركة الجاية

363   إعداد وإعداد لإعدادها يطول شرحه

364   والتبن علو الجبال من تحتها مَيّه ..

365   والشعب عمال بيغنج لسه من جرحه

ولما تعبوا خدونى وكنت من غير دار 366
للنار .. وللتغطيه قالوا إنها مجاذيب هامش20 367
وصحافه تدَّن ولا بطانه ورا مزمار 368
يامعرصين اختشوا مجاذيب وفيها نجيب 369

انا عارف انى هاموت موته ما متها حد 370
وساعتها هايقولوا لا قبله ولا بعدُه 371
وبطانه بتقول يا عينى مات فى عمر الورد 372
وعصابه بتقول خُلُصْنا منه .. مين بعده 373

يا نيك يا نيك يا ليل ! 374
يا نيك يا نيك يا عين 375

بكتب يا عالم وانا عارف انى هاموت 376
فى منفى ولاً فى زنزانه اهو كله تابوت ... ! 377
ولو ما متش اهى علقه بالجمله تفوت 378
تهون يا ويل ولا تسكتشى ع النيك اقلام 379

يا مصرى قم وصحى النوم واقرا الاخبار 380
الدنيا صحيت الا احنا كدا بالمندار 381
شوف الصهاينه على ترابنا واقفين زنهار 382
حلاوتها ماتشات الكوره على خط النار 383
يانكسه جايه أُوف سايت ناموا الحكام 384

تقول كدا يقولوا مشاغب ده ولا عميل 385
عميل لمين وانتوا العملا لاسرائيل 386

بعد التحيه يا شهدى والذى منه .. هامش21 387
ها اوصيك وصيه تصونها زى نن العين 388
ولما اموت احكى عنى وقول لهم "إنه .. 389
مصرى ابن مصرى وكس ام اللى ماله عنين 390

ابويا مات مصرى ثاير .. بس عاش فيَّه 391
ابويا عايش .. أبويا تاره لسَّه مامتش 392
ابويا كافح وكان عنده الكفاح غيَّه 393
واللى ابوه زى ابويا يبقى ما اتيتمش 394

انا ابويا جدع .. قصدى ابويا كان 395

396	وعاش غريب فى الوطن .. ياقسوة الغربة
397	وترابنا من عهد خوفو بيحضن الجدعان
398	مبروك عليك التراب يا نازل التربه !"
399	يابنى انا جعت واتعريت وشوفت الويل
400	وشربت أيامى كاس ورا كاس طرشت المر
401	يابنى بحق التراب وبحق حق النيل
402	لو جعت زيى ولو شنقوك ما تلعن مصر
403	اكره واكره واكره بس حب النيل
404	وحب مصر اللى فيها مبدأ الدنيا
405	دى مصر يا شهدى فى الجغرافيا ما لها مثيل
406	وفى التاريخ عمرها ما كانت التانيه
407	يعنى ها تطلع كده الأول باذن الله
408	فى الشعر والنثر والطيران وما شئتم
409	يعنى ها تطلع كده راجل باذن الله
410	مش م الخنافس تخاف من هجمة الفانتوم
411	إياك تقول م العذاب "هذا جناه ابى"
412	ما كنت اقولها وكان أوْلى "أبويا جناه"
413	أبويا مجنى عليه زيى .. وياما غبي
414	قال ع القتيل انه قاتل .. آه يا شهدى آه
415	آه يابنى يا ورده لسه منوره ع الغصن
416	إوعى الخيانه يا كبدى إوعى م الاندال
417	الفن اصبح خيانه والخيانه فن
418	شوف الشوارع وقوللى فيها كام تمثال
419	بلدنا فيها الكرم حتى للظوغلي
420	لاظوغلى مين .. واللّه ما اعرف ..
421	نظرة يا عرابي
422	عارف عرابى يا شهدى .. والنبى تقوللي
423	على رأى عمك شكوكو " أحَّـه يا خرابى"
424	سبع سنين يابنى ما اعرف .. ياترى عيان^{هامش22}
425	عريان .. جعان .. ولاً ميت ولاً لسَّـه حيْ
426	سبع سنين يابنى فى الغربه وانا انسـان

427   مش أعمى .. لكن بفتش فى النهار ع الضيّ

428   يابنى يا دمى يا صبرى اللى زهق م الصبر

429   الله يجازى اللى جاب لى فى الشباب داءين

430   سُكَّر فى دمى .. وفوقه جاب لى داء السكُر

431   وحاش طبيبى .. وانا محتاج يا شهدى اتنين

432   عيان يا شهدى واديك شايف وليلى طويل

433   وتصحى يابنى تلاقينى م الألم سهران

434   يا حمَّى للصبح .. آه يا ليل يا عين يا ليل

435   ياخساره .. آدى الجدع سكران ومش سكران

436   يشرب ويشرب عشان ينسى ولا بينسي

437   الصلب والشنق والهول اللى ماله علاج هامش23

438   ياللى نسيتوا قولولى ازاى قتيل ينسي

439   ولاً انتوا برضو اللى قالوا "إصلبوا الحلاَّج"

440   قالولى بيعُه .. قالولى يابنى "بيع ابنك"

441   وجَوَّعونى يا شهدى فى بلاد برَّه

442   قالولى "ها تموت" و قلت اموت عشان خطرك

443   وموتونى وانا عايش متين مره

444   خاطرك كبير عندى يابنى وكله يرخصلك

445   وانت وانا للتراب .. نرخص ونفدى مصر

446   يا مصر كإدى تمن يرخص عشان خاطرك

447   لو حتى قالوا التمن يا مصر هوه القبر

448   سبع سنين يابنى يا نارى من المنفي

449   سبع سواقى بتنعى لم طافولى نار

450   وجيت يا بنى وقالوا كان فى مستشفي

451   ونارى ماتنطفى الا بأخد التار

452   قالوا انتهى .. قالوا يعنى خلاص بقى مجنون

453   يا شهدى مجنون بمصر وكس أُم الطب

454   الطب من عهد كاس سقراط بقى ملعون

455   الطب هو الجنون .. بس الجنون مش طب

456   يا نيك يا نيك يا ليل

457 يا نيك يا نيك يا عين

458 اخـش بيت الأدب القى الأدب ممنوع
459 تدخل ورايا المباحث شئ مش معقول
460 يمين شمال بتراقبنى والكسوف مرفوع
461 لولا الملامه لا ياخدوا عينه م البول

462 يحللوها يلاقوها م الفصيلة "جيم"
463 وف أى خانه يحطونى ولو "شيعى"
464 ومش مهم .. المهم أدخل فى سين وجيم
465 وشيعى وقت اللزوم اهى تنقرى شـيوعي

466 مافيش لا شيعى ولا شيوعى ولا دياولو
467 فيه لسه فهرس طويل فيه الخانات ألوان
468 ومحقق اعمى وديب قاعد وبيناولوا
469 عميانى و ادبح ويا خساره ع الخرفان

470 قاعد قبالى جنابه يبص ويسجّل
471 كحيت انا لمين .. ضحكت لمين .. شاورت لمين
472 والتانى قاعد وعينه نت ع الصندل
473 يمكن اكون بادى شفره لحد م القعدين

474 وبيلعبوا معايا قال .. والنقره بالنقره
475 قال يعنى فاهمين وأذكيه ميتخموش
476 طب موشى ليه ناكنا من جوه ومن بره
477 لما انتوا أذكيه ولا انتو ما تنكسـفوش

478 شوفوا اليهود فين يا عالم روحوا راقبوهم
479 بلاش تراقبوا الغلابه حتى فى المراحيض
480 يا ديول اليهود مهما ها تحموهم
481 بكره نشوفكم نسا زى النسا بتحيض

482 الغمز واللمز والاشـارات دى شغلتكم
483 دا شعب ما يتغلب الا بغدر وغش
484 ومادام فهمناكوا .. يعنى كشفنا لعبتكم
485 نلعب بقى احنا والأذكى اكيد هايقش

486 أقرا فى بيت الادب أجدع كلام ينقال

متتابعات على الكُــسْ أُمِّيّاتْ

ليه تولدينا لحوت ! .. طب يبقى مين أنور 642

او يبقى مين لاعور .. ويبقى مين "ياسر" 643

وقبلهم كان مين .. وبعدهم كان مين .. وكلهم "كوهين" ! 644

ومين يصدق ايه .. وازاى وامتى وليه ؟! 645

حبل وسقط وحبل .. اخطف وشبه ودجّل 646

والنكسه ورا نكسه .. والوكسه ورا وكسه 647

وكلهم شرحه .. هتلر وتيتو وفرانكو 648

لو حتى كان عنتر .. ولا هارون الرشيد 649

حسين ونيكسون وفيصل .. بودجورنى وبرجنيف 650

رئيس زعيم أو ملك .. والكل ع الزمبلك 651

عشان كده الثورات .. طول عمرها بتخيب 652

والنصب م الحكومات .. ع الشعب بالتنصيب ! 653

عشان كدا كل شعب .. جواه مكوّع شعب 654

حتى اليابان شعبين .. حتى الزنوج شعبين 655

واحد اصيل مسكين .. والتانى جاى تهجين 656

قرود وراكبه الخيول .. طب مين هايقدر يقول .. 657

...

يا نيك يا نيك يا ليل .. 714

يا نيك يا نيك يا عين ! 715

[هوامش]

هامش 2 حط مطرح مخرج اى حد فى اى مكان !

هامش 3 حط مطرح " النص " أى ميثاق من مواثيق الثوره حتى ورقة الطلاق .. نقصد ورقة اكتوبر !!

هامش 4 كل مصر مجرد استوديو للنيك الاندماجى العالمى

هامش 5 إعكس " الكنت " تطلع " نكت " و " تنك " .. صدفه ؟!

هامش 6 أى لبوه وأى ابن لبوه فى بلد " المكاتب " المتناكه !

هامش 7 يجب ان يذكر فى حياتى او بعد موتى خاصةً بعد تشنيع الجرائد والمجلات . انه قد تزوج صاحب الكس أميات من ممثله - وفيه فرق بين ممثله ومومسله - بعد ان مُنعت زوجته الروسيه وابنه منها من دخول مصر . ثم اتضح ان الممثله ابنه شقيق رئيس القلم المخصوص (أيام الملكية) ومدير عام الجوازات والجنسيه فيما بعد !!

هامش 8 لاتنسى دورها السرّى كدسيسه للمخابرات بعلم عمها رئيس المخابرات وقلم مكافحه الشيوعيه !

هامش 9 زى الامير خالد - أو أى واحد من اثرياء البترول .

هامش 10 صاحب الكس اميات لم يعَيّن حتى الأن منذ عودته من روسيا فى سنه 1946 !! ممنوع يعمل او ياكل عيش !!

هامش 11: نجيب محفوظ - وكان صاحب الكس اميات من اوائل من عَرَّفوا المثقفين العرب بنجيب محفوظ فى الخمسينات !

هامش 12 شهدى عطيه الشافعى - مناضل وطنى مصرى .. قتل فى المعتقل لا لأنه شيوعى فقط ولكن لانه مصرى وطنى اساساً وقبل كل شئ ، ولذلك لم يُقتل جميع الشيوعيين فى مصر ..! وانما خرج منهم معرّصون كثيرون كما لم يُقتل جميع الاخوان المسلمين وانما قُتل الوطنيون المصريون منهم من امثال سيد قطب و غيره . اذن لاتهم الخانة فى الفهرس أو الجدول او تفنيطة التهم .. المهم هو قتل اى عنصر وطنى بأية خانة !

هامش 13 العباسية .. قضى صاحب هذه الكس اميات فيها ستة شهور ... .

هامس 14 المره الأولى كانت بفوطه والثانيه بحبل ! .. وهنا يظهر مفعول دسيسه بنت شقيق رئيس قلم مكافحة الشيوعيه السابق ذكرها ! .. مع ملاحظة ان هذه الكس اميات مكتوبه فى عهد عبد الناصر وانه قرأها شخصيا .. ولدى الدوائر المسؤلة علم بتفاصيلها وقد نشرت آخر ساعه فى الاسابيع الاخيرة تحقيقات عما يحدث فى مصر - من وراء ضهر الشعب - للعناصر الوطنية فى مستشفيات الامراض العقلية !! !

هامش 15 كان عبد الناصر حيا - وكنت مغفلا وحسن النيه ولاتسبوا الموتى فانهم قد أفضوا الى ما قدموا .. كما يقول الحديث الشريف !.. مهما كان لاتجعلوا من الموتى شماعة تعلِّق عليها كل الملابس القذره فرابسو يغسل اكثر بياضا !!

هامش 16 تصفيه العناصر الوطنيه فى كل موقع تصيب أيضاً ضابط المخابرات المصرى الوطنى وضابط المباحث المصرى الوطنى وأى عنصر وطنى حتى الكبابجى الوطنى ! فإذا كان ما حدث لصاحب الأميات فى العاسسه من افانين التعذيب والتدمير قد حدث بعلم المخابرات المصريه فتلك مصيبه وإن كان قد حدث من خلف ظهرها فالمصيبه ألعنْ ! .. والذين يحاولون اليوم ان يجعلوا من عبد الناصر شماعه للأوساخ - بعد موته - هم على استعداد لأن يجعلوا من أنور السادات شماعه لأوسخ الأوساخ فيما لو أصبح موشى ديان غداً رئيسا لمصر المتناكه التى لا تتعلم من التجارب ، ثم انهم يحاولون إحلال نظام فردى محل نظام فردى .. وتظل الطاحونه دائره على الوطنيين !

هامش 17 تحت يد النائب العام السابق تحقيق شامل لتفاصيل هذه الأميات .. وقد اغلق التحقيق من فوق لأنه يمس رؤوساً كبيره !! .. ويمس أسراراً .. ولأن رؤوسنا بلا ثمن .. مع اننا ولاد تسعة أشهر كلنا !!

هامش 18 يمين بالله لو كانوا ناكونى كنت قلت .. فيها إيه ؟ .. دا حتى المتناكين بيقولوا إنها زى شكة الدبوس !!

ملحوظه 1 أنا بديلكوا وثيقة تاريخية من الخمسينات لحد الآن .. بأقولها وانشروها بأى وسيلة فى حياتى أو بعد موتى، عشان خاطر فريد ابنى وشهدى ابنى، لاتظلموا الموتى وان طال المدى. "إنى أخاف عليكموا أن تلتقوا" .. زى ماقال أبو العلاء المعرى .

هامش 19 كتب هذا بعد نكسـة 1967 وقبل نكسـة كسـينجر 1974 !! أى بين النكستين !!

هامش 20 مستشفى المجانين .. المجاذيب .. العباسيه ! ..

هامش 21 شهدى ابن صاحب الأميات من الزوجه الروسيه ساشا كورساكوفا

هامش 22 حُرم الشـاعر من ابنه سبع سنوات واكثر .. منعوه هو وامه من دخول مصر ثم دخلا بعد يأس !!

هامش 23 الشاعر "يعالج" حتى الآن من اثار التعذيب فى جولة العباسيه عام 1969 من القلب والكبد والسكر والضغط والانحدار التدريجى الى العمى والكلى وورم الساقين ونشر العظام .. وهو فى نفس الوقت "تحت التحفظ" !!

هامش 24 مناضل وطنى وكاتب مصرى اخوانى .. اعدم !

...

هامش 31 الماسونيه هى الدين السرى أو التنظيم السرى أو الحكومه السريه الخفيه لليهود ومنذ اقدم العصور منذ السبى الاول فى بابل وهى وراء جميع حكومات العالم بلا اسـتثناء .. وانظمتها بلا اسـتثناء بلعبة الخطف والتشبيه !!

Notes

Notes to Introduction

1. al-ʿAqqād (1952), 'Taqdīr Brūtūkūlāt Ḥukamāʾ Ṣihyūn: li-al-Ustādh al-Kabīr ʿAbbās Maḥmūd al-ʿAqqād', p. 12.

2. For a review of the textual history of *The Protocols* in Europe, see Boym (1999), 'Conspiracy Theories and Literary Ethics: Umberto Eco, Danilo Kiš and The Protocols of Zion'.

3. For al-ʿAqqād's views on Zionism and Communism, see, respectively, 'al-Munazzama al-Shayṭāniyya' (The Satanic Organization), *al-Akhbār*, 24 October 1955 and 'al-Madhāhib al-Haddāma Tahdim Nafsahā' (Destructive Ideologies Destroy Themselves), *Majallat al-Azhar*, August 1959, both of which are collected in al-ʿAqqad (2014 [1964]), *Yawmiyāt*, pp. 147–8, 217–21. He would author book-length polemics on both groups: *al-Ṣahyūniyya al-ʿĀlamiyya* (World Zionism) (1968) and *Lā Shuyūʿiyya wa-Lā Istiʿmar* (Neither Communism nor Colonialism) (1957). al-ʿAqqād also held conspiracist views on Existentialism and related movements: see, for example, 'al-Wujūdiyya: al-Jānib al-Marīḍ Minhā' (Existentialism: Its Pathological Dimension), in which he claims that 'a Jewish finger [i.e. hand] is behind every doctrine that belittles moral values and aims to demolish the rules upon which human society has been founded in every time period', *Bayn al-Kutub wa-al-Nās*, p. 22. On his view of history as a conflict between 'giants' or 'great men', see: 'Rūḥ al-Insān fī Ṣirāʿ al-Jabābira', *Akhbār al-Yawm*, 25 June 1955.

4. Hofstadter (1996), 'The Paranoid Style in American Politics', *The Paranoid Style in American Politics, and Other Essays*.

5. Gray (2010), *Conspiracy Theories in the Arab World: Sources and Politics*.

6. The two definitive works on this topic remain Jacquemond (2008), *Conscience of the Nation: Writers, State, and Society in Modern Egypt* and Mehrez (2008),

Egypt's Culture Wars: Politics and Practice. The insights of these two studies inform the present monograph throughout, but see in particular Chapter 4 for a closer look at a sonorous clash between members of the cultural and political fields.

7. The politics and aesthetics of *adab al-iltizām* or *littérature engagée* in Arabic have been the topic of considerable critical attention. See in particular the essays assembled in Pannewick and Khalil (2015), *Commitment and Beyond: Reflections on/of the Political in Arabic Literature since the 1940s*, as well as the seminal work of Verena Klemm (1998), *Literarisches Engagement im arabischen Nahen Osten: Konzepte und Debatten.*

8. Hofstadter (1996), pp. 29, 32

9. For a review of such polemics, see Landau (1996), 'Muslim Opposition to Freemasonry'.

10. Cheikho, *al-Sirr al-Maṣūn*, vol. 6, p. 50:

في اطراف الارض نملك غاياتْ   جمعيتنا مشهورا بكثر الزوات

فيها خيخان وكاهن نسا وبناتْ   فيها حجّاج وأُمرا وباشا وقيصر

فيها ملوك وفايض صندوقتنا الف كيس   ومنزيدا في كل دقيقة حتى ما تخيسْ

والمقصود ذل الروسا ومحو القسيسْ   وبعد قطع المشايخ جنس المضرْ

11. On the history of Freemasonry in Egypt and the Levant, see Landau (1965), 'Prolegomena to a Study of Secret Societies in Modern Egypt'; Sommer (2015), *Freemasonry in the Ottoman Empire: A History of the Fraternity and its Influence in Syria and the Levant*; and Wissa (1989), 'Freemasonry in Egypt 1798–1921: A Study in Cultural and Political Encounters'.

12. 'Fourth generation warfare', or the use of information and communication technologies by foreign powers to influence public opinion, has been a term much touted by President ʿAbd al-Fattāḥ al-Sīsī in recent years; the notion of a secret 'geophysical weapon' was propounded by General Ḥusām Suwaylam on Egyptian television (Shams El Din, 'A Year of Conspiracies', *Mada Masr*, 27 December 2015, available at <www.madamasr.com/sections/politics/year-conspiracies>, last accessed 1 October 2016). The use of narcotics, in particular hashish, as a vector of insidious foreign hegemony occurs in *Shaʿb Allāh al-Mukhtār* (God's Chosen People, 1956), a play by Ali Ahmad Bakathir, in which a character credits David Ben Gurion with founding 'a special ministry for smuggling hashish into Egypt' (p. 59). This understanding of hashish as a foreign plot is also expounded in Aḥmad, *al-Ḥashīsh Mamnūʿ!* (Hashish is Forbidden!, 1953), which is, however, remarkable for virtually no mention of Israel. On chewing gum as an Israeli conspiracy, see Ghoussoub (2000),

'Chewing Gum, Insatiable Women, and Foreign Enemies: Male Fears and the Arab Media'. On conspiracist interpretations of 'rumours' (*ishāʿāt*) in Egyptian regime rhetoric, see Koerber, 'Istiqrāʾ al-Ishāʿa: Bināʾ al-Khuṭūra wa-Ṭuqūs al-Mukāfaḥa', *Jadaliyya*, 27 January 2014, available at <www.jadaliyya.com/pages/index/16154/المكافحة-وطقوس-الخطورة-بناء_الإشاعة-استقراء>, last accessed 1 October 2016.

13. Mahfouz (1984), *al-Tanẓīm al-Sirrī*, pp. 17–19. This 'unconventional' use of love ditties by hidden enemies of the nation is given more elaborate expression in ʿĪsa (1964), *al-Shāʾiʿāt wa-Kayfa Nuwājihuhā* (Rumors and How We can Confront Them), a book published by the Arab Socialist Union (p. 67).

14. Swedenburg (2000), 'Saʿida Sultan/Danna International: Transgender Pop and the Polysemiotics of Sex, Nation, and Ethnicity on the Israeli–Egyptian Border'.

15. Al-Tūnisī (1961), *al-Khaṭar al-Yahūdī*, p. 85. This is most likely a mistaken reference to the chapter on Khālid b. Yazid in the *Kitāb al-Bukhalāʾ*. The *Ḥiyal al-Luṣūṣ* (The Tricks of Thieves) is considered lost. See Pellat, 'al-Djāḥiẓ', in *Encyclopedia of Islam, Second Edition*.

16. Al-Tūnisī (1961), *al-Khaṭar al-Yahūdī*, p. 89.

17. Al-Zuʿbī (1972), *al-Māsūniyya fī al-ʿArāʾ*, p. 7. Cf. 'al-Maqāma al-Būʿiziyya', pp. 227–45.

18. Writing on European and American missionary (mis)readings of local trickster types as Satan, Lewis Hyde (1998) suggests that 'the erasure of trickster figures, or the unthinking confusion of them with the Devil, only serves to push the ambiguities of life into the background', *Trickster Makes this World: Mischief, Myth, and Art*, p. 10.

19. Collins, 'Introduction: Towards the Morphology of a Genre', *Apocalypse: The Morphology of a Genre*, pp. 1–19; emphasis in the original.

20. Cook (2005), *Contemporary Muslim Apocalyptic Literature*, pp. 15–35; Filiu (2011), *Apocalypse in Islam*, pp. xxii–xiv, xx, 85–95 and *passim*.

21. Stewart (1999), 'Conspiracy Theory's Worlds', p. 14; capitalisation in the original.

22. Freud (1996 [1911]), 'Psychoanalytic Notes upon an Autobiographical Account of a Case of Paranoia (*Dementia Paranoides*)', *Three Case Histories*, p. 154.

23. These structural similarities between paranoia and psychoanalysis have been perhaps most forcefully argued for by Farrell (1998), *Freud's Paranoid Quest: Psychoanalysis and Modern Suspicion*. See also Melley (2000), *Empire of Conspiracy: The Culture of Paranoia in Postwar America*, pp. 23–5.

24. Jameson (1991), *Postmodernism*, p. 37.

25. See, for example, Eco (1992), 'Overinterpreting Texts', *Interpretation and Overinterpretation*, p. 48.

26. Felski (2015), *The Limits of Critique*; Sedgwick (2003), 'Paranoid Reading and Reparative Reading, Or, You're So Paranoid, You Probably Think this Essay is About You', *Touching Feeling: Affect, Pedagogy, Performativity*.

27. Latour, *Reassembling the Social: An Introduction to Actor-Network-Theory*, p. 45. See especially Chapter 2 for Latour's full argument about what constitutes an 'actor' in his Actor-Network-Theory.

28. Namely, 'Gamal' (Abdel Nasser) and 'Naguib' (Mahfouz/Surur) in Naguib Surur's *Kuss-ummiyyāt* (see Chapter 2), the father–son pair 'al-Namarsī' in Gamal al-Ghitani's *Ḥikāyāt al-Khabiʾ* (Chapter 4), and Naʿim/Naʿim in Mohammad Rabie's *ʿĀm al-Tinnīn* (Chapter 5). See also n53 below.

29. For a discussion of the concept of 'gossip literature' (*adab al-namīma*) as proposed by Fārūq ʿAbd al-Qādir, see Chapter 4 of the present monograph.

30. Hofstatder (1996), 'The Paranoid Style', p. 36.

31. See Chapter 3, Part I of Said (1994), *Orientalism*.

32. Felski (2015), *The Limits of Critique*, pp. 40–51.

33. al-Ḥakīm (1995 [1955]), *Īzīs, Tawfīq al-Ḥakīm: al-Muʾallafāt al-Kāmila*, pp. 875–6.

34. For an important study of how 'conspiracy theory' has emerged within the last half-century as an object of discourse, analysis, and panic in the United States, see Bratich (2008), *Conspiracy Panics: Political Rationality and Popular Culture*.

35. Mahfouz (2008), *Karnak Café*, p. 24.

36. Rabie (2012), *ʿĀm al-Tinnīn*, p. 111.

37. An important work that seeks to address the critical dearth on comparative studies in conspiracy theories is Butter et al. (2014), *Conspiracy Theories in the Middle East and the United States: A Comparative Approach*.

38. Fenster (2012), 'Foreword', *Conspiracy Theory in Latin Literature*, p. ix.

39. Freud, 'Psychoanalytic Notes'.

40. Melley (2000), *Empire of Conspiracy: The Culture of Paranoia in Postwar America*.

41. Fenster (2008), *Conspiracy Theories: Secrecy and Power in American Culture*, p. 103.

42. Sedgwick, 'Paranoid Reading', p. 144.

43. Sedgwick, 'Paranoid Reading', p. 128; emphasis in the original. Stewart (1999) strikes a similar note when she says of conspiracy theory: 'Think of it not as a prefabricated ideology (as if abstract, exegetical ideas were what ruled the world) but as a practice. An obsessive and skeptical practice of scanning and speculating

from the realm of the concrete, undeniable, tangible detail to the realm of the final word, the system that makes sense of inchoate sensibilities and moments of strange convergence. It's a practice born of a world that cries out for interpretation' ('Conspiracy Theory's Worlds', p. 16).

44. Felski (2015), *The Limits of Critique*, p. 20.

45. For this critique of Hofstadter, see: Anderson (1996), 'Conspiracy Theories, Premature Entextualization, and Popular Political Analysis', p. 96; Fenster (2008), *Conspiracy Theories*, pp. 31–42; Melley (2000), *Empire of Conspiracy*, p. 13.

46. Hofstadter (1996), 'The Paranoid Style', p. 4; emphasis added.

47. The most egregious offender in this arena is surely Daniel Pipes (1996), *The Hidden Hand: Middle East Fears of Conspiracy*, a work whose polemical and partisan nature is belied by the neo-conservatism of its author, that is, a political movement committed to carrying out some of the very conspiracies that the work would so perversely enjoy denying. On the perversity of such a position, see Chapter 3 for our discussion of Sonallah Ibrahim's *al-Lajna*, particularly as regards the Committee members' delight in repeating/denying conspiracy theories.

48. Abū ʿUthmān (2013), 'The Art of Keeping Silent', *Sobriety and Mirth: A Selection of the Shorter Writings of al-Jāhiz*, p. 130.

49. On al-Jāhiz's writings on *al-nābita*, see al-Qādī (1993), 'The Earliest "Nābita" and the Paradigmatic "Nawābit"', *Studia Islamica*, pp. 27–66. Although al-Qādī exculpates al-Jāhiz from the charge of 'paranoia' (p. 51), she presents a close reading of his polemics that is highly attentive to the Basrite's affects: 'SURPRISE' (p. 43), 'CONTEMPT' (p. 45), 'ANGER' (p. 47), 'FEAR' (p. 48). Based on al-Qādī's description, al-Jāhiz's polemics would appear to us to be, if not 'paranoid' in Hofstadter's sense, then certainly 'paranoid' in the looser sense suggested by Sedgwick. The fear al-Jāhiz expresses about *al-nābita*'s infiltration of elite circles, as well as its nefarious influence over the masses, has a more extreme analogy in medieval heresiographical tracts along the lines of Muhammad b. Mālik al-Hammādī's *Kashf Asrar al-Bātiniyya wa-Asrār al-Qarāmita*, an eleventh-century exposé on the secret society of the Qarmatians, written by an undercover researcher who had penetrated their ranks.

50. See Irwin, 'An Orientalist Mythology of Secret Societies', *Orientalism and Conspiracy: Politics and Conspiracy Theory in the Islamic World*, pp. 71–86.

51. ʿInān's key works in this genre are *Tārīkh al-Jamʿiyyāt al-Sirriyya wa-al-Harakāt al-Haddāma* (1926), *Tārīkh al-Muʾāmarāt al-Siyāsiyya* (1928), and *al-Hākim*

bi-Amr Allāh wa-Asrār al-Daʿwa al-Fāṭimiyya (1937). ʿInān may also have been one of the first authors to use the expression *naẓariyyat al-muʾāmara*, although the context suggests less 'conspiracy theory' than a specific 'theory of conspiracy' in the dramatic disappearance of al-Ḥākim bi-Amr Allāh: 'Hal Qutil al-Ḥākim bi-Amr Allāh am Ikhtafā?' (1937), p. 128.

52. See especially *Ma Hunālik* (1896), Ibrāhīm al-Muwayliḥī's illuminating account of the Ottoman/Egyptian security services in the late nineteenth century: 'For twenty years, these spies have been actively submitting their reports and taking up the Sultan's precious time, yet we have never heard of them uncovering a single conspiracy (*muʾāmara*), exposing a corrupt gang (*ʿaṣaba*), or revealing an evil society (*jamʿiyya*). For [all their reports] are lies piled upon lies, slander upon slander' (p. 146). The translation here is my own, although the entire work has been translated by Roger Allen as *Spies, Scandals, and Sultans: Istanbul in the Twilight of the Ottoman Empire* (2008).

53. It is unfortunate that we should leave out an extended discussion of the 'micro-novels' of Saʿd al-Khādim (1932–2003), such as *Min Riḥlat Ūdīsiyūs al-Miṣrī* (1979), which features a paranoid or schizophrenic protagonist as well as criticisms of the Egyptian regime's rule by conspiracism. As the literature of conspiracy abounds with uncanny doubles and doppelgangers, it is worth pointing out that the aforementioned author should not be confused with a different Saʿd al-Khādim (1913–87), who was a pioneering painter and author of such conspiracist (and ostensibly non-fiction) works as *al-Muʾāmarat al-Istiʿmāriyya ʿalā Turāthina al-Fannī* (Colonialist Conspiracies against our Artistic Heritage) (1966) and *al-Fann wa-l-Istiʿmār al-Ṣahyūnī* (Art and Zionist Colonialism) (1974). Space has also left us no choice but to omit a discussion of the brilliant and bizarre 'novels' of the outsider artist Muḥammad Rabīʿ (1975–2008), not to be confused with the Muḥammad Rabīʿ (b. 1978) we shall discuss in Chapter 5. See especially his *ʿUmūm al-Layālī al-Latī* (2000) and *Muʾāmara ʿalā al-Sayyida Ṣunʿ Allāh* (2002).

Notes to Chapter 1

1. Kāmil (1953), *Maḥkamat al-Thawra*, vol. 1, p. 10.
2. Abū al-Fath (1991), *Gamāl ʿAbd al-Nāṣir*, p. 143. The Free Officers also referred to themselves as a 'movement'.
3. Abū al-Fath (1991), *Gamāl ʿAbd al-Nāṣir*, pp. 141–5; al-Aswānī, 'Qaḍiyyat Raʾfat Shalabī: Awwal Ḍaḥiyya li-Qānūn Taḥdīd al-Milkiyya'.
4. The transcript for Sadat's address is available in numerous online sources. See,

for example, 'Thawrat 23 Yūlyū', *al-Maʿrifa*, available at <www.marefa.org/index.php/ثورة_23_يوليو>, last accessed 6 October 2016. For the audio, see Amānī Rajab, 'Bi-l-Fidiyū: Taʿarraf ʿalā Qiṣṣat Bayān "Thawrat 23 Yulyū"', *al-Dustūr*, 23 July 2016, available at <www.dostor.org/1127816>, last accessed 6 October 2016.

5. 'Idhāʿa Hāmma li-l-Liwāʾ Muḥammad Najīb Bīk', *al-Akhbār*, 25 July 1952.

6. Kāmil, *Maḥkamat al-Thawra*, pp. 20–45.

7. Ibid., p. 23.

8. '200 Alf Miṣrī Yaḥtashidūn fī Mīdān al-Jumhūriyya', *al-Ahrām*, 16 September 1953.

9. On the fragility, squabbles, and infighting that characterized the July regime from its inception, see Gordon (1992), *Nasser's Blessed Movement: Egypt's Free Officers and the July Revolution*, pp. 12–13, 79–80, *passim*, and Kandil (2012), *Soldiers, Spies, and Statesmen: Egypt's Road to Revolt*, especially Chapters 1 and 2.

10. Kāmil, *Maḥkamat al-Thawra*, pp. 46–7, 369–73.

11. On these courts and their political and historical context, see Brown, *The Rule of Law in the Arab World: Courts in Egypt and the Gulf* (1997), pp. 76–83, and Gordon, *Nasser's Blessed Movement*, Chapter 3.

12. For an account of the 'running drama' of these radio performances, see Litvin (2011), *Hamlet's Arab Journey: Shakespeare's Prince and Nasser's Ghost*, p. 38.

13. Kīra (ed.) (1953–4), *Muḥākamāt al-Thawra: al-Maḍbaṭa al-Rasmiyya li-Maḥāḍir Jalasāt Maḥkamat al-Thawra*.

14. Kira (ed.), *Muḥākamāt al-Thawra*, p. 8.

15. Kamil, *Maḥkamat al-Thawra*, p. 53.

16. See Evens (2009), 'Rumor, the Breath of Kings, and the Body of Law in *2 Henry IV*', pp. 1–24; Gross (1994), 'The Rumor of Hamlet', pp. 43–66; Neubauer (1999), *The Rumour: A Cultural History*, pp. 74–9, *passim*.

17. Kira (ed.), *Muḥākamāt al-Thawra*, pp. 331–83.

18. Litvin (2011), *Hamlet's Arab Journey*.

19. This notion of cultural or stylistic 'homologies' has too rich an intellectual history to explore in depth here, but two of the more pedagogical expositions remain: Hebdige (2007), *Subculture: The Meaning of Style*, Chapter 9, and Willis (2014), *Profane Culture*.

20. On the question of 'effects' and its difficulties for the study of mass media, particularly in Egypt, see Abu-Lughod (2005), *Dramas of Nationhood: The Politics of Television in Egypt*, p. 26.

21. Ihsan Abdel Quddous, *al-Jamʿiyya al-Sirriyya allatī Taḥkum Miṣr'*, *Rūz al-Yūsuf*, 22 March 1954.

22. Besides the works discussed in this chapter, notable plays that dealt with conspiracy include several by Tawfiq al-Hakim (*Īzīs*, 1955; *Maṣīr Ṣurṣār*, 1965; *Bank al-Qalaq*, 1967), Mīkhāʾīl Rūmān (*al-Wāfid*, 1965; *al-Khiṭāb*, 1965), and ʿAlī Sālim (*il-Nās illī fī il-Sama il-Tāmina*, 1963). Reviews of these plays can be found in Badawi (1987), *Modern Arabic Drama in Egypt*.

23. The letter is reproduced in Salāma (2013), *al-Khurūj ʿan al-Naṣṣ fī ʿAlāqat Bākathīr wa-l-Masraḥ al-Miṣrī*, pp. 135–6.

24. Cited in Salama, *al-Khurūj ʿan al-Naṣṣ*, p. 136.

25. On these rumours and others, see Sadat (1953), 'Ṣafaḥāt Majhūla min Kitāb al-Thawra'. In addition, many of the Free Officers themselves had been members of the Muslim Brotherhood: Kandil, *Soldiers, Spies, and Statesmen*, pp. 36–8.

26. Bakathir (1988), *Ilāh Isrāʾīl*.

27. See, for example, *Shaylūk al-Jadīd* (1945), *Imbarāṭūriyya fī al-Mazād* (1953), and *Shaʿb Allāh al-Mukhtātar* (1955).

28. The play was published in four parts on the website *Rābiṭat Udabāʾ al-Shām* (odabasham.net), beginning in August 2006. Retrieved from: <web.archive. org/web/20071012120815/http://odabasham.net/show.php?sid=7537>, <web. archive.org/web/20071012120820/http://odabasham.net/show.php?sid= 7593>, <web.archive.org/web/20071012120825/http://odabasham.net/show. php?sid=7648>, and <web.archive.org/web/20071012120831/http://odabash am.net/show.php?sid=7715>.

29. For a review of this novel, see Mehrez, *Egypt's Culture Wars*, Chapter 3.

30. Bakathir (1979), *Ḥabl al-Ghasīl*, p. 92.

31. Ibid., p. 96.

32. Salama (2013), *al-Khurūj ʿan al-Naṣṣ*, p. 37, *passim*.

33. Abdel Nasser's remarks are paraphrased by author Fatḥī Ghānim, then a member of the review committee of the Modern Theater (*al-masraḥ al-ḥadīth*), in his negative reader report on Bakathir's play. The report is reproduced in Salāma, *al-Khurūj ʿan al-Naṣṣ*, pp. 146–7. Cf. Abdel Nasser's remarks on 'a reactionary party' (*ḥizb rajʿī*) in 'Munāqashat Jamāl ʿAbd al-Nāṣir maʿa Aʿḍāʾ al-Lajna al-Tanfīdhiyya wa-l-Amāna al-ʿĀmma ḥawla Khiṭṭat al-ʿAmal al-Jadīda li-l-Tanẓīm al-Siyāsī', p. 25.

34. Salāma (2013), *al-Khurūj ʿan al-Naṣṣ*, p. 11.

35. Ibid.

36. See the reader report by Fatḥī Ghānim, reproduced in Salāma (2013), *al-Khurūj*

ᶜan al-Naṣṣ, pp. 146–7, and the review by Maḥmūd Amīn al-ᶜĀlam, 'Mādhā Yuqaddimuhu Bākathīr ᶜalā "Ḥabl al-Ghasīl"', *al-Muṣawwir*, 20 August 1965, reproduced in Salāma, *al-Khurūj ᶜan al-Naṣṣ*, pp. 157–63.

37. For readings along these lines, see Badawi (1987), *Modern Arabic Drama in Egypt*, pp. 161–3; Cohen-Mor (1992), *Yusuf Idris: Changing Visions*, p. 116; Clarissa Burt (2001), 'The Tears of a Clown: Yusuf Idris and Postrevolutionary Egyptian Theater', *Colors of Enchantment: Dance, Music, and the Visual Arts of the Middle East*, pp. 62–7; Muḥammad (1994), *al-Masraḥ wa-l-Sulṭa fī Miṣr min 1952 ilā 1970*, pp. 164–72.

38. On Nasser's invocation of Pirandello's play, see Litvin (2011), *Hamlet's Arab Journey*, pp. 62–3.

39. On these various applications of *takhṭīṭ*, see, for example: ᶜAbd al-ᶜAzīz Muḥammad al-Zakī, 'Ḥawla al-Takhṭīṭ al-Ishtirākī li-l-Thaqāfa', *al-Majalla*, 103, 1 July 1965, pp. 31–5; Khayrī Ḥamad, 'al-Takhṭīṭ: Ṭarīq al-Insān al-ᶜArabī fī Ṣināᶜat Tārīkhihi, *al-Thaqāfa*, 50, 30 June 1964, pp. 8–11; Ibrāhīm ᶜIṣmat Mutāwiᶜ, 'al-Takhṭīṭ fī Ẓill al-Ishtirākiyya', *al-Thaqāfa*, 99, 10 June 1965, pp. 24–6; Farīd al-Mizāwī, 'Ishtirākiyyatunā wa-l-Takhṭīṭ al-Khulqī li-l-Aflām', *al-Thaqāfa*, 100, 17 June 1965, pp. 42–6; Surur (1957), 'Takhṭīṭat fī al-Masraḥ al-Miṣrī', *al-Ādāb*, pp. ẓ–m.

40. Meijer (2002), *The Quest for Modernity: Secular Liberal and Left-Wing Political Thought in Egypt, 1945–1958*, p. 7.

41. Meijer, *The Quest for Modernity*, pp. 176–85.

42. Mitchell (2002), *Rule of Experts: Egypt, Techno-Politics, Modernity*.

43. See Shams El Din, 'A Year of Conspiracies', *Mada Masr*, 27 December 2015, available at <www.madamasr.com/sections/politics/year-conspiracies>, last accessed 1 October 2016.

44. On an alleged meeting between Ṣalāḥ Naṣr, head of the Egyptian General Intelligence Directorate from 1957 to 1967, and the astrologer Ḥasan al-Shīmī ('al-ᶜAbqarī al-Falakī'), see Khūrshīd (1988), *Shāhida ᶜalā Inḥirāfāt Ṣalāḥ Naṣr*, pp. 34–6. More recently, the oneiromantic enthusiasms of President ᶜAbd al-Fattāḥ al-Sīsī have been met with much mockery: 'Leaked Sisi Audio Stirs Sarcasm', *Mada Masr*, 12 December 2013, available at <www.madamasr.com/news/leaked-sisi-audio-stirs-sarcasm>, last accessed 1 October 2016.

45. The portions of the play that are discussed here are reproduced in al-Tuhāmī (1997), 'Shillat Yūsuf Idrīs', pp. 86–9. The title *Shillat al-Ghad* was mentioned by Idris in an interview with Rashād Kāmil, 'Iᶜtirāfāt Muthīra fī al-Ghurfa Raqam 619', *Ṣabāḥ al-Khayr*, 16 July 1981.

46. This is the opinion of the text's editor, al-Tuhāmi (1997), 'Shillat Yūsuf Idrīs', p. 89.

47. Yūsuf Idrīs, 'Naḥw Masraḥ Miṣrī', *al-Kātib*, 34, January 1964, pp. 67–79; 'Naḥw Masraḥ Miṣrī (2): Radd ᶜalā al-Mustawribīn wa Bidāyat al-Taᶜarruf ᶜalā Malāmiḥinā', *al-Kātib*, 35, February 1964, pp. 109–20; and 'Naḥw Masraḥ Miṣrī (3)', *al-Kātib*, 36, March 1964, pp. 86–97.

48. For a discussion of Idris's theories and their reception, see Badawi (1987), *Modern Arabic Drama in Egypt*, pp. 156–7.

Notes to Chapter 2

1. Surur (1956), 'al-Ḥidhāʾ', p. 25.

2. The most notable of these include his trilogy, *Yāsīn wa-Bahiyya* (1965), *Āh yā Layl yā Qamar* (1968), and *Qūlū li-ᶜAyn al-Shams* (1976).

3. See, for example, Rajāʾ al-Naqqāsh, 'Iḥdharū Hādhā al-Adab al-Badhīʾ', *al-Ahrām*, 22 April 2007.

4. The observation is that of journalist Aḥmad al-Gammāl ('Taksīr al-Qulal', *al-Ahrām*, 9 October 2014), who even cites some of the verses himself on the pages of the flagship state-owned newspaper *al-Ahrām*.

5. Surur's remarks may be found in an endnote to the version of the *Kuss-ummiyyāt* edited by his son Shuhdī (*malḥūẓa* 1). See below for a discussion of this and other versions of the poems. For the opinions of al-Naqqāsh and Kazem, see al-Naqqāsh (2007), 'Iḥdharū Hādhā al-Adab al-Badhīʾ', and Ṭalāl Fayṣal, 'Ummiyyāt Nagīb Surūr: al-Istithnāʾ alladhī Yuʾakkid al-Qāᶜida', *Akhbār al-Adab*, 21 April 2012.

6. The most notable attempt to sanitise Surur occurred with the publication of his 'complete works' by the state-sponsored General Egyptian Book Organization (GEBO) in the 1990s. See Surur, *al-Aᶜmāl al-Kāmila*, ed. ᶜIṣām al-Dīn Abū al-ʿUlā (1993–7).

7. Al-Naqqāsh, 'Iḥdharū Hādhā al-Adab al-Badhīʾ', and Fārūq ᶜAbd al-Qādir, '*Minēn Agīb Nās*?! Wa-Darāwīsh Nagīb Surūr', pp. 100–17.

8. This view is represented by a number of voices in Ṭalāl Fayṣal's ficto-historical novel, *Surūr* (2013). See especially p. 351, where the *Kuss-ummiyyāt* are imagined as having been peformed simply in jest among a gathering of Cairo's cultural stars.

9. See the bibliography of Surur's works in Surur (2006), *Luzūm mā Yalzam*, p. 160 (*al-Ummiyyāt*).

10. This information is based on the testimony of Surur's fellow student Abū Bakr

Yūsuf, 'Nagīb Surūr: Ma²sāt al-ᶜAql', *Jamaliya*, 21 October 2006, available at <www.jamaliya.com/ShowPage.php?id=398>, last accessed 25 September 2016. Citations here refer to the version reproduced in Khayrī (2009), *Dūn Kīkhūtih al-Miṣrī: Dirāsa ᶜIlmiyya Wathāᵓiqiyya li-Ḥayāt wa-Fikr Nagīb Surūr*, pp. 207–22.

11. Ibid., p. 216.

12. Rajāᵓ al-Naqqāsh, 'Ma²sāt Fannān Miṣrī fī Būdābist', *al-Jumhūriyya*, 5 July 1964. References here are to the version reproduced in Khayrī, *Dūn Kīkhūtih al-Miṣrī*, pp. 223–6.

13. Ibid., 224–5.

14. See Chapter 4 of the present monograph.

15. Al-Naqqāsh (1964), 'Ma²sāt Fannān Miṣrī fī Būdābist', pp. 223–4.

16. Yūsuf, 'Najīb Surūr: Ma²sat al-ᶜAql', p. 216. Article republished in the book Ḥāzim Khayrī, *Dūn Kīkhūtih al-Miṣrī: Dirāsa ᶜIlmiyya Wathāᵓiqiyya li-Ḥayāt wa-Fikr Nagīb Surūr* (Cairo: al-Majlis al-Aᶜlā li-l-Thaqāfa, 2009).

17. Al-Naqqāsh (1964), 'Ma²sāt Fannān Miṣrī fī Būdābist', p. 226.

18. 'Taᶜallamtu fī Mūskū', *al-Jīl*, 14 August 1964. Republished in Khayrī (2009), *Dūn Kīkhūtih al-Miṣrī*, pp. 227–35.

19. 'Najīb Surūr Yaqūl: Lā Urīd an Amūt "Karwata"', *al-Jumhūriyya*, 16 December 1965. Republished in Khayrī (2009), *Dūn Kīkhūtih al-Miṣrī*, pp. 237–8.

20. 'Risāla min Fannān Ḥāᵓir', *al-Kawākib*, 10 December 1968. Republished in Khayrī (2009), *Dūn Kīkhūtih al-Miṣrī*, pp. 241–2.

21. Khayrī (2009), *Dūn Kīkhūtih al-Miṣrī*, p. 290. Two endnotes to the *Kussummiyāt* specify that the poet spent '6 months' in al-ᶜAbbāsiyya in '1969' (S1· line 192, *hāmish* 13 and line 437, *hāmish* 23). See below for a description of the manuscripts and numbering of lines.

22. Naguib Surur, 'Risāla ilā Yūsuf Idrīs', *Adab wa-Naqd*, 34, December 1987, pp 117–30. Reprinted in Khayrī, *Dūn Kīkhūtih al-Miṣrī*, pp. 257–72.

23. Surur does not specify who.

24. Naguib Surur, 'Risāla ilā Yūsuf Idrīs', in Khayrī (2009), *Dūn Kīkhūtih al-Miṣrī*, p. 266.

25. Ibid., pp. 267–8.

26. See the following section of this chapter for more on the relationship between Surur and al-Maᶜarrī. On the epithet 'my imam', see Dhikrī (2013), *Shiᶜr Najīb Surūr: al-Turāth wa-l-Wāqiᶜ wa-ᵓĀfāq al-Maᶜnā*, p. 92.

27. Ḥijāzī (1970), 'Anqidhū Najīb Surūr'. Curiously, Ṭalāl Fayṣal's ficto-historical novel, *Surūr* (2013), gives the incorrect date of 20 January 1969 (p. 150),

perhaps to suggest that Ḥijāzī's intervention had something to do with Surur's abduction.

28. See, for example, Fayṣal (2012), '*Ummiyyāt* Najīb Surūr'.

29. Fahīm (2006), '‘An Najīb Surūr: Lam Yamut Baṭalan, wa-lākin Māt Baḥthan ‘an al-Buṭūla!', *Luzūm mā Yalzam*, p. 23.

30. In his letter to Yusuf Idris, Surur also mentions a third hospital, Bahmān ('Risāla ilā Yūsuf Idrīs', p. 270), although this is the only reference to this institution that we have encountered in his or other accounts.

31. Jubayr (2006), 'Risāla ilā al-Jīl al-Jadīd', *Brūtūkūlāt Hukamāʾ Rīsh*, p. 9.

32. Shuhdī Surūr's website, wadada.net, is no longer available. The poems were previously accessible at <www.wadada.net/surur/ummiyyat/ummiyyat.doc>; at the time of writing, they may be accessed via the Internet Archive's 'Way Back Machine': <web.archive.org/web/20060115115336/http://www.wadada. net/surur/ummiyyat/ummiyyat.doc>, last accessed 30 July 2016. A copy of Shuhdī Surūr's document can also be accessed at the online encyclopedia *al-Maʿrifa*: <http://www.marefa.org/sources/index.php/نجيب_سرور_-_لكسميات>, last accessed 30 July 2016.

33. Recording S2, which covers only portions of the *Kuss-ummiyyāt*, was made available in seven parts by Shuhdī Surūr on his now defunct website, wadada. net: <www.wadada.net/surur/ummiyyat/01_menen_agib_nas.mp3>, <www. wadada.net/surur/ummiyyat/02_tab_3leia_eltalaq.mp3>, <www.wadada.net/ surur/ummiyyat/03_ayuha_elwaqifun.mp3>, <www.wadada.net/surur/umm iyyat/11_wasiet_shohdy.mp3>, <www.wadada.net/surur/ummiyyat/12_akh osh_bet_eladab.mp3>, <www.wadada.net/surur/ummiyyat/13_beram_duf3h. mp3>, and <www.wadada.net/surur/ummiyyat/14_iqra2_yasheikh_quffaa. mp3>. Compilations of these files may be found at numerous online locations, such as <soundcloud.com/ahmed-hossam-17/53mqcwqohlbf>, last accessed 30 July 2016, and <www.youtube.com/watch?v=nsrt6r4O2_A>, last accessed 30 July 2016. Recording S3 differs considerably from S1 and S2, and although the voice is distorted, we are of the opinion that the reciter is indeed Naguib Surur. We have been unable to determine the source, although a digital version is available online in five parts at <soundcloud.com/oq9hbco90wnz/5-1a>, <soundcloud.com/oq9hbco90wnz/2-5a>, <soundcloud.com/oq9hbco90wnz/3-5a>, <soundcloud.com/oq9hbco90wnz/4-5a>, and <soundcloud.com/oq9hbco 90wnz/5-5a>, last accessed 30 July 2016.

34. Line numbers have been assigned in order to facilitate reading, although they do not occur in the original document (S1).

35. 'The Door-Knocker', literally 'the guy who knocked on the door' (*illī ʾaraʿ l-bāb*), is a pun on the name of Pharaoh Menkaura (*manqaraʿ*).
36. Larkin (1992), 'A Brigand Hero of Egyptian Colloquial Literature', p. 59.
37. Cachia (2000), 'Folk Themes in the Works of Najīb Surūr', p. 204 n21.
38. See Cachia (1977), pp. 91–2.
39. Cachia, 'Folk Themes', p. 196.
40. See especially lines 11–16 of the *mawwāl* of Adham al-Sharqāwī (Larkin 1992: 60), and line 491 of the *Kuss-ummiyyāt*.
41. Stetkevych (1989), 'Arabic Hermeneutical Terminology: Paradox and the Production of Meaning', p. 82.
42. Stetkevych, 'Intoxication and Immortality: Wine and Associated Imagery in al-Maʿarri's Garden', *Critical Pilgrimages: Studies in the Arabic Literary Tradition*, pp. 38–43.
43. Surur's invective against *nēk* and *niyāka* has eerie similarities with the memoirs of Freud's famous 'paranoiac', Dr Daniel Paul Schreber, who explains his use of these same profanities in the following way: 'The expression "*outward* f…g contrary to the Order of the World," refers to my observations that the taking up of putrid matter by pure rays is connected with a kind of voluptuous sensation for them. The choice of the word "f…g" is not due to my liking for vulgar terms, but having had to listen to the words "f…k" and "f…g" thousands of times, I have used the term for short in this little note to indicate the behavior of rays which was contrary to the Order of the World' (Schreber (2000), *Memoirs*, p. 175; emphasis in original).
44. See in particular the three novels discussed in Chapter 5, where these profanities constitute a central element in the anti-conspiracy lament.
45. This latter word is a pun on the words *mumaththila* ('actress') (pronounced *mumassila* in Egyptian Colloquial Arabic) and *mūmis* ('prostitute').
46. Surur (1987), 'Risāla ilā Yūsuf Idrīs', p. 263.
47. Republished in 2007 by Dār al-Shurūq.
48. Fārūq ʿAbd al-Qādir criticized Surur, and dismissed the entirety of his literary work, in part for what he perceived as the latter's inability to move beyond the critical concepts of power and hegemony developed in the days of feudalism and colonialism. See ʿAbd al-Qādir, '*Minēn Agīb Nās*?! Wa-Darāwīsh Najīb Surūr', p. 104, *passim*.
49. Collins, 'Introduction: Towards the Morphology of a Genre', pp. 6–7.
50. Surur (1977), 'ʿAlāmat Istifhām Ḥāʾira ḥawl Mawt Sayyid Darwīsh', *Hākadhā Qāl Juḥā*, pp. 70–6.

51. Surur (1977), 'Thaqāfat al-Saḥ al-Daḥ Imbū', *Hākadhā Qāl Juḥā*, p. 100.

52. Ibid., p. 108.

53. Ibid., p. 106.

54. '"The telluric serprent simply stands for the occult serpent Kundalini. The goddess reposes, coiled, and sleeps her eternal sleep. Like a vortex or a whirlpool, like the first half of the syllable om."

    "But what secret does the serpent refer to?"

    "To the telluric currents."

    "What are the telluric currents?"

    "A great cosmological metaphor, which refers to the serprent."' (Umberto Eco, *Foucault's Pendulum*, p. 448).

55. See, for example, the endnotes to lines 246, 515, and 527, which have been marked in Shuhdi's Surur's (S1) edition as *malḥūẓa* 1, *hāmish* 34, and *hāmish* 35, respectively.

56. Surur (2008), *Taḥt ʿAbāʾ at Abī al-ʿAlāʾ*.

57. Ibid., pp. 161–9, *passim*.

58. El-Shamy (1982), 'Belief Characters as Anthropomorphic Psychosocial Realities: The Egyptian Case', pp. 7–36.

59. See, for example, the argument made by Sonallah Ibrahim in defence of his use of obscene imagery in 'ʿAlā Sabīl al-Taqdīm' (2003 [1986]), p. 16.

60. See, for example, 'Risāla ilā Yūsuf Idrīs', p. 265, and *Taḥt ʿAbāʾ at Abī al-ʿAlāʾ*, pp. 124–5.

61. The poet performs a pun on the expression *ḥālat gīm* ('State G'), used to announce an emergency – hence our translation 'E for emergency'. The second pun conflates *shīʿī* ('Shiite') with *shuyūʿī* ('communist').

62. The process of top-down conspiracist 'suggestion' occurs also in the case of Sonallah Ibrahim's protagonist in *al-Lajna*, discussed in Chapter 3. Compare also with the plight of Amgad Ṣalāḥ in Youssef Rakha's *Kitab al-Ṭughrā* – discussed in Chapter 5 – whose conspiracist fantasies undergo a process of 'canonisation' under the duress of the mental asylum.

63. The letter is one of two published in Khayrī (2009), *Dūn Kīkhūtih al-Miṣrī*, pp. 165–72.

64. Muḥammad Khalīfa al-Tūnisī, 'al-Khaṭar al-Yahūdī: Brūtūkūlāt Shuyūkh Ṣihyūn al-ʿUlamāʾ', p. 1,654, and subsequent issues.

65. The play is not listed in the quite comprehensive bibliography of Surur's works compiled in Khayrī (2009), *Dūn Kīkhūtih al-Miṣrī*, pp. 281–2. However, Surur is cited as its director on the website of Ali Ahmad Bakathir operated by ʿAbd

al-Ḥakīm al-Zabīdī, <www.bakatheer.com/a3mal_details.php?id=149>, last accessed 1 October 2016.

66. Schreber (2000), *Memoirs*, p. 100.

67. Ibid. In an article on the novelistic work of Thomas Pychon, Leo Bersoni (1989) also remarks on the the prevalence of 'doubles' in paranoid fiction, which he views in part as a function of the paranoiac's obsession with seeking out 'other orders behind the visible' ('Pynchon, Paranoia, and Literature', pp. 105–9). We may also note a strange resonance with the practice of 'subsitute king' in ancient Mesopotamia. See Bottéro (1992), *Mesopotamia: Writing, Reasoning, and the Gods*, Chapter 9.

Notes to Chapter 3

1. Estimates on the number of dead vary. According to Human Rights Watch, 'at least 817 and likely more than 1,000' were killed. See 'All According to Plan: The Rab'a Massacre and Mass Killings of Protestors in Egypt', *Human Rights Watch*, 12 August 2014, available at <www.hrw.org/report/2014/08/12/all-according-plan/raba-massacre-and-mass-killings-protesters-egypt>, last accessed 1 October 2016.

2. Aḥmad Manṣūr and Sonallah Ibrahim, 'al-Riwāʾī al-Kabīr Ṣunᶜ Allāh Ibrāhīm fī Ḥiwār li-l-*Yawm al-Sābiᶜ*', *al-Yawm al-Sābiᶜ*, 24 August 2013, available at <www.youm7.com/story/2013/8/24/الروائي-الكبير-صنع-الله-إبراهيم-في-حوال-ـلـ-«»اليوم-السابع»->, last accessed 1 October 2016. See also Starkey (2016), *Sonallah Ibrahim: Rebel with a Pen*, pp. 30–1, 215–16.

3. See Chip Rossetti, '"Baffling and Disappointing"; On the "Authoritarian Turn" of the Egyptian Intelligentsia', available at <arablit.org/2014/09/12/baffling-and-disappointing-on-the-authoritarian-turn-of-the-egyptian-intelligentsia>.

4. See, for example, Ursula Lindsey, 'Et Tu Sonallah?' (arabist.net/blog/2013/8/25/et-tu-sonallah); Marcia Lynx Qualey, '… and Sonallah Ibrahim?' (arablit.org/2013/08/27/and-sonallah-ibrahim); Marcia Lynx Qualey, 'Re-reading Sonallah Ibrahim' (arablit.org/2014/01/12/re-reading-sonallah-ibrahim); Elliott Colla, 'Revolution on Ice' (www.jadaliyya.com/pages/index/15874/revolution-on-ice); and Ahmed El Shamsy, 'Sisi, Nasser, and the Great Egyptian Novel' (muftah.org/sisi-nasser-the-great-egyptian-novel/#.V1x33jWHhD5).

5. All translations in the present chapter are drawn from Constable and St Germain (trans) (2001), *The Committee: A Novel*, except where otherwise indicated. References to the Arabic text are based on the edition published by Dār al-Mustaqbal al-ᶜArabī in 1997.

6. Constable and St. Germain (trans) (2001), *The Committee*, p. 156. Cf. p. 120 in the Arabic edition.

7. See below for our discussion of Felski (2015), *The Limits of Critique*.

8. al-Musawi (2007), 'Engaging Globalization in Modern Arabic Literature', pp. 320–1. For other readings of *al-Lajna* as political critique, see Radwan (2008), 'A Place for Fiction in the Historical Archive', *Critique: Critical Middle Eastern Studies*, pp. 79–95; and Stone (2010), 'Georg Lukács and the Improbable Realism of Ṣunᶜ Allah Ibrāhīm's *The Committee*', pp. 136–47.

9. The Arabic has *al-barīʾat al-maẓhar* ('seemingly innocent'), p. 23. Constable and St Germain have rendered this as 'slender', which does not sufficiently capture the protagonist's accusatory tone.

10. The Arabic has *umīṭ al-lithām* ('I lift the veil'), p. 61. Constable and St Germain have rendered this as 'offer a solution to' (p. 75), which unfortunately glosses over the specific metaphor that structures the protagonist's act of interpretation.

11. Bersoni (1989), 'Pynchon, Paranoia, and Literature', p. 102.

12. Felski (2015), *The Limits of Critique*.

13. Ibid., p. 30.

14. Felski (2015), *The Limits of Critique*, p. 93; emphasis in the original. The 'detective', in turn, is the product of much larger traditions of suspicious readers in literature and history. Carlo Ginzburg (1992), for example, traces the emergence of what he calls the 'evidential' or 'conjectural paradigm' from ancient Mesopotamian practices of divination, to Sufi *firāsa*, to European Renaissance medicine, to Giovanni Morelli, Sherlock Holmes, and Sigmund Freud: 'Clues: Roots of an Evidential Paradigm', *Clues, Myths, and the Historical Method*, pp. 96–125.

15. The 2 November 1976 issue of *Le Monde diplomatique*, which the protagonist cites as the source for his information on the Trilateral Commission (p. 22), also contains an article on economic 'diversification', and is perhaps whence the author has derived this term. See Pauwels (1976), 'Les voies de la diversification industrielle', p. 24.

16. Felski (2015), *The Limits of Critique*, pp. 59–60.

17. Sedgwick (2003), 'Paranoid Reading and Reparative Reading', pp. 134–44.

18. Ibid., p. 138.

19. Thus, *pace* El-Ariss (2012), there is nothing 'new' about exposure as a critical strategy. That the present novel – the work of an author of the 'sixties generation' – places its faith in the liberating effects of exposure indicates that recent literary acts of *faḍḥ* can hardly be said to comprise a radical departure

from 'old' literature, at least in this respect. See Tarek El-Ariss (2012), 'Fiction of Scandal', pp. 510–31.

20. Silverstein (2002), 'An Excess of Truth: Violence, Conspiracy Theorizing and the Algerian Civil War', pp. 643–74.

21. Silverstein (2002), 'An Excess of Truth', p. 656.

22. Ibid., p. 649.

23. See Mehrez (1994), 'Sonallah Ibrahim and the (Hi)story of the Book', *Egyptian Writers between History and Fiction: Essays on Naguib Mahfouz, Sonallah Ibrahim, and Gamal al-Ghitani*, pp. 46–51.

24. Gamal al-Ghitani, 'Hādhā al-Rajul Khaṭar ᶜalā al-Shaᶜb wa-l-Dawla', *al-Akhbār*, 5 August 2013.

Notes to Chapter 4

1. ᶜAbbās (2011), 'Liwāṭ', *Halaka al-Fājir: Malḥamat Thawrat 25 Yanāyir*, pp. 235–49. Originally published in May 2002, according to the author's footnote (p. 235).

2. For a full report on the case, see Human Rights Watch (2004), *In a Time of Torture: The Assault on Justice in Egypt's Crackdown on Homosexual Conduct*.

3. ᶜAbbās, 'Liwāṭ', p. 249.

4. Human Rights Watch, *In a Time of Torture*, p. 2.

5. Ibid., p. 24.

6. Ibid., pp. 23–4.

7. Muḥammad ᶜAbd al-Nabī (2017 [2016]), *Fī Ghurfat al-ᶜAnkabūt*, p. 155.

8. Ibid., p. 156.

9. Constable and St Germain (trans.), *The Committee*, p. 75.

10. As, for example, when the protagonist says that the Coca-Cola bottle 'is just the right size to fit up anyone's ass' (19). On metaphors of homosexuality as foreign invasion in Arabic literature, see Hanadi Al-Samman (2008), , pp. 270–310; Guth (1995), 'The Function of Sexual Passages in some Egyptian Novels of the 1980s', *Love and Sexuality in Modern Arabic Literature*; Lagrange (2006), 'Male Homosexuality in Modern Arabic Literature', *Imagined Masculinities: Male Identity and Culture in the Modern Middle East*.

11. See Rogin (1992), 'JFK: The Movie', pp. 500–5.

12. According to the author's colophon, the twin novels were written over a period of eleven years (1990–6 and 1998–2001, respectively), yet they were most likely meant to be published as one book. Al-Ghitani underwent heart surgery in the period between the two novels, preventing him from writing them together.

To our knowledge, they have not been the object of any critical attention, with the exception of Al-Musawi, who briefly discusses the first novel, and ʿAbd al-Qādir, whose review of both novels is brashly polemical. Al-Musawi (2003), *The Postcolonial Arabic Novel: Debating Ambivalence*, pp. 302–5; al-Qādir (2003), *Fī al-Riwāya al-ʿArabiyya al-Muʿāṣira*, pp. 145–83. See also Mona Zaki's English translation of one chapter from *Ḥikāyāt al-Muʾassasa* (which she translates as *The Stories of the Establishment*) in *Banipal* 13 (2002), pp. 11–16.

13. Al-Ghitani (2002), *Ḥikāyāt al-Muʾassasa*, pp. 143–4. As noted above, the two novels (*Ḥikāyāt al-Muʾassasa* and *Ḥikāyāt al-Khabīʾa*) were originally intended to be published as one. The two incidents cited here would appear to echo in turn a motif deployed by al-Ghitani in previous works such as 'Wa fīmā Yalī mā Jarā li-l-Ḥalabī', *Risālat al-Baṣāʾir fī al-Masāʾir* (1995), pp. 446–8.

14. Saleh (1999), 'The Woman as a Locus of Apocalyptic Anxiety in Medieval Sunnī Islam', *Myths, Historical Archetypes and Symbolic Figures in Arabic Literature: Towards a New Hermeneutic Approach*, p. 134, n48.

15. Besides *lūṭī* ('sodomite', 'pederast', or '(active) homosexual'), Fayrūz is frequently characterized as a '(sexual) deviant' (*shādhdh* [*jinsiyyan*]), or someone who suffers from '(sexual) deviance' (*shudhūdh* [*jinsī*]). The term, often without the qualifier 'sexual' (*jinsī*) attached, almost always refers to homosexuality, even if other patterns of behaviour outside of the heterocentric norm might sometimes be connoted. Depending on one's perspective, *shādhdh* falls ethically somewhere between the polemical and the polite: polemical, because it pronounces a value judgement, and polite, because in its obscurity it avoids the graphic and grotesque. The history of the term, which has been the object of numerous studies (for example, Al-Samman 2008), is of little importance here: the novel vividly portrays the behaviour, the act, the practice, the orientation, the desire, and so forth, that *shādhdh* and its near synonyms are meant to express.

16. For a fuller discussion of this term, see the Introduction of the present monograph.

17. Baudrillard (1990), *Seduction*, p. 85.

18. Manẓūr (2008), *Lisān al-ʿArab*, v. 13, p. 318:

وقد فَتَنَ وافْتَتَنَ، جعله لازماً ومتعدّياً، وفَتَّنَه تفتيناً فهو مفتَّنٌ أي مفتون جدّاً. والفتون أيضاً: الافتتان، يتعدّى ولا يتعدّى، ومنه قولهم: قلبٌ فاتِنٌ أي مُفْتَتِنٌ.

19. Ibid., p. 318:

والمفتونُ الفتنةُ، وهو مصدر كالمحلوف والمعقول.

20. Baudrillard, *Seduction*, p. 81.

21. *Ḥikāyāt al-Muʾassasa*, p. 214.

22. *Ḥikāyāt al-Muʾassasa*, p. 226.
23. *Ḥikāyāt al-Muʾassasa*, p. 219.
24. Emphasis added. The saying occurs in a number of sources. See, for example, the *tafsīr* of al-Suyūṭī, *al-Durr al-Manthūr fī al-Tafsīr bi-l-Maʾthūr* (*sūra* 4:95).
25. *Ḥikāyāt al-Muʾassasa*, pp. 225–6, *passim*.
26. ʿAbd al-Qādir alternatively calls this genre 'the literature of "you know who, dear neighbor"' (*adab iyyāka aʿnī fa-smaʿī yā gāra*), that is, 'innuendo'. *Fī al-Riwāya al-ʿArabiyya al-Muʿāṣira*, p. 176.
27. Ibid., p. 147.
28. Ibid., p. 176.
29. Such a reading returns the novel to the older meaning of the word *ḥikāyāt* (tales, stories) in its title, namely, popular oral performances, as opposed to 'higher' or more canonical forms, a meaning that for medieval littérateurs like al-Jāḥiẓ (776– 868) held connotations of mimicry and miming. See Pellat, Bausani, Boratav, Ahmad, and Winstedt (2012), 'Ḥikāya', *Encyclopaedia of Islam, Second Edition*.
30. al-Qādir, *Fī al-Riwāya al-ʿArabiyya al-Muʿāṣira*, p. 148.
31. Ibid., 152.
32. Baudrillard, *Seduction*, p. 85.
33. On 'dialogic' aspects of al-Ghitani's fiction, see Mehrez (2008), *Egypt's Culture Wars: Politics and Practice*, p. 64, and Al-Musawi, *The Postcolonial Arabic Novel*, p. 44. For 'metafictional' dimensions of his work, see Al-Musawi, *The Postcolonial Arabic Novel*, pp. 265–72, and Azouqa (2011), 'Gamāl al-Ghīṭānī's *Pyramid Texts* and the Fiction of Jorge Luis Borges: A Comparative Study', pp. 1–28.
34. Many of the rumours about Faruq Husni were the topic of an instalment of ʿĀdil Ḥammūda's sensationalist television programme *Kull Rijāl al-Raʾīs* (All the President's Men), broadcast on 17 August 2011, and available at <http://www.youtube.com/watch?v=drmN-NmZN4k>. Ḥammūda nonetheless sought to downplay the charges of sexual deviance.
35. See Hosni's biography, 'al-Sīra al-Dhātiyya', available at <www.fineart.gov.eg/arb/cv/cv.asp?IDS=655>, last accessed 15 September 2015.
36. Abāẓa, 'Wujūm', p. 13.
37. Rajab Al-Banna, 'Bidāyat Maʿraka Jadīda', *al-Ahrām*, 18 October 1987, p. 7.
38. Muḥammad ʿAbd al-Munʿim, 'al-Muḥārib al-Aḥmaq', *al-Ahrām*, 20 October 1987.
39. ʿAbd al-Qādir Shahīb, 'Ḍajja ḥawla Wazīr al-Thaqāfa: Hujūm ḍidd Wazīr am ḍidd Jīl?', *Rūz al-Yūsuf*, 26 October 1987, p. 10.

40. Nāṣir Ḥusayn, 'Hādhā al-Wazīr al-Shābb', *Rūz al-Yūsuf*, 26 October 1987, p. 55.

41. 'Fārūq Ḥusnī li-Bawwābat al-Ahrām: Lastu Shādhdhan wa-Ṣafwat al-Sharīf warā' al-Shā'i'a', *Bawwābat al-Ahrām*, 16 June 2011, available at <gate.ahram.org.eg/News/83576.aspx>, last accessed 15 September 2015.

42. On these rumours, see, for example, Fadi Salah, 'New Libel Charges against Controversial Salafi Preacher', *Daily News Egypt*, 25 December 2012, available at <www.dailynewsegypt.com/2012/12/25/new-libel-charges-against-controversial-salafi-preacher>, last accessed 15 September 2015, and Magdī al-Gallād's interview with Mamdūḥ al-Laythī on the programme *Anta wa-Ḍamīrak*, which aired 1 August 2011, available at <http://www.youtube.com/watch?v=r5EpP6ShJAQ>.

43. *Ḥikāyāt al-Mu'assasa*, p. 141.

44. Al-Sharqāwī's reconciliation with the minister is recounted in 'Kursī al-Thaqāfa wa-Ghaḍab al-Mustawzirīn', *Rūz al-Yūsuf*, 26 October 1987, pp. 47–8. Al-Sharqawi passed away on 10 November 1987.

45. Huwayda Ṣāliḥ, 'Faḍā'iḥ "Wīkīlīks" wa-"Klīnīks" al-Ghīṭānī', *al-Yawm al-Sābi*ᶜ, 25 December 2010.

46. Mehrez, *Egypt's Culture Wars*, p. 6.

47. See also Jacquemond, *Conscience of the Nation*.

48. Ṣāliḥ, 'Faḍā'iḥ "Wīkīlīks" wa-"Klīnīks" al-Ghīṭānī'.

49. 'Al-Ghīṭānī: Jā'izat al-Dawla la Tamnaḥuhā al-Wizāra', *al-Maṣrī al-Yawm*, 28 June 2007.

50. With a sideways smirk, al-Ghitani told reporters that he had 'been following the works of the artist Farouk Hosni since the '80s' and that he could notice 'a development in the use of colors and in the manifestation of form'. The interview is available at <www.youtube.com/watch?v=mAtPzrZ9d3Q>, last accessed 10 October 2016.

51. Himself a painter, Farouk Hosni was often referred to in the press as '*al-wazīr al-fannān*' ('the artist-minister').

52. Zaki (2002), 'Excerpt from the Novel *To the Presidential Floor* with Translator's Note', p. 14.

53. Abd al-Wāḥid (2005), *Muthaqqafūn taḥt al-Ṭalab*, p. 319.

54. Ṣāliḥ, 'Faḍā'iḥ "Wīkīlīks" wa-"Klīnīks" al-Ghīṭānī'.

55. Mehrez, *Egyptian Writers between History and Fiction*, p. 61; emphasis in the original.

Notes to Chapter 5

1. Boym (1999), 'Conspiracy Theories and Literary Ethics: Umberto Eco, Danilo Kiš and The Protocols of Zion', p. 100.
2. Boym (1999), 'Conspiracy Theories and Literary Ethics', p. 100.
3. Hutcheon (1994), *Irony's Edge: The Theory and Politics of Irony*, p. 11.
4. On 'generations' in Egyptian literature, see, for example, Kendall (2006), Ramadan (2012), and Jacquemond (2008).
5. Hafez (2010), 'The New Egyptian Novel: Urban Transformation and Narrative Form'.
6. On these authors, see, for example, Abdel-Messih (2009), 'Hyper Texts: Avant-gardism in Contemporary Egyptian Narratives'; El-Ariss, 'Fiction of Scandal' (2012) and *Trials of Arab Modernity* (2013); Elsadda, *Gender, Nation, and the Arabic Novel*, chapter 9; Mehrez, *Egypt's Culture Wars*, chapter 7.
7. El-Ariss, 'Fiction of Scandal'.
8. See Hilary Plum, 'A Conversation with Youssef Rakha', available at <www.musicandliterature.org/features/2015/3/6/a-conversation-with-youssef-rakha>, last accessed 10 October 2016.
9. The formal semblance between Eco's *Foucault's Pendulum* and Rakha's novel is most striking. There are, in addition, certain formal parallels between Pynchon's magnum opus (*Gravity's Rainbow*, 1973) and Rakha's *kitāb*: as variations on the 'encyclopedic' as defined by Northrop Frye (2006: 295), gleeful derisions of contemporary social 'types', and rich repositories of inventively obscure language, both come near to achieving a form of Menippean satire. The novel also evokes Paul Auster's Quinn in *City of Glass* (1985) who, after wandering around Manhattan, discovers that his daily walks, traced on a map, spell out the phrase 'Tower of Babel'. This tribute to New York's polyvocality and multiculturalism is mimicked in Mustafa al-Shurbagi's discovery of the *ṭughrā*, the subtle political-semantic matrix behind his journeys, that also stands in for a cherished, if fatally threatened, cosmopolitanism. *Naked Lunch* (1959) by William S. Burroughs also reverberates in Mustafa's occasional, but fetishistically detailed, detours into drug subculture (p. 121) and his musings on the link between cocaine and paranoia (p. 128). The Islamist manifestation of the *kitāb*'s Conspiracy also mimes the conspiratorial 'Islam Inc.' of *Naked Lunch* – a tribute that is more explicit in Rakha's English-language fiction. See, for example, Youssef Rakha, 'Thus Spoke Che Nawwarah: Interview with a Revolutionary', *Kenyon Review Online*, available at: <www.kenyonreview.org/

kr-online-issue/2013-winter/selections/youssef-rakha-342846>, last accessed 15 September 2015.

10. *Rabīᶜ* (<spring456.blogspot.com>; later *Muḥammad Rabīᶜ* at <moham-madrabie.net>, since discontinued) and *Wassaᶜ Khayālak*, about which see below.

11. Personal communication with the author, 20 June 2013.

12. 'Bisu' (*bīsū*) is sometimes explained as the pseudo-diminutive form of Iblīs ('Satan'); *wassaᶜ khayālak* may also be translated as 'widen your shadow', that is, 'live large'.

13. Naji, *al-Mudawwināt: Min al-Būst ilā al-Twīt* (Blogs: From Post to Tweet).

14. The novel also extends into cyberspace with several brilliant video collages by the author. Available at <www.youtube.com/watch?v=AtX-Utu7wa4>, <www.youtube.com/watch?v=edqMrHlVt-0>, <www.youtube.com/watch?v=9gBrdMRnQUQ>.

15. Perhaps, too, his father's name Nayif (*nāyif*) gestures to 'naïve', 'knave', the knight errant = Hamlet or Quixote, both prototypes for radical conspiracist suspicion, as we have seen in previous chapters.

16. Mustafa derives this noun from the verb in the colloquial expression *aṭallaᶜ maytīnak* ('I'll screw you up', lit. 'I'll raise your dead ones'). Rakha's *mayyitīn* are Surur's *mitnākīn*.

17. Al-Sīsī has sometimes been given this epithet by supporters in the press, although his name (*al-sīsī*) is rather infelicitously homophonous with 'pony' (*sīsī*).

18. The novel provides a fascinating etymology of the word *maᶜarraṣ/muᶜarriṣ*, which in contemporary Egyptian slang, from Surur to the bloggers of recent years, denotes a 'kiss-ass', 'boot-licker', or 'sell-out' (although more literally, a 'pimp'). Originally, the novel informs us, a *muᶜarriṣ* was an individual who constructed roofs of buildings out of *ᶜaraṣāt* or '(wooden) planks' – in other words, a kind of engineer. Through a subtle pun, the novel places Naᶜim's work as an engineer (*muᶜarriṣ*) as coextensive with the reign of Sadat, who is remembered by detractors as *il-miᶜarraṣ* ('the sell-out' or 'kiss-ass') for his obsequious relationship with the governments of Israel and the United States.

19. The touchstone work on this literature remains Bosworth (1976), *The Mediaeval Islamic Underworld*.

20. The book is described on its cover as a *riwāya* ("novel"), although it contains illustrations that suggest something more akin to a graphic novel, or a new hybrid literary form.

21. For a recent elaboration on the cyborg ethos, newly articulated as a practice of 'becoming-with' 'companion species', see Haraway (2008), *When Species Meet*.

22. Rakha (2012), 'In Extremis: Literature and Revolution in Contemporary Cairo (An Oriental Essay in Seven Parts)', p. 161.

Notes to Epilogue

1. Furet (2001), *Interpreting the French Revolution*, pp. 53–4.

2. See, for example, Mai Shams El-Din, 'A Year of Conspiracies', *Mada Masr*, 27 December 2015, available at <www.madamasr.com/sections/politics/year-conspiracies>, last accessed 1 October 2016; Dalia Rabie, 'Unholy Terrors: A Box of Tomatoes, a Hip-Hop Group and the Supreme Council of the World', *Mada Masr*, 11 September 2015, available at <www.madamasr.com/sections/politics/unholy-terrors-box-tomatoes-hip-hop-group-and-supreme-council-world>, last accessed 1 October 2016; and Heba Afify, 'Four Years of Paranoia', *Mada Masr*, 2 February 2015, available at <www.madamasr.com/sections/politics/four-years-paranoia>, last accessed 1 October 2016.

3. On *brigands*, see Lefebvre (1989), *The Great Fear of 1789: Rural Panic in Revolutionary France*; on *balṭagiyya*, see Ghannam (2012), 'Meanings and Feelings: Local Interpretations of the Use of Violence in the Egyptian Revolution', pp. 32–6. On rumours of kidnapped children, see Farge and Revel (1991), *The Vanishing Children of Paris: Rumor and Politics before the French Revolution*; this may be compared with incidents that occurred during the Egyptian revolution: in May 2011, for example, a church was stormed and ransacked, and at least a dozen people killed, in the working-class neighbourhood of Imbaba in Cairo, after rumours circulated both locally and online that a Muslim girl was being held captive inside. The scenario repeated itself in the Delta village of Mīt Bashar in February 2012. Such incidents are discussed in Mahmoud (2015), *Religious Difference in a Secular Age: A Minority Report*, pp. 111–14. The literature on conspiracy theory in the French Revolution is enormous; for an overview, see Hofman (1993), 'Opinion, Illusion, and the Illusion of Opinion: Barruel's Theory of Conspiracy', pp. 27–60.

4. Ashour (2013), *Athqal min Raḍwā* and *al-Ṣarkha* (2015).

5. *Athqal min Raḍwā*, p. 207.

6. On Tawfīq ʿUkāsha as a 'trickster', see Armbrust (2013), 'The Trickster in Egypt's January 25th Revolution', pp. 834–64.

7. A witty satire of the revolution's conspiracy theories was performed by the comedian MonaTov (Mūnā-tūf) in the sixth and final episode of her

unfortunately short-lived YouTube programme: <www.youtube.com/watch?v=9Tlf3LaqD2E>. Mockeries of Egyptian conspiracy theories have been a regular feature of Bassem Youssef's intermittently broadcast programme, *Al-Bernameg* (*il-Birnāmig*) (2011–14).

8. *Athqal min Raḍwā*, p. 211.

Bibliography

ᶜAbbās, Muḥammad. *Halaka al-Fājir: Malḥamat Thawrat 25 Yanāyir* (Cairo: Maktabat Jazīrat al-Ward, 2011).

ᶜAbd al-Nabī, Muḥammad. *Fī Ghurfat al-ᶜAnkabūt* (Cairo: Dār al-ᶜAyn li-l-Nashr, 2016).

ᶜAbd al-Qādir, Fārūq. 'Minēn Agīb Nās?! Wa-Darāwīsh Nagīb Surūr', *Adab wa-Naqd*, 15, 1 September 1985, pp. 100–17.

—. *Fī al-Riwāya al-ᶜArabiyya al-Muᶜāṣira* (Cairo: Dār al-Hilāl, 2003).

ᶜAbd al-Wāḥid, Muḥammad. *Muthaqqafūn taḥt al-Ṭalab* (Cairo: Dār Gharnāṭa, 2005).

Abdel-Messih, Marie-Thérèse. 'Hyper Texts: Avant-gardism in Contemporary Egyptian Narratives', *Neohelicon* 36 (2009), pp. 515–23.

Abū al-Fatḥ, Aḥmad. *Gamāl ᶜAbd al-Nāṣir* (Cairo: al-Maktab al-Miṣri al-Ḥadīth, 1991).

Abū Rayya, Yūsuf. *Laylat ᶜUrs* (Cairo: al-Hayʾa al-Miṣriyya al-ᶜĀmma li-l-Kitāb, 2002), trans. R. Neil Hewison, *Wedding Night* (Cairo: AUC Press, 2006).

Abu-Lughod, Lila. *Dramas of Nationhood: The Politics of Television in Egypt* (Chicago: University of Chicago Press, 2005).

Aḥmad, Marzūq. *al-Hashīsh Mamnūᶜ!* (Cairo: Sharikat al-Tawzīᶜ al-Miṣriyya, 1953).

Anderson, Jon W. 'Conspiracy Theories, Premature Entextualization, and Popular Political Analysis', *The Arab Studies Journal* 4:1 (1996), pp. 96–102.

al-ᶜAqqād, ᶜAbbās Maḥmūd. *Bayn al-Kutub wa-l-Nās* (Cairo: Dār al-Maᶜārif, 1952).

—. *Lā Shuyūᶜiyya wa-Lā Istiᶜmār* (Cairo: Dār al-Hilāl, 1957).

—. 'Taqdīr Brūtūkūlāt Ḥukamāʾ Ṣihyūn: li-al-Ustādh al-Kabīr ᶜAbbās Maḥmūd al-ᶜAqqād', in Muḥammad Khalīfa al-Tūnisī (ed. and trans.), *al-Khaṭar al-Yahūdī: Brūtūkūlāt Ḥukamāʾ Ṣahyūn* (Beirut: Dār al-Kitāb al-ᶜArabī, 1961 [1951]), pp. 11–16.

—. *al-Ṣahyūniyya al-ᶜĀlamiyya* (Cairo: Maktabat Gharīb, 1968).

—. *Yawmiyāt*. (Cairo: Muʾassasat Hindāwī li-l-Taʿlīm wa-l-Thaqāfa, 2014 [1964]).

Armbrust, Walter. 'The Trickster in Egypt's January 25th Revolution', *Comparative Studies in Society and History* 55:4 (2013), pp. 834–64.

Ashour, Radwa [= Raḍwā ʿĀshūr]. *Athqal min Raḍwā* (Cairo: Dār al-Shurūq, 2013).

—. *al-Ṣarkha* (Cairo: Dār al-Shurūq, 2015).

al-Aswānī, Ṣalāḥ. 'Qaḍiyyat Raʾfat Shalabī: Awwal Ḍaḥiyya li-Qānūn Taḥdīd al-Milkiyya', *al-Wafd*, 25 July 1992.

al-ʿĀyidī, Aḥmad. *An Takūn ʿAbbās al-ʿAbd* (Cairo: Dār Mīrīt, 2003), trans. Humphrey Davies, *Being Abbas el Abd* (Cairo: AUC Press, 2009).

Azouqa, Aida O. 'Gamāl al-Ghīṭānī's *Pyramid Texts* and the Fiction of Jorge Luis Borges: A Comparative Study', *Journal of Arabic Literature* 42:1 (2011), pp. 1–28.

Badawi, M. M. *Modern Arabic Drama in Egypt* (Cambridge: Cambridge University Press, 1987).

Bakathir, Ali Ahmad (= ʿAlī Aḥmad Bā Kathīr). *Shaylūk al-Jadīd* (Cairo: Maktabat Miṣr, n.d. [1945]).

—. *Imbarāṭūriyya fī al-Mazād* (Cairo: Maktabat Miṣr, n.d. [1953]).

—. *Shaʿb Allāh al-Mukhtār* (Cairo: Dār Miṣr li-l-Ṭibāʿa, n.d. [1956]).

—. *al-Tawrā al-Ḍāʾiʿa* (Cairo: Maktabat Miṣr, n.d. [1967])

—. *Sīrat Shujāʿ* (Cairo: Dār al-Maʿārif, 1957 [1954]).

—. *Ḥabl al-Ghasīl* (Cairo: Maktabat Miṣr, 1979 [1965]).

—. *Mismār Juḥā* (Cairo: Maktabat Miṣr, 1985 [1951]).

—. *Ilāh Isrāʾīl* (Cairo: Maktabat Miṣr, 1988 [1957]).

—. *Sirr al-Ḥākim bi-Amr Allāh* (Cairo: Maktabat Miṣr, 1989 [1948]).

—. *Libās al-ʿIffa* (published online at *Rābiṭat Udabāʾ al-Shām*, 2006 [1966]), available at <web.archive.org/web/20071012120815/http://odabasham.net/show.php?sid=7537>, last accessed 10 October 2016.

Al-Banna, 'Bidāyat Maʿraka Jadīda', *al-Ahrām*, 18 October 1987.

Baudrillard, Jean. *Seduction*, trans. Brian Singer (Montreal: New World Perspectives, 1990).

Bersoni, Leo. 'Pynchon, Paranoia, and Literature', *Representations* 25 (winter 1989), pp. 105–9.

Bosworth, Clifford Edmund. *The Mediaeval Islamic Underworld: The Banū Sāsān in Arabic Society and Literature* (Leiden: E. J. Brill, 1976).

Bottéro, Jean. *Mesopotamia: Writing, Reasoning, and the Gods* (Chicago: University of Chicago Press, 1992).

Boym, Svetlana. 'Conspiracy Theories and Literary Ethics: Umberto Eco, Danilo

Kiš and The Protocols of Zion', *Comparative Literature* 51:2 (spring 1999), pp. 97–122.

Bratich, Jack Z. *Conspiracy Panics: Political Rationality and Popular Culture* (Albany: State University of New York Press, 2008).

Brown, Nathan J. *The Rule of Law in the Arab World: Courts in Egypt and the Gulf* (Cambridge: Cambridge University Press, 1997).

Burt, Clarissa. 'The Tears of a Clown: Yusuf Idris and Postrevolutionary Egyptian Theater', in Sherifa Zuhur (ed.), *Colors of Enchantment: Dance, Music, and the Visual Arts of the Middle East* (Cairo: AUC Press, 2001).

Butter, Michael et al. *Conspiracy Theories in the Middle East and the United States: A Comparative Approach* (Boston: De Gruyter, 2014).

Cachia, Pierre. 'The Egyptian "Mawwāl": Its Ancestry, Its Development, and Its Present Forms, *Journal of Arabic Literature* 8 (1977), pp. 77–103.

—. 'Folk Themes in the Works of Najīb Surūr', *Arabic and Middle Eastern Literatures* 3:2 (2000), pp. 195–204.

Cheikho, Louis (= Lawīs Shaykhū). *al-Sirr al-Maṣūn fī Shīʿat al-Farmasūn*, 6 vols (Beirut: al-Maṭbaʿa al-Kāthūlīkiyya li-l-Ābāʾ al-Yasūʿiyyīn, 1909–11).

Cohen-Mor, Dalya. *Yusuf Idris: Changing Visions* (Potomac: Sheba Press, 1992).

Collins, John J. 'Introduction: Towards the Morphology of a Genre', in John J. Collins (ed.), *Apocalypse: The Morphology of a Genre* (Missoula: Scholars Press, 1979), pp. 1–19.

Cook, David. *Contemporary Muslim Apocalyptic Literature* (Syracuse: Syracuse University Press, 2005).

Dhikrī, Maḥmūd Aḥmad. *Shiʿr Najīb Surūr: al-Turāth wa-l-Wāqiʿ wa-ʾĀfāq al-Maʿnāʾ* (Cairo: al-Hayʾa al-ʿĀmma li-Quṣūr al-Thaqāfa, 2013).

Eco, Umberto. *Foucault's Pendulum*, trans. William Weaver (London: Picador, 1990 [1988]).

—. 'Overinterpreting Texts', in Stefan Collini (ed.), *Interpretation and Overinterpretation* (Cambridge: Cambridge University Press, 1992), pp. 45–66.

Eissa, Ibrahim (= Ibrāhīm ʿĪsā). *Maqtal al-Rajul al-Kabīr* (Cairo: n.p., 1999).

El-Ariss, Tarek. 'Fiction of Scandal', *Journal of Arabic Literature* 43 (2012), pp. 510–31.

—. *Trials of Arab Modernity: Literary Affects and the New Political* (New York: Fordham University Press, 2013).

Elsadda, Hoda. *Gender, Nation, and the Arabic Novel: Egypt 1892–2008* (Edinburgh: Edinburgh University Press, 2012).

El-Shamy, Hasan M. 'Belief Characters as Anthropomorphic Psychosocial Realities: The Egyptian Case', *al-Kitāb al-Sanawī li-ᶜIlm al-Ijtimāᶜ* 3 (1982), pp. 7–36.

Evens, Meredith. 'Rumor, the Breath of Kings, and the Body of Law in *2 Henry IV*', *Shakespeare Quarterly* 60:1 (2009), pp. 1–24.

Fahīm, Shawqī. 'ᶜAn Najīb Surūr: Lam Yamut Baṭalan, wa-lākin Māt Baḥthan ᶜan al-Buṭūla!', in Naguib Surur, *Luzūm mā Yalzam* (Cairo: Dār al-Shurūq, 2006), pp. 7–25.

Farge, Arlette and Jacques Revel. *The Vanishing Children of Paris: Rumor and Politics before the French Revolution*. (Cambridge, MA: Harvard University Press, 1991).

Farrell, John. *Freud's Paranoid Quest: Psychoanalysis and Modern Suspicion* (New York: New York University Press, 1998).

Fayṣal, Ṭalāl. *Surūr* (Cairo: Dār al-Kutub Khān, 2013).

Felski, Rita. *The Limits of Critique* (Chicago: University of Chicago Press, 2015).

Fenster, Mark. *Conspiracy Theories: Secrecy and Power in American Culture* (Minneapolis: University of Minnesota Press, 2008).

—. 'Foreword', in Victoria Emma Pagán, *Conspiracy Theory in Latin Literature* (Austin: University of Texas Press, 2012), pp. ix–xi.

Filiu, Jean-Pierre. *Apocalypse in Islam* (Berkeley: University of California Press, 2011).

Freud, Sigmund. 'Psychoanalytic Notes upon an Autobiographical Account of a Case of Paranoia (*Dementia Paranoides*)', in Philip Rieff (ed. and trans.), *Three Case Histories* (New York: Simon & Schuster, 1996 [1911]), pp. 103–86.

Frye, Northrop. *Anatomy of Criticism: Four Essays* (Toronto: University of Toronto Press, 2006).

Furet, François. *Interpreting the French Revolution* (Cambridge: Cambridge University Press, 2001).

Ghannam, Farha. 'Meanings and Feelings: Local Interpretations of the Use of Violence in the Egyptian Revolution', *American Ethnologist* 39:1 (2012), pp. 32–6.

al-Ghitani, Gamal (= Jamāl al-Ghīṭānī). *Risālat al-Baṣāʾ ir fī al-Maṣāʾir* (Cairo: al-Hayʾa al-Miṣriyya al-ᶜĀmma li-l-Kitāb, 1995).

—. *Ḥikāyāt al-Khabīʾa* (Cairo: Dar al-Shurūq, 2002).

—. *Ḥikāyāt al-Muʾassasa* (Cairo: Dār al-Shurūq, 2002).

—. 'Hādhā al-Rajul Khaṭar ᶜalā al-Shaᶜb wa-l-Dawla', *al-Akhbār*, 5 August 2013.

Ghoussoub Mai. 'Chewing Gum, Insatiable Women, and Foreign Enemies: Male Fears and the Arab Media', in Mai Ghoussoub and Emma Sinclair-Webb (eds), *Imagined Masculinities: Male Identity and Culture in the Modern Middle East* (London: Saqi, 2000), pp. 227–35.

Ginzburg, Carlo. *Clues, Myths, and the Historical Method* (Baltimore: The Johns Hopkins University Press, 1992).

Gordon, Joel. *Nasser's Blessed Movement: Egypt's Free Officers and the July Revolution* (New York: Oxford University Press, 1992).

Gray, Matthew. *Conspiracy Theories in the Arab World: Sources and Politics* (New York: Routledge, 2010).

Gross, Kenneth. 'The Rumor of Hamlet', *Raritan*, 14:2 (1994), pp. 43–66.

Guth, Stephen. 'The Function of Sexual Passages in some Egyptian Novels of the 1980s', in R. Allen, H. Kirkpatrick, and E. de Moor (eds), *Love and Sexuality in Modern Arabic Literature* (London: Saqi Books, 1995), pp. 123–30.

Hafez, Sabry. 'The New Egyptian Novel: Urban Transformation and Narrative Form', *New Left Review* 64 (July–August 2010), pp. 47–62.

al-Ḥakīm, Tawfiq. *Maṣīr Ṣurṣār* (Cairo: Maktabat Miṣr, 1965).

—. *Bank al-Qalaq* (Cairo: Maktabat Miṣr, 1967).

—. *Īzīs*, in *Tawfīq al-Ḥakīm: al-Muʾallafāt al-Kāmila* (Beirut: Maktabat Lubnān, 1995 [1955]), pp. 845–80.

al-Ḥammādī, Muḥammad b. Mālik. *Kashf Asrar al-Bāṭiniyya wa-Asrār al-Qarāmiṭa*, ed. Muḥammad Zāhid al-Kawtharī (Cairo: al-Maktaba al-Azhariyya li-l-Turāth, 1995).

Haraway, Donna. *When Species Meet* (Minneapolis: University of Minnesota Press, 2008).

Hebdige, Dick. *Subculture: The Meaning of Style* (London: Routledge, 2007 [1979]).

Hijāzī, Ahmad ʿAbd al-Muʿṭī, 'Anqidhū Najīb Surūr', *Rūz al-Yūsuf*, 25 May 1970.

Hofman, Amos. 'Opinion, Illusion, and the Illusion of Opinion: Barruel's Theory of Conspiracy', *Eighteenth-Century Studies* 27:1 (autumn 1993), pp. 27–60.

Hofstadter, Richard. 'The Paranoid Style in American Politics', in Richard Hofstadter, *The Paranoid Style in American Politics, and Other Essays* (Cambridge, MA: Harvard University Press, 1996), pp. 3–40.

Human Rights Watch. *In a Time of Torture: The Assault on Justice in Egypt's Crackdown on Homosexual Conduct* (New York: Human Rights Watch, 2004).

Hutcheon, Linda. *Irony's Edge: The Theory and Politics of Irony* (New York: Routledge, 1994).

Hyde, Lewis. *Trickster Makes this World: Mischief, Myth, and Art* (New York: Farrar, Straus & Giroux, 1998).

Ibn Manẓūr, *Lisān al-ʿArab* (Beirut: Dār Ṣādir, 2008).

Ibrahim, Sonallah (= Ṣunʿ Allāh Ibrāhīm). *al-Lajna* (Cairo: Dār al-Mustaqbal al-ʿArabī, 1997 [1981]), trans Charlene Constable and Mary S. St. Germain, *The Committee: A Novel* (Syracuse: Syracuse University Press, 2001).

'ʿAlā Sabīl al-Taqdīm', in Sonallah Ibrahim, *Tilka al-Rāʾiḥa, wa-Qiṣaṣ Ukhrā* (al-Minyā: Dār al-Hudā li-l-Nashr wa-l-Tawzīʿ, 2003 [1986]), pp. 11–21.

Idris, Yusuf (= Yūsuf Idrīs). 'Naḥw Masraḥ Miṣrī', published in three parts as: 'Naḥw Masraḥ Miṣrī', *al-Kātib* 34 (January 1964), pp. 67–79; 'Naḥw Masraḥ Miṣrī (2): Radd ʿalā al-Mustawribīn wa Bidāyat al-Taʿarruf ʿalā Malāmiḥinā', *al-Kātib* 35 (February 1964), pp. 109–20; and 'Naḥw Masraḥ Miṣrī (3)', *al-Kātib* 36 (March 1964), pp. 86–97.

—. *al-Farāfīr* (Cairo: Maktabat Miṣr, 1964).

—. *al-Mukhaṭṭaṭīn* (Cairo: Maktabat Miṣr, 1969).

—. 'Shillat Yūsuf Idrīs', ed. Ayman al-Tuhāmī, *Rūz al-Yūsuf*, 24 March 1997, pp. 86–9.

ʿInān, ʿAbd Allāh. *Tārīkh al-Jamʿiyyāt al-Sirriyya wa-l-Ḥarakāt al-Haddāma* (Cairo: Idārat al-Hilāl, 1926).

—. *Tārīkh al-Muʾāmarāt al-Siyāsiyya* (Cairo: Idārat al-Hilāl, 1928).

—. 'Hal Qutil al-Ḥākim bi-Amr Allāh am Ikhtafā?', *al-Risāla*, 186, 25 January 1937.

—. *al-Ḥākim bi-Amr Allāh wa-Asrār al-Daʿwa al-Fāṭimiyya* (Cairo: Dār al-Nashr al-Ḥadīth, 1937).

Irwin, Robert. 'An Orientalist Mythology of Secret Societies', in Arndt Graf, Schirin Fathi, and Ludwig Paul (eds), *Orientalism and Conspiracy: Politics and Conspiracy Theory in the Islamic World* (London: I. B. Tauris, 2011), pp. 71–86.

ʿĪsa, Muḥammad Ṭalʿat. *al-Shāʾiʿāt wa-Kayfa Nuwājihuhā* (Cairo: Maktabat al-Qāhira al-Ḥadītha, 1964).

Jacquemond, Richard. *Conscience of the Nation: Writers, State, and Scoiety in Modern Egypt* (Cairo: AUC Press, 2008).

al-Jāḥiz, Abū ʿUthmān. 'The Art of Keeping Silent', in *Sobriety and Mirth: A Selection of the Shorter Writings of al-Jāhiz*, trans. Jim Colville (New York: Routledge, 2013), pp. 123–36.

Jameson, Fredric. *Postmodernism, Or the Cultural Logic of Late Capitalism* (Durham, NC: Duke University Press, 1991).

Jubayr, ʿAbdū. 'Risāla ilā al-Jīl al-Jadīd', in Naguib Surur, *Brūtūkūlāt Ḥukamāʾ Rīsh* (Cairo: Dār al-Shurūq, 2006), pp. 7–16.

Kāmil, Rashād. 'Iʿtirāfāt Muthīra fī al-Ghurfa Raqam 619', *Sabāh al-Khayr*, 16 July 1981.

Kandil, Hazem. *Soldiers, Spies, and Statesmen: Egypt's Road to Revolt* (London: Verso, 2012).

al-Khādim, Saʿd (1913–87). *al-Muʾāmarat al-Istiʿmāriyya ʿalā Turāthina al-Fannī* (Cairo: al-Dār al-Qawmiyya, 1966).

—. *al-Fann wa-l-Istiʿmār al-Ṣihyūnī* (Cairo: al-Hayʾa al-Miṣriyya al-ʿĀmma li-l-Kitāb, 1974).

al-Khādim, Saʿd (1932–2003). *Min Riḥlat Ūdīsiyūs al-Miṣrī* (Cairo: al-Dār al-Miṣriyya li-l-Tibāʿa wa-l-Nashr wa-l-Tawzīʿ, 1979).

Kāmil, ʿĀdil. *Malik min Shuʿāʿ Shuʿāʿ* (Cairo: Maktabat Miṣr, 1945).

Kāmil, Amīn Ḥasān. *Maḥkamat al-Thawra*, v. 1 (Cairo: Matbaʿat Miṣr, 1953).

Kendall, Elisabeth. *Literature, Journalism and the Avant-Garde: Intersection in Egypt* (London: Routledge, 2006).

Khayrī, Ḥāzim. *Dūn Kīkhūtih al-Miṣrī: Dirāsa ʿIlmiyya Wathāʾiqiyya li-Ḥayāt wa-Fikr Nagīb Surūr* (Cairo: al-Majlis al-Aʿlā li-l-Thaqāfa, 2009).

Khūrshīd, Iʿtimād. *Shāhida ʿalā Inḥirāfāt Ṣalāḥ Naṣr* (Cairo: Muʾassasat Āmūn al-Ḥadītha li-l-Ṭabʿ wa-l-Nashr, 1988).

Kīra, Kamāl (ed.). *Muḥākamāt al-Thawra: al-Maḍbata al-Rasmiyya li-Maḥāḍir Jalasāt Maḥkamat al-Thawra*, 6 vols (Cairo: Maktab Shuʾūn Maḥkamat al-Thawra, 1953–4).

Klemm, Verena. *Literarisches Engagement im arabischen Nahen Osten: Konzepte und Debatten* (Würzburg: Ergon, 1998).

Lagrange, Frédéric. 'Male Homosexuality in Modern Arabic Literature', in M. Ghoussoub and E. Sinclair-Webb (eds), *Imagined Masculinities: Male Identity and Culture in the Modern Middle East* (London: Saqi Books, 2006), pp. 169–98.

Landau, Jacob M. 'Prolegomena to a Study of Secret Societies in Modern Egypt', *Middle Eastern Studies* 1:2 (January 1965), pp. 135–86.

—. 'Muslim Opposition to Freemasonry', *Die Welt des Islams* 36:2 (July 1996), pp. 186–203.

Larkin, Margaret. 'A Brigand Hero of Egyptian Colloquial Literature', *Journal of Arabic Literature* 23:1 (1992), pp. 49–64.

Latour, Bruno. *Reassembling the Social: An Introduction to Actor-Network-Theory* (New York: Oxford University Press, 2005).

Lefebvre, Georges. *The Great Fear of 1789: Rural Panic in Revolutionary France* (New York: Schocken Books, 1989).

Litvin, Margaret. *Hamlet's Arab Journey: Shakespeare's Prince and Nasser's Ghost* (Princeton: Princeton University Press, 2011).

Mahfouz, Naguib (= Najīb Maḥfūẓ). *al-Tanẓīm al-Sirrī* (Cairo: Maktabat Miṣr, 1984).

—. *al-Karnak* (CairoMaktabat Miṣr, 1974), trans. Roger Allen, *Karnak Café* (New York: Anchor Books, 2008).

Mahmoud, Saba. *Religious Difference in a Secular Age: A Minority Report* (Princeton: Princeton University Press, 2015).

Mehrez, Samia. *Egyptian Writers between History and Fiction: Essays on Naguib Mahfouz, Sonallah Ibrahim, and Gamal al-Ghitani* (Cairo: AUC Press, 1994).

—. *Egypt's Culture Wars: Politics and Practice* (London: Routledge, 2008).

Meijer, Roel. *The Quest for Modernity: Secular Liberal and Left-Wing Political Thought in Egypt, 1945–1958* (London: RoutledgeCurzon, 2002).

Melley, Timothy. *Empire of Conspiracy: The Culture of Paranoia in Postwar America* (Ithaca: Cornell University Press, 2000).

Mitchell, Timothy. *Rule of Experts: Egypt, Techno-Politics, Modernity* (Berkeley: University of California Press, 2002).

Muḥammad, Fāṭima Yūsuf. *al-Masraḥ wa-l-Sulṭa fī Miṣr min 1952 ilā 1970* (Cairo: al-Hayʿa al-Miṣriyya al-ʿĀmma li-l-Kitāb, 1994).

ʿAbd al-Munʿim, Muḥammad, 'al-Muḥārib al-Aḥmaq', *al-Ahrām*, 20 October 1987.

al-Musawi, Muhsin J. *The Postcolonial Arabic Novel: Debating Ambivalence* (Leiden: Brill, 2003).

—. 'Engaging Globalization in Modern Arabic Literature: Appropriation and Resistance', *Modern Language Quarterly* 68:2 (June 2007).

al-Muwayliḥī, Ibrāhīm. *Ma Hunālik* (Cairo: Maṭbaʿat al-Muqaṭṭam, 1896), trans. Roger Allen, *Spies, Scandals, and Sultans: Istanbul in the Twilight of the Ottoman Empire* (Lanham: Rowman and Littlefield Publishers, 2008).

Naji, Ahmed (= Aḥmad Nājī). *Rūjirz* (Cairo: Dār Malāmiḥ, 2007).

—. *Sabʿa Durūs Mustaqā min Aḥmad Makkī* (2009), available at <www.goodreads.com/ebooks/download/6472987-7>, last accessed 10 October 2016.

—. *al-Mudawwināt: Min al-Būst ilā al-Twīt* (Cairo: Arabic Network for Human Rights Information, 2010).

—. *Istikhdām al-Ḥayā* (Cairo: Manshūrāt Marsūm Dār al-Tanwīr, 2014), trans. Benjamin Koerber, *Using Life* (Austin: University of Texas Press, 2017).

al-Naqqāsh, Rajāʾ. 'Iḥdharū Hādhā al-Adab al-Badhīʾ', *al-Ahrām*, 22 April 2007.

Nasser, Gamal Abdel. 'Munāqashat Jamāl ʿAbd al-Nāṣir maʿa Aʿḍāʾ al-Lajna al-Tanfīdhiyya wa-l-Amāna al-ʿĀmma ḥawla Khiṭṭat al0ʿAmal al-Jadīda li-l-Tanẓīm al-Siyāsī', *al-Ṭalīʿa*, 3, March 1965, p. 25.

Neubauer, Hans-Joachim. *The Rumour: A Cultural History* (London: Free Association Books, 1999).

Orwell, George. *1984* (New York: Houghton Mifflin Harcourt, 2017 [1949]).

Pagán, Victoria Emma. *Conspiracy Theory in Latin Literature* (Austin: University of Texas Press, 2012).

Pannewick, Friederike and Georges Khalil (eds). *Commitment and Beyond: Reflections on/of the Political in Arabic Literature since the 1940s* (Wiesbaden: Reichert Verlag, 2015).

Pauwels, Jean-pierre. 'Les voies de la diversification industrielle', *Le Monde diplomatique*, 2 November 1976, p. 24.

Pellat, Charles. 'al-Djāḥiẓ', in P. Bearman, Th. Bianquis, C. E. Bosworth, E. van Donzel, and W. P. Heinrichs (eds), *Encyclopaedia of Islam, Second Edition*, edited by Brill Online, 2012.

Pipes, Daniel. *The Hidden Hand: Middle East Fears of Conspiracy* (New York: St Martin's Press, 1996).

Pynchon, Thomas. *Gravity's Rainbow* (New York: The Viking Press, 1973).

al-Qāḍī, Wadād. 'The Earliest "Nābita" and the Paradigmatic "Nawābit"', *Studia Islamica* 78 (1993), pp. 27–66.

Rabīʿ, Muḥammad (1975–2008). *ʿUmūm al-Layālī al-Latī* (2000), available at <www.goodreads.com/ebooks/download/8471875>, last accessed 10 October 2016.

—. *Muʾāmara ʿalā al-Sayyida Ṣunʿ Allāh* (2002), available at <www.goodreads.com/ebooks/download/8471931>, last accessed 10 October 2016.

Rabie, Mohammad (= Muḥammad Rabīʿ, b. 1978). *Kawkab ʿAnbar* (Cairo: Dār al-Kutub Khān, 2010).

—. *ʿĀm al-Tinnīn* (Cairo: Dār al-Kutub Khān, 2012).

—. *ʿUṭārid* (Cairo: Dār al-Tanwīr, 2014), trans. Robin Moger, *Otared* (New York: Hoopoe, 2016).

Radwan, Noha. 'A Place for Fiction in the Historical Archive', *Critique: Critical Middle Eastern Studies* 17:1 (spring 2008), pp. 79–95.

Rakha, Youssef (= Yūsuf Rakhā). *Kitāb al-Ṭughrā: Gharāʾib al-Tārīkh fī Madīnat al-Mirrīkh* (Cairo: Dār al-Shurūq, 2011), trans. Paul Starkey, *The Book of the Sultan's Seal: Strange Incidents from History in the City of Mars* (New York: Interlink Books, 2015).

—. 'In Extremis: Literature and Revolution in Contemporary Cairo (An Oriental Essay in Seven Parts)', *Kenyon Review* 34:3 (2012), pp. 151–66.

—. *al-Tamāsīḥ* (Beirut: Dār al-Sāqī, 2013), trans. Robin Moger, *The Crocodiles: A Novel* (New York: Seven Stories Press, 2014).

Ramaḍān, Sumayya. *Awrāq al-Narjis* (Cairo: Maktabat Madbūlī, 2002), trans. Marilyn Booth (Cairo: AUC Press, 2006).

Ramadan, Yasmine. 'The Emergence of the Sixties Generation in Egypt and the Anxiety over Categorization', *Journal of Arabic Literature* 43 (2012), pp. 409–30.

Rogin, Michael. 'JFK: The Movie', *The American Historical Review* 97:2 (April 1992), pp. 500–5.

Rūmān, Mīkhāʾīl. *al-Wāfid*, in *al-Layla Naḍḥak, al-Wāfid* (Cairo: Majallat al-Masraḥ, 1966 [1965]).

—. *al-Khiṭāb*, in *al-Masraḥ* (May 1967 [1965]).

Said, Edward. *Orientalism* (New York: Vintage Books, 1994).

Salāma, ʿAbīr. *al-Khurūj ʿan al-Naṣṣ fī ʿAlāqat Bākathīr wa-l-Masraḥ al-Miṣrī* (Cairo: al-Majlis al-Aʿlā li-l-Thaqāfa, 2013).

Saleh, Walid. 'The Woman as a Locus of Apocalyptic Anxiety in Medieval Sunnī Islam', in Angelika Neuwirth, et al. (eds), *Myths, Historical Archetypes and Symbolic Figures in Arabic Literature: Towards a New Hermeneutic Approach* (Stuttgart: Franz Steiner Verlag, 1999), pp. 123–45.

Sālim, ʿAlī. *il-Nās illī fī il-Sama il-Tāmina* (Damascus: Wizārat al-Thaqāfa, 1966 [1963]).

Al-Samman, Hanadi. 'Out of the Closet: Representations of Homosexuals and Lesbians in Modern Arabic Literature', *Journal of Arabic Literature* 39 (2008), pp. 270–310.

Schreber, Daniel P. *Memoirs of My Nervous Illness* (New York: New York Review Books, 2000).

Sedgwick, Eve Kosofsky. 'Paranoid Reading and Reparative Reading, Or, You're So Paranoid, You Probably Think this Essay is About You', in *Touching Feeling: Affect, Pedagogy, Performativity* (Durham, NC: Duke University Press, 2003), pp. 123–51.

—. *Epistemology of the Closet* (Berkeley: University of California Press, 2008).

Silverstein, Paul A. 'An Excess of Truth: Violence, Conspiracy Theorizing and the Algerian Civil War', *Anthropological Quarterly* 75:4 (autumn, 2002), pp. 643–74.

Sommer, Dorothe. *Freemasonry in the Ottoman Empire: A History of the Fraternity and its Influence in Syria and the Levant* (New York: I. B. Tauris, 2015).

Starkey, Paul. *Sonallah Ibrahim: Rebel with a Pen* (Edinburgh: Edinburgh University Press, 2016).

Stetkevych, Jaroslav. 'Arabic Hermeneutical Terminology: Paradox and the Production of Meaning', *Journal of Arabic Literature*, 48:2 (1989), pp. 81–96.

Stetkevych, Suzanne. 'Intoxication and Immortality: Wine and Associated Imagery in al-Maᶜarri's Garden', in Fedwa Malti-Douglas (ed.), *Critical Pilgrimages: Studies in the Arabic Literary Tradition* (Austin: Dept of Oriental and African Languages and Literatures, University of Texas at Austin, 1989), pp. 29–48.

Stewart, Kathleen. 'Conspiracy Theory's Worlds', in George E. Marcus (ed.), *Paranoia within Reason: A Casebook on Conspiracy as Explanation* (Chicago: University of Chicago Press, 1999), pp. 13–19.

Stone, Chris. 'Georg Lukács and the Improbable Realism of Ṣunᶜ Allah Ibrāhīm's *The Committee*', *Journal of Arabic Literature* 41 (2010), pp. 136–47.

Surur, Naguib (= Najīb Surūr). 'al-Ḥidhāʾ', *al-Risāla al-Jadīda*, 29, 1 August 1956, p. 25.

—. 'Takhṭīṭat fī al-Masraḥ al-Miṣrī', *al-Ādāb* 5:1 (1957), pp. *zāʾ-mīm*.

—. *Yāsīn wa-Bahiyya* (Cairo: Majallat al-Masraḥ, 1965).

—. *Āh yā Layl yā Qamar* (Cairo: Dār al-Kitāb al-ᶜArabī, 1968).

—. *Qūlū li-ᶜAyn al-Shams* (Cairo: Maktabat Madbūlī, 1976).

—. *Hākadhā Qāl Juḥā* (Cairo: Dār al-Thaqāfa al-Jadīda, 1977).

—. 'Risāla ilā Yūsuf Idrīs', *Adab wa-Naqd* 34, December 1987, pp. 117–30.

—. *al-Aᶜmāl al-Kāmila*, vol. 4, ed. ᶜIṣām al-Dīn Abū al- 'Ulā (Cairo: al-Hayʾa al-Miṣriyya al-ᶜĀmma li-l-Kitāb, 1993–7).

—. *Luzūm mā Yalzam* (Cairo: Dār al-Shurūq, 2006).

—. *Riḥla fī Thulāthiyyat Najīb Maḥfūẓ* (Cairo: Dār al-Shurūq, 2007).

—. *Taḥt ᶜAbāʾat Abī al-ᶜAlāʾ* (Cairo: al-Majlis al-Aᶜlā li-l-Thaqāfa, 2008).

Swedenburg, Ted. 'Saᶜida Sultan/Danna International: Transgender Pop and the Polysemiotics of Sex, Nation, and Ethnicity on the Israeli–Egyptian Border', in Walter Armbrust (ed.), *Mass Mediations: New Approaches to Popular Culture in the Middle East and Beyond* (Berkeley: University of California Press, 2000), pp. 88–119.

al-Taymūriyya, ᶜĀʾisha. *Natāʾij al-Aḥwāl fī al-Aqwāl wa-al-Afᶜāl* (Cairo: al-Hayʾa al-Miṣriyya al-ᶜĀmma li-l-Kitāb, 2002 [1887]).

al-Tūnisī, Muḥammad Khalīfa, 'al-Khaṭar al-Yahūdī: Brūtūkūlāt Shuyūkh Ṣihyūn al-ᶜUlamāʾ', *al-Risāla*, 856, 28 November 1949, p. 1,654,

—. *al-Khaṭar al-Yahūdī: Brūtūkūlāt Ḥukamāʾ Ṣahyūn* (Beirut: Dār al-Kitāb al-ᶜArabī, 1961).

Willis, Paul E. *Profane Culture* (Princeton: Princeton University Press, 2014).

Wissa, Karim. 'Freemasonry in Egypt 1798–1921: A Study in Cultural and Political

Encounters', *Bulletin of the British Society for Middle Eastern Studies* 16:2 (1989), pp. 143–61.

Zaki, Mona. 'The Stories of the Establishment', *Banipal* 13 (2002), pp. 11–16.

Al-Zuʿbī, Muḥammad ʿAlī. *al-Māsūniyya fī al-ʿArāʾ* (Beirut: Maṭabiʿ Maʿtūq Ikhwān, 1972).

Index

EU Authorised Representative:

Easy Access System Europe Mustamäe tee 50, 10621 Tallinn, Estonia

gpsr.requests@easproject.com

Printed and bound by CPI Group (UK) Ltd, Croydon, CR0 4YY

04/06/2026

02127501-0001